Textbook 2

2

课本（下册）

Zoom In: Elementary Chinese in 60 Hours

60 小时突破初级中文

主　编：LIQUN SU（苏立群）
副主编：WEI-SAN SU（胡未三）
编写者：LIQUN SU（苏立群）
WEI-SAN SU（胡未三）
王　岩
ZHANG, GAO（张杲）

MP3
www.sinolingua.com.cn

SinolinguA
华语教学出版社

First Edition 2021

ISBN 978-7-5138-2062-2

Published by Sinolingua Co., Ltd
24 Baiwanzhuang Street, Beijing 100037, China
Tel: (86) 10-68320585 68997826
Fax: (86) 10-68997826 68326333
http://www.sinolingua.com.cn
E-mail: hyjx@sinolingua.com.cn
Facebook: www.facebook.com/sinolingua
Printed by Beijing Hucais Culture Communication Co., Ltd.

Printed in the People's Republic of China

前言 Preface

During my twenty years of teaching at SOAS (School of Oriental and African Studies, University of London), I began to develop an interest in different ways of teaching Chinese as a written language. My book *Mastering Chinese Characters: A Modern Approach* was published in 2014 by the Commercial Press. I've now compiled a new series of textbooks which is an update called the *Zoom In* series (including *Elementary Chinese in 60 Hours* 1 & 2, *Intermediate Chinese in 118 Hours* 1 & 2, *Advanced Chinese in 337 Hours* 1 & 2 with accompanying workbooks).

The traditional way to teach written Chinese has been to take each character apart and trace the roots of its radicals to their sources. Though being well-accepted by Chinese students who are already familiar with their own history and culture, this approach has not been particularly effective for foreign students learning the language from scratch. In hindsight, this strategy was perhaps both too academic and too localised. It tended to assume the student possessed a basic knowledge of China such as its national and folkloric heritage, its geography, social values and codes of behaviour.

In an attempt to avoid similar pitfalls, it became something of an obsession of mine to figure out an alternative way to inspire and support foreign students in a way which does not require prior knowledge of Chinese. The resulting series of textbooks is an attempt at this more intuitive approach, that employs fresh visual tools. Since both pictures and sound are regular components of Chinese characters, we have included a cartoon to match each character, supported by a short piece of text in English which students are encouraged to read aloud. Whatever proved most helpful to the class or individual ended up on these pages, as I believe the priority should always be given to practical use over established convention.

In accordance with the Chinese saying, "Give a man a fish and you feed him for a day; teach a man to fish and you feed him for a lifetime. Knowledge is the best charity," the book encourages students to follow the method and pursue their own learning goals as far as their interest dictates.

The first 15 lessons are dedicated to character learning while the later lessons include two parts."Part 1

Combining Characters" is about making words or phrases. All 170 characters learned in the first 15 lessons are used to form words and phrases. "Part II Compose Sentences" is about using words and phrases to form five sentences. The first three sentences are simple and the last two are longer and more difficult. After finishing the whole book, students should be able to know 1,250 words or phrases and read 510 simple sentences, while those with strong language ability could master as many as 850 sentences.

An exercise book is also designed to help students memorize Chinese characters and word combinations as well as helping to construct sentences with those words. The book also provides a story of some 4,500 words for students to read.

This series has been used in the classroom for two years. Students could spend 1.5 hours per week in a total of twenty weeks (30 hours) to learn 170 Chinese characters.

In the West there exists tremendous interest in learning Chinese. In order to follow this trend, I would suggest a couple of things: Firstly, to remind Chinese language teachers that a spoken language and its written form are intimately connected. In other words, to teach the spoken language, it is paramount to teach reading and writing at the same time. Secondly, our attention should be given more to children and teenagers, for whom Chinese has become one of the most popular subjects at school. It is with this age group in mind that we hope to take on a serious subject in a relaxed and playful manner.

As this volume is soon to be put into publication, I would like to express my particular gratitude to Richard Pilgrim for his outstanding contribution to proofreading the English part. Special thanks go to Mr. Kevin Munns for his recording of the English in the book. His high standard of English has greatly helped improve the book!

David Su Liqun

前言 Preface

任教英国伦敦大学亚非学院（School of Oriental and African Studies, University of London）的20年期间，我一直都在寻找一种向欧美学生介绍汉字的方法。“突破中文”系列教材是在《汉字图解学习手册》（Mastering Chinese Characters: A Modern Approach，商务印书馆2014）的基础上运用更新思路编写的。该系列教材共分六个级别：《60小时突破初级中文（上、下册）》、《118小时突破中级中文（上、下册）》和《337小时突破高级中文（上、下册）》，每个级别含课本和练习册各一册。

《60小时突破初级中文（下册）》课本的第一部分（字篇，第一课到第十五课）学习汉字。

在对外汉语教学的数十年中，曾不断有人尝试过以“图片解析汉字”的方法来编写教材，不过总体来说收效不明显，原因是这些书对汉字的解释过于“学术化”与“地域化”。“学术化”是指“以文解文，以字解字”，忽略了学习者是外国人，他们对中国是“零知识”；“地域化”是指著书者大多对欧美受众群体的社会及价值观缺乏切身的了解，因而，在文化的沟通和语言的表达两个方面都受到了局限。这套“突破中文”系列教材尽量避免这些短处，而采用的方法是：第一，把学生领回到甲骨文、金文和籀文时代——对这个久远的时光隧道本书不是用“引证”和“六书”去充填，而是通过卡通画的形象并结合汉字后面的故事把这些字“激活”来启发、引导学生；第二，采用了以“声”加深学生对“形”记忆的特殊模式，即每一个汉字都设计了“把汉字说出来”的一条，就是用一句地道的英文把这个汉字的形、声、义都归纳、融合进去，达到“只要记得住这句话，就知道这个字的意思、写法和发音”的目的。此外，课本还提供了书写的笔顺，鼓励学习者“唱字”，“横竖撇捺，点勾折提”边写边唱。

课本的第二部分（词句篇，第十六课到第三十课）是学习汉字的组构功能，即以字组词、以词组句、以句组段、以段组章的规律。

解释这个规律之前，需要先把这套书何以取名“Zoom In（趋真向实法则）”或称“Natural Flow（自然顺序法，简称‘序法’）”做一个说明。

什么是这个“趋真向实法则”（或“自然顺序法”）呢？众所周知，大自然里有两个相互独立又相互制约的元素，一个是时间，一个是空间。宇宙中的万物在穿过时间隧道时都在改变其空间的位置；所以这个“自然顺序法”是时间先于空间，而时间自身的顺序是由无限的长到有限的短，空间自身的顺序是由无限的大到有限的小。人类的生活也不例外，这两个元素的规则影响着我们的万千世界。耐人寻味的是这个“自然顺序法”从数千年以前就反射到中华民族的语言（汉语）中，汉语的“序法”规则就是建立在这个基础之上的。

具体来说，两个或两个以上的汉字首尾相接的法则，在表达时间时是“由长到短”，表达空间时是由“大到小”。更具体来说，这个“序法（自然顺序法）”反映到汉语的字词与句子的组构方面，都是从广义到狭义，从整体到局部，从一般到具体，从前到后，从上到下，等等。

中国古代的智者说：“给人一条鱼，你只喂他一天；教给一个人会钓鱼，你就养活了他一辈子；授人以技能是最好的助人方式。”基于汉语这种简单易懂的“序法”，课本的第二部分（第十六课到第三十课）就是把这个“序法”用在“以字组词，以词组句”上——教授学习者钓鱼的技能！

于此，课本里后十五课的内容都是使用第一部分学习的 170 个初级汉字去组构词、短语的，而且，每个汉字都给出五个使用该汉字的句子，其中前三句比较简单，后两句相对长些、复杂些。在本书的最后一课结束的时候，学生能够认读 1250 个单词或短语，可以掌握 510 个简单句子；对于那些语言能力强的人，可以达到 850 个句子。此外，复本还配有练习册，提供记忆汉字和字词扩充及中英句子互翻的练习。为了增加学生的成就感，本书还附有一篇长达 4500 个汉字的小说供学生阅读欣赏。

《60 小时突破初级中文（下册）》（含课本及练习册）从完成初稿到最终提交用了两年多的时间，其间，它已被作为课堂教材试用过多次。粗粗统计的结果是，如果学生每周上课或自学 1.5 小时，经过 20 周共 30 个小时的学习，通过初等高阶水平的考试是绰绰有余的。

苏立群

目录 Contents

字篇

附录

字篇

Radical/Component 口 mouth 吧 Grammatical Code ba 179

Grammatical Code ba 吧

口 (mouth) + 巴 (reptile/snake) = code of a guessing or suggestion

Catchphrase

I SUGGEST you leave me alone because I am a poisonous snake. The SUGGESTION particle is 吧 ba.

Stroke order

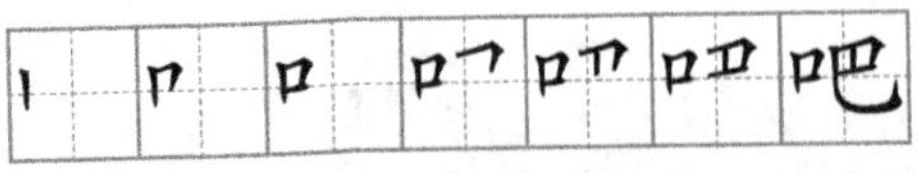

Radical/Component 白 white 白 WHITE bái 180

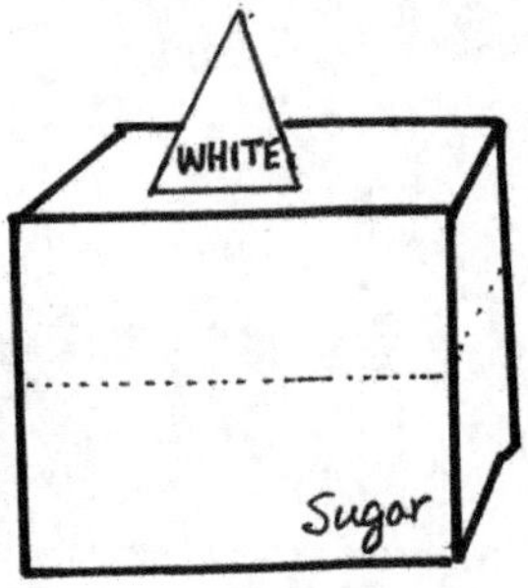

WHITE bái 白

Ancient form 

丿 (mark) + 日 (sunlight) = white

Catchphrase

Here is a package of WHITE sugar. WHITE is 白 bái.

Stroke order

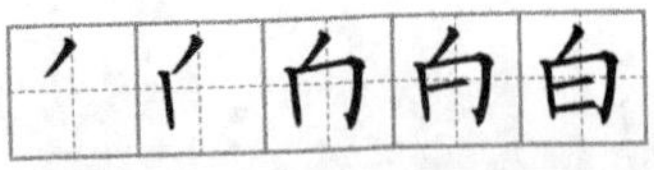

Radical/Component 一 the first stroke 百 HUNDRED bǎi 181

HUNDRED bǎi 百

Ancient form 

一 (one) +  (white food/two zeros) = hundred

Catchphrase

This package of the white sugar is one HUNDRED grams. HUNDRED is 百 bǎi.

Stroke order

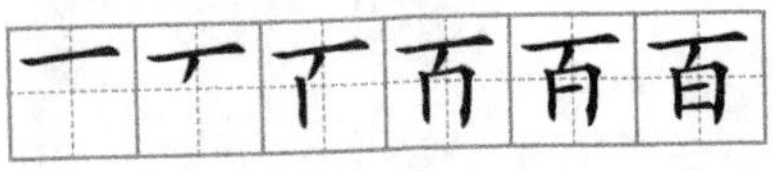

Radical/Component 王 jade　班 GROUP bān　182

GROUP bān 班

Ancient form

王 (jade) + 刂 (saw/knife) + 王 (jade) = group

Catchphrase

Two pieces of jade form a GROUP, made by a saw cutting a square block of jade in two. GROUP is 班 bān.

Stroke order

一 二 干 王 王 玎 玎 玔 玔 班

Radical/Component 巾 turban　帮（幫*）HELP bāng　183

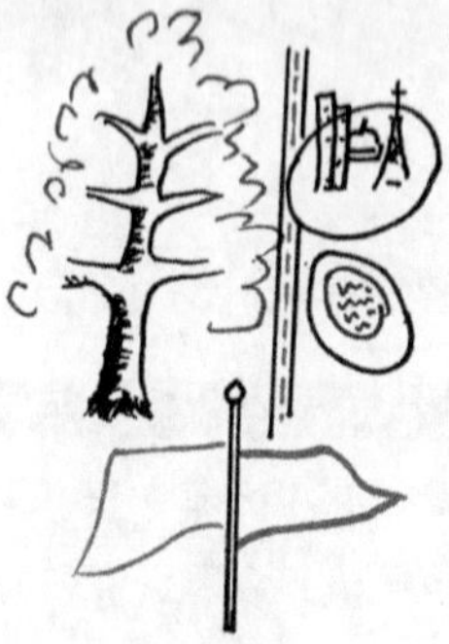

HELP bāng 帮

Traditional form 幫

丰 (woods) + 阝 (town) + 巾 (cloth linking) = help

Catchphrase

Making a connection between the forest and the city can HELP improve the environment. HELP is 帮 bāng.

Stroke order

一 二 三 丰 邦 邦 邦 帮 帮

* 为便于各地区学生使用，如果这个汉字有繁体字，就在此处括弧内标明。

* The traditional form of the character, if any, is included for the reader's reference through the textbook.

Radical/Component 扌 hand　报（報）REPORT bào　184

REPORT bào 报

Ancient form　Traditional form 報

手 (hand) + 𠬝 (slavery labour) = report

Catchphrase

When an official REPORTs to his superior, it is customary for him to bow his head in obeisance. REPORT is 报 bào.

Stroke order

一 十 扌 扌 扌 报 报

Radical/Component 田 field 备（備）PREPARE bèi 185

PREPARE bèi 备

Ancient form Traditional form 備

文 (tools) + 田 (field/box) = a box with all needs

Catchphrase

I have packed my basket and am fully PREPAREd for my mission. PREPARE is 备 bèi.

Stroke order

Radical/Component 匕 person/knife 比 COMPARE bǐ 186

COMPARE bǐ 比

Ancient form

two people

Catchphrase

Two rival ballerinas COMPARE their beauty. COMPARE is 比 bǐ.

Stroke order

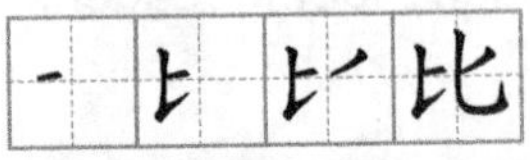

Radical/Component 竹 bamboo 笔（筆）BRUSH/PEN bǐ 187

BRUSH/PEN bǐ 笔

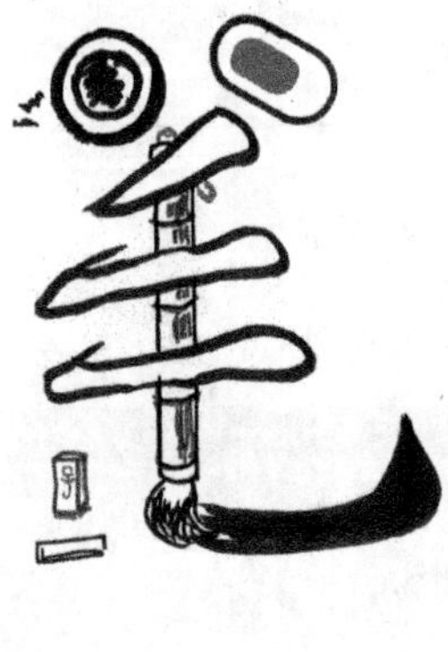

Ancient form Traditional form 筆

竹 (bamboo) + 毛 (hair) = brush/pen

Catchphrase

Beautiful calligraphy comes not only from your artistic eye but also from the way you hold the bamboo writing BRUSH in a straight line, with fully absorbed ink. BRUSH/PEN is 笔 bǐ.

Stroke order

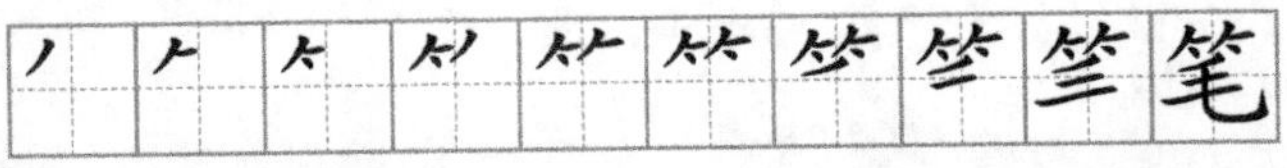

Radical/Component ⻌ walk　边（邊）EDGE/SIDE biān　188

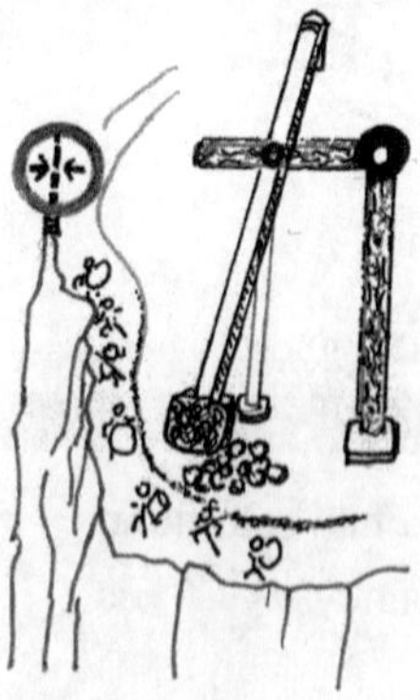

EDGE/SIDE biān 边

Ancient form　Traditional form 邊

(walk) + (moved by force) = edge/side

Catchphrase

In ancient times, criminals were forced to go to the country's EDGE for hard and dangerous work. EDGE/SIDE is 边 biān.

Stroke order

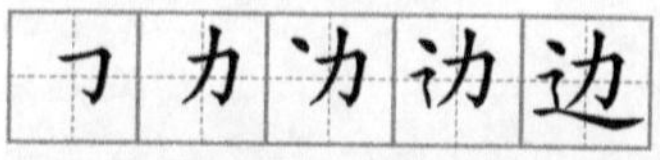

Radical/Component 衣 cloth　表 APPEARANCE/SURFACE biǎo　189

APPEARANCE/SURFACE biǎo 表

Ancient form

(hair) + (hat & dress) = appearance/surface

Catchphrase

A person's APPEARANCE often reflects his inner life. APPEARANCE/SURFACE is 表 biǎo.

Stroke order

Radical/Component 刂 knife　别（別）DON'T/GOODBYE bié　190

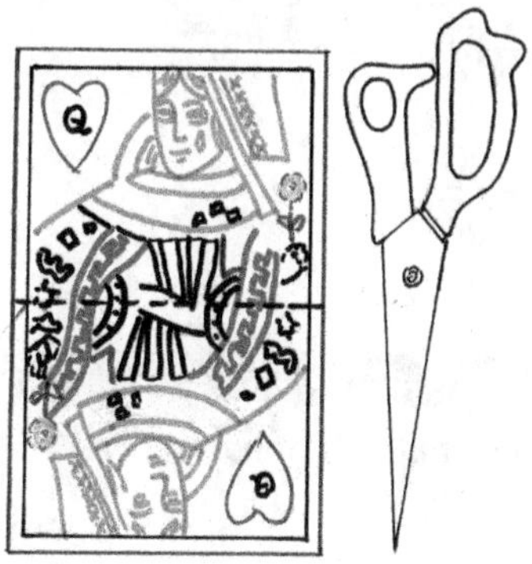

DON'T/GOODBYE bié 别

Ancient form　Traditional form 別

另 (body/another) + 刂 (knife) = don't/goodbye

Catchphrase

Part One: Please DON'T cut me in half! DON'T is 别 bié.
Part Two: GOODBYE, my twin! GOODBYE is 别 bié.

Stroke order

Radical/Component 宀 roof 宾（賓）GUEST bīn 191

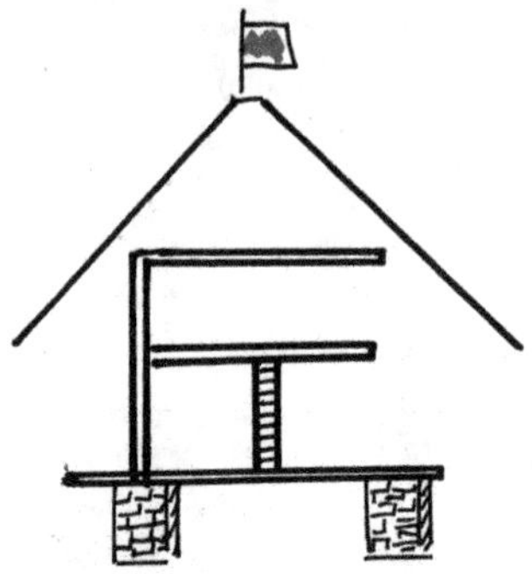

GUEST bīn 宾

Ancient form Traditional form 賓

宀 (roof) + 兵 (soldier/weapons) = guest

Catchphrase

If a soldier is your GUEST, you should provide him with good accommodation because soldiers protect our country. GUEST is 宾 bīn.

Stroke order

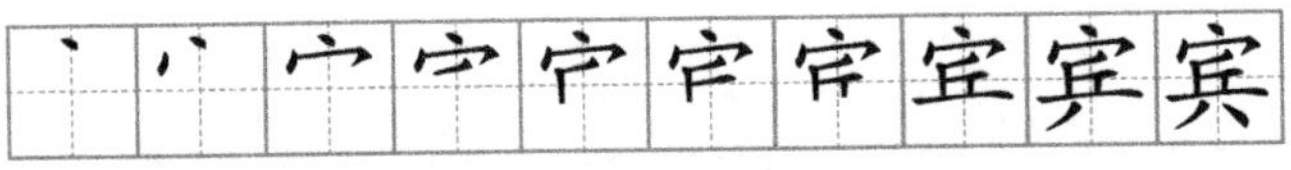

Radical/Component 疒 sickness 病 SICK bìng 192

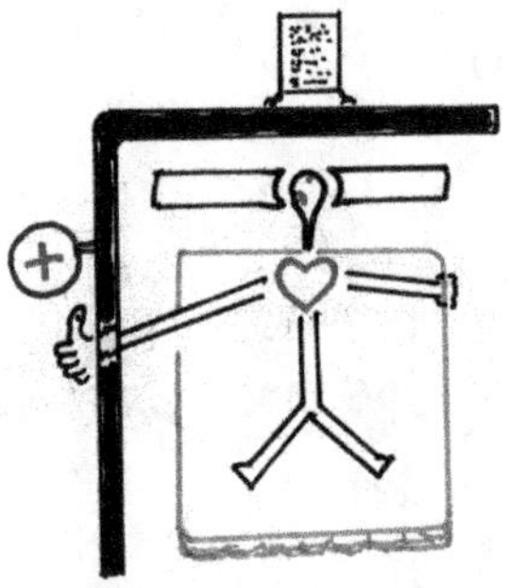

SICK bìng 病

Ancient form

疒 (bed with two handles) + 丙 (A patient lies down forceless) = sick

Catchphrase

A SICK man lies down on the hospital bed; he holds the edge of the bed with one hand, and stretches out the other hand to let his relatives know he is OK. SICK is 病 bìng.

Stroke order

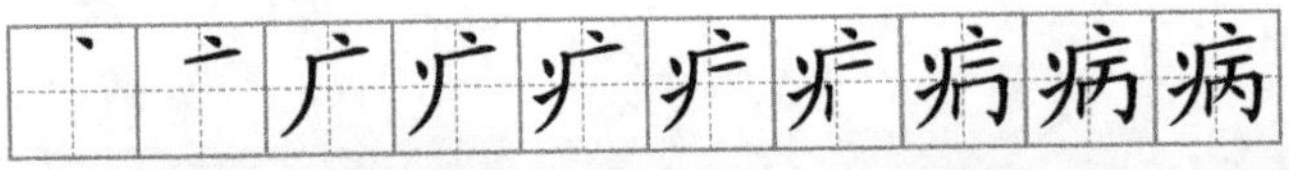

Radical/Component 止 held pace 步 PACE/STEP bù 193

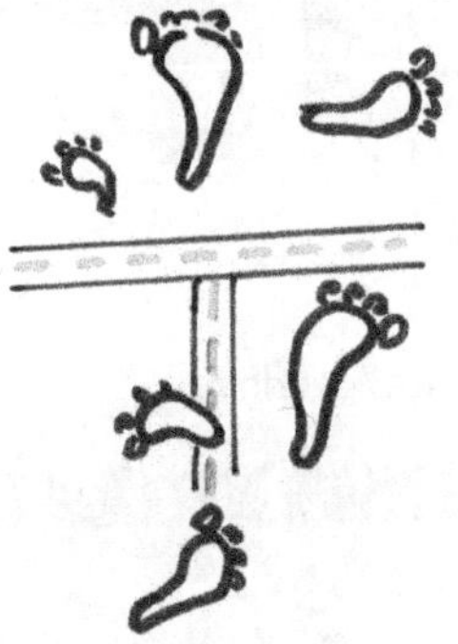

PACE/STEP bù 步

Ancient form

止 (stop) + 少 (few)= pace/step

Catchphrase

A person PACEs all round the T junction, but still cannot find the right direction. PACE/STEP is 步 bù.

Stroke order

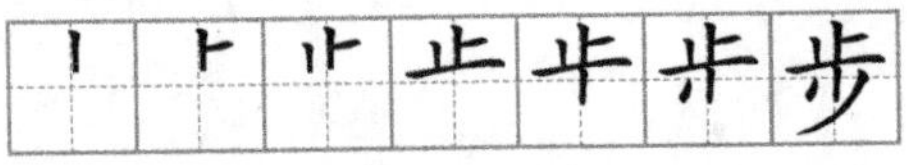

Radical/Component 丿 the first stroke 长（長）LONG cháng ; GROW zhǎng 194

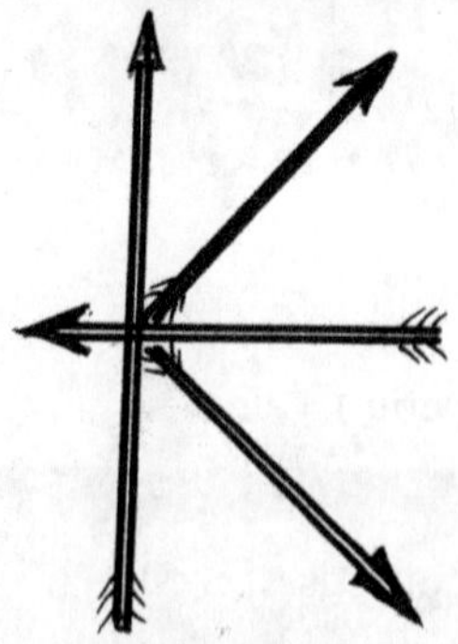

LONG cháng; **GROW** zhǎng 长

Ancient form Traditional form 長

Catchphrase

Four LONG arrows point in different directions. LONG is 长 cháng.
*Another meaning GROW is 长 zhǎng.

Stroke order

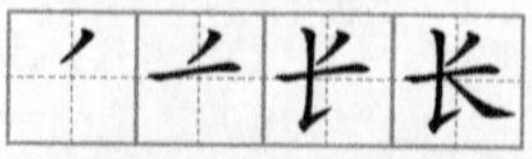

Radical/Component 巾 scarf/dress 常 OFTEN cháng 195

OFTEN cháng 常

Ancient form

尚 (fashion hat and head) + 巾 (scarf/dress) = often

Catchphrase

This lady OFTEN wears a fashionable hat and scarf. OFTEN is 常 cháng.

Stroke order

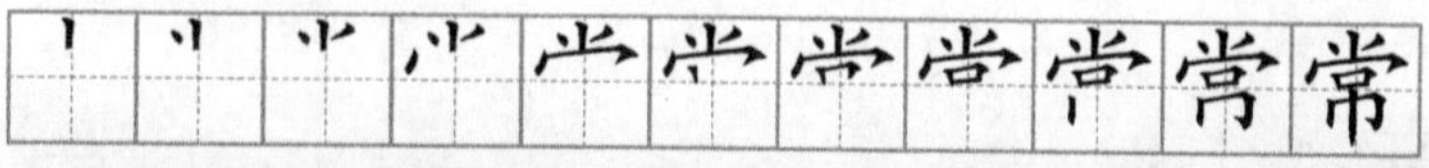

Radical/Component 土 land/farmland 场（場）OPEN SPACE/MW chǎng 196

OPEN SPACE/MW chǎng 场

Ancient form Traditional form 場

土 (land) + 昜 (sun & shadow/change) = open space

Catchphrase

A public facility should have an OPEN SPACE with sun and shade. OPEN SPACE/MW is 场 chǎng.

Stroke order

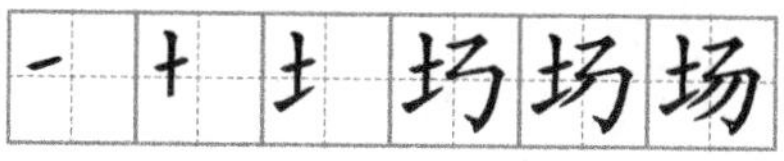

Radical/Component 口 mouth　唱 SING chàng　197

SING chàng 唱

Ancient form 

口 (opened mouth) + 昌 (prosperity) = sing

Catchphrase

A mouth SINGs a song to celebrate prosperity. SING is 唱 chàng.

Stroke order

Radical/Component 穴 cave　穿 PENETRATE/WEAR chuān　198

PENETRATE/WEAR chuān 穿

Ancient form 

穴 (cave) + 牙 (teeth) = penetrate/wear

Catchphrase

Teeth PENETRATE food like a cave penetrates a hill. PENETRATE/WEAR (clothes) is 穿 chuān.

Stroke order

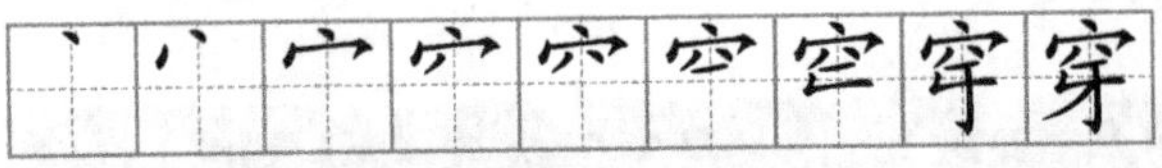

Radical/Component 木 wood　床 BED chuáng　199

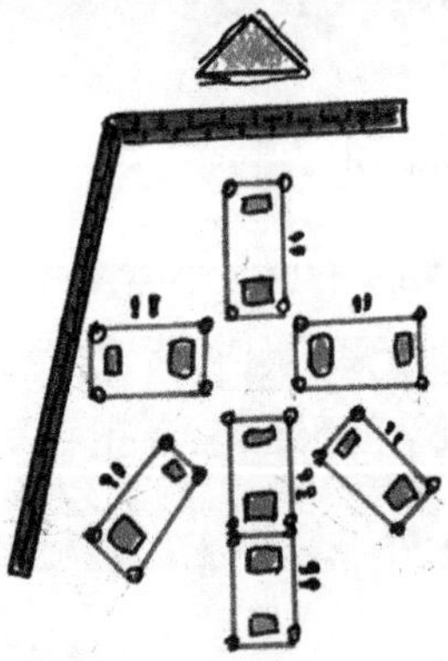

BED chuáng 床

Ancient form 

广 (abroad) + 木 (wood) = bed

Catchphrase

Six wooden BEDs are in the hospital. BED is 床 chuáng.

Stroke order

Radical/Component 欠 lack　次 SECOND-RATE/MW cì　200

SECOND-RATE/MW cì　次

Ancient form

冫 (mouth water)+ 欠 (lack energy) = second-rate/MW

Catchphrase

This athlete was so tired, he didn't win this time. People said he was becoming SECOND-RATE. SECOND-RATE/MW is 次 cì.

Stroke order

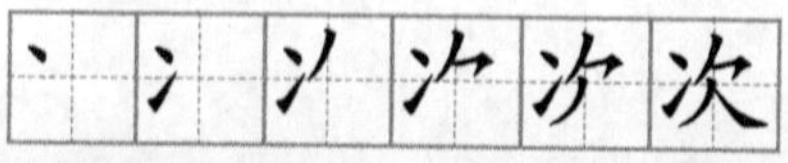

Radical/Component 人 person　从（從）FOLLOW/FROM cóng　201

FOLLOW/FROM cóng　从

Ancient form　Traditional form 從

人 (person) + 人 (person) = follow/from

Catchphrase

One person FOLLOWs another one. FOLLOW/FROM is 从 cóng.

Stroke order

Radical/Component 金 gold　错（錯）MISTAKE cuò　202

MISTAKE cuò　错

Ancient form　Traditional form 錯

金 (gold) + 昔 (in the past) = mistake

Catchphrase

Take the gold before sunset — it would be a MISTAKE to wait. MISTAKE is 错 cuò.

Stroke order

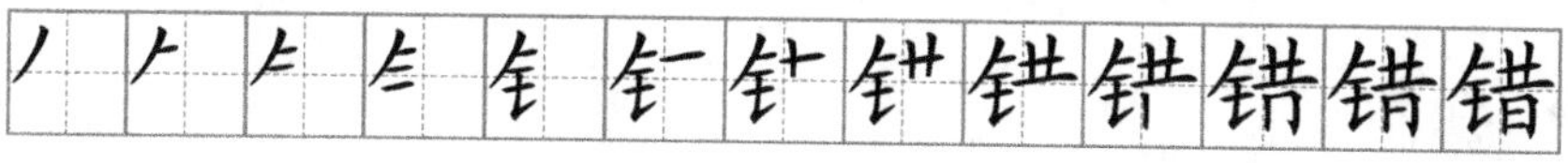

Radical/Component 亻 man 但 BUT dàn 203

BUT dàn 但

Ancient form

(man) + (sunrise) = but

Catchphrase

The beautiful sun has risen over the horizon BUT this man has no work to do. BUT is 但 dàn.

Stroke order

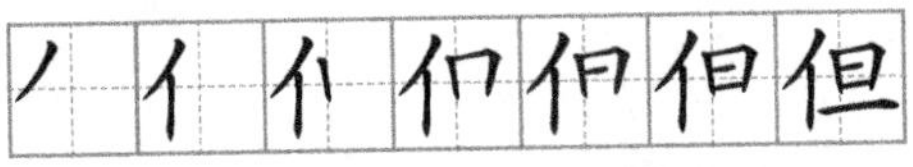

Radical/Component 虫 insect 蛋 EGG dàn 204

EGG dàn 蛋

Ancient form

疋 (the part of body between legs) + 虫 (insect/ovum) = egg

Catchphrase

Is this hen waiting for a fresh EGG to come out? EGG is 蛋 dàn.

Stroke order

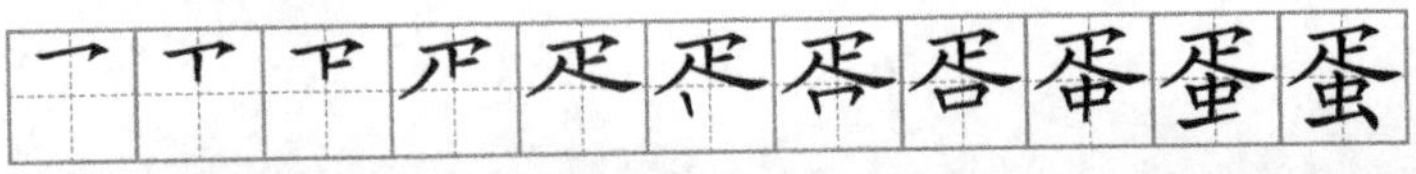

Radical/Component 刂 knife 到 ARRIVE/REACH dào 205

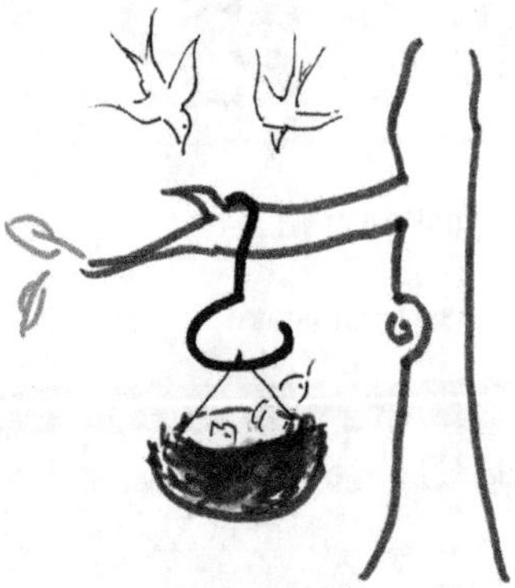

ARRIVE/REACH dào 到

Ancient form

至 (birds head to nets) + 刂 (knife/person) = arrive/reach

Catchphrase

The parent birds ARRIVE at the nest many times a day to feed their young. ARRIVE/REACH is 到 dào.

Stroke order

Radical/Component 辶 walk　道 WAY/ROAD dào　206

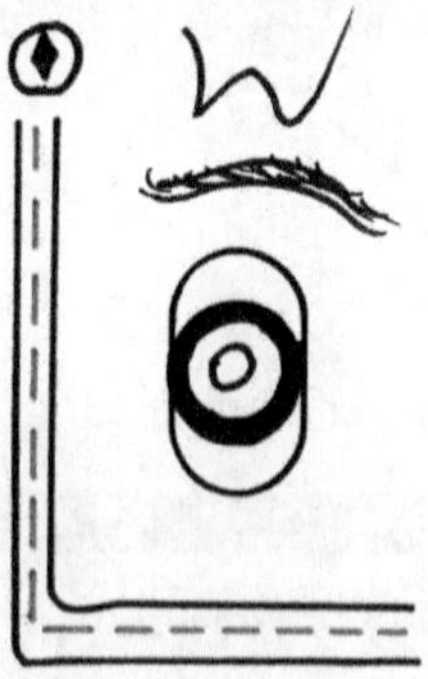

WAY/ROAD dào 道

Ancient form

辶 (walk) + 首 (head) = way/road

Catchphrase

Do not turn your head away from the path when walking in the WAY of the Dao. The WAY/ROAD is 道 dào.

Stroke order

丶 丷 䒑 䒑 䒑 首 首 首 首 首 道 道

Radical/Component 彳 street/step　得 GET dé; Grammatical Code de; MUST/HAVE TO děi　207

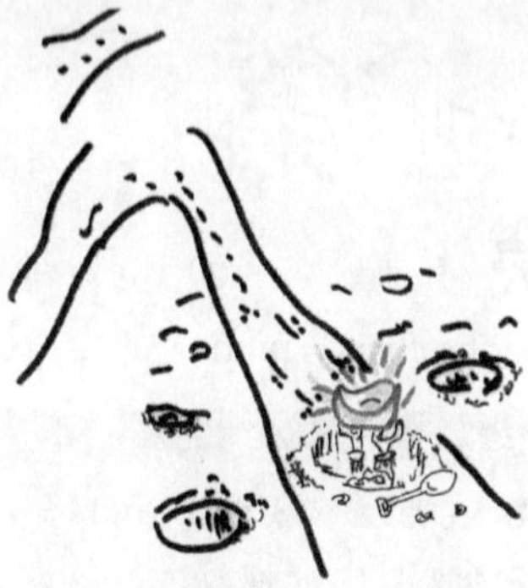

GET dé; **Grammatical Code** de; **MUST/HAVE TO** děi 得

Ancient form

彳(street/step) + (shell/money) + (hand) = get/obtain

Catchphrase

Following the road you will GET a treasure to hold. GET is 得 dé. 得 de is also a grammatical code meaning as the result of an action. 得 děi means MUST/HAVE TO.

Stroke order

丿 彡 彳 彳 彳 彳 彳 得 得 得 得

Radical/Component ⺮ bamboo　等 WAIT děng　208

WAIT děng 等

Ancient form

⺮ (bamboo) + 寺 (temple) = wait

Catchphrase

If you keep up your meditation outside the temple and WAIT for the bamboo to grow tall, you will be a kung fu master. WAIT is 等 děng.

Stroke order

丿 𠂉 𠃋 ⺮ ⺮ ⺮ 笁 笁 笙 笙 等 等

Radical/Component 丷 foot　弟 YOUNGER BROTHER dì　209

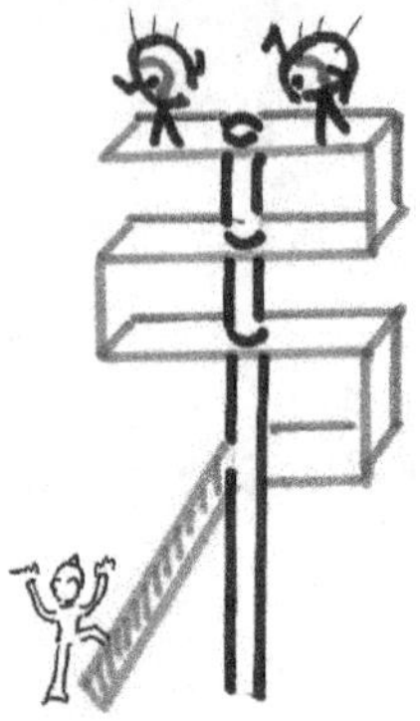

YOUNGER BROTHER dì 弟

Ancient form

(family tree) + (to circle down) = younger brother

Catchphrase

Two brothers have climbed to the top floor and are waving to their YOUNGER BROTHER. YOUNGER BROTHER is 弟 dì.

Stroke order

丶	丷	䒑	当	弚	弟	弟

Radical/Component ⺮ bamboo　第 Prefix of Ordinal Number dì　210

Prefix of Ordinal Number dì 第

Ancient form

(bamboo) + (climb/younger brother) = prefix

Catchphrase

The two brothers have climbed to the NUMBER 3 floor and planted two bamboo trees on top. The Prefix of Ordinal Number is 第 dì.

Stroke order

丿	𠂉	𥫗	𥫗	𥫗	⺮	笃	笃	笃	第	第

Radical/Component 忄 heart　懂 UNDERSTAND dǒng　211

UNDERSTAND dǒng 懂

Ancient form

(heart/mind) + (plant/eyes) + (heavy) = understand

Catchphrase

If the mind UNDERSTANDs how heavy the loads are, it can alleviate some of the burdens. UNDERSTAND is 懂 dǒng.

Stroke order

丶	丷	忄	忄	忄	忄	忄	恾	恾	愂	愅	愅	愅	懂	懂

Radical/Component 力 force 动（動）MOVEMENT dòng 212

MOVEMENT dòng 动

Ancient form Traditional form 動

云 (cloud) + 力 (force) = movement

Catchphrase

Clouds are pushed along by the MOVEMENT of the air. MOVEMENT is 动 dòng.

Stroke order

一 二 云 云 动 动

Radical/Component 戶 door 房 BUILDING fáng 213

BUILDING fáng 房

Ancient form

(window) + (square-shape/place) = building

Catchphrase

Various types of square BUILDINGs are common in rural areas. BUILDING is 房 fáng.

Stroke order

丶 ⺈ ⺕ 户 户 房 房 房

Radical/Component 丨 first stroke 非 NON-/WRONG fēi 214

NON-/WRONG fēi 非

Ancient form

two people standing back to back

Catchphrase

When two people argue, each is likely to think that the other is WRONG. NON-/WRONG is 非 fēi.

Stroke order

丨 ⺆ ⺕ ⺕ 非 非 非 非

Radical/Component 口 mouth 啡 COFFEE (second character) fēi 215

COFFEE (second character) fēi 啡

Ancient form

口 (mouth) + 非 (non-/wrong)

Catchphrase

Humankind has made something which was non-drinkable into wonderful COFFEE. COFFEE (2nd character) is 啡 fēi.

Stroke order

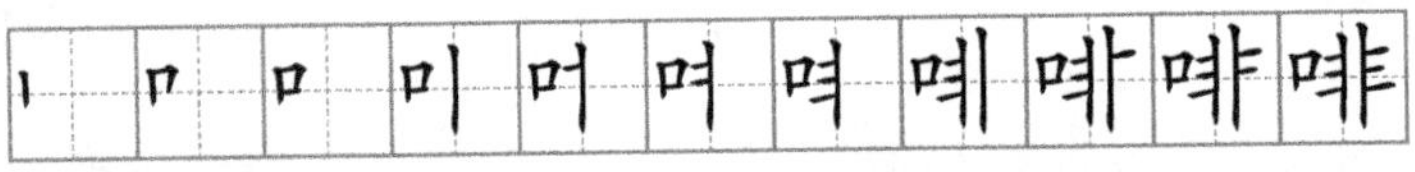

Radical/Component 二 the first two strokes 夫 ADULT MAN fū 216

ADULT MAN fū 夫

Ancient form

Catchphrase

The ADULT MAN is delivering water and food to his family. ADULT MAN is 夫 fū.

Stroke order

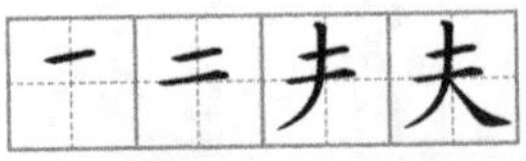

Radical/Component 口 mouth 告 INFORM/TELL gào 217

INFORM/TELL gào 告

Ancient form

牛 (cow) + 口 (mouth) = inform/tell

Catchphrase

Cows cannot speak, therefore they cannot INFORM us of their feelings. INFORM/TELL is 告 gào.

Stroke order

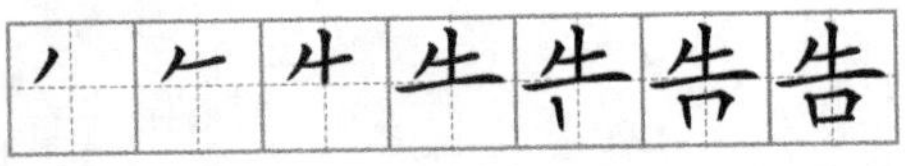

Radical/Component 口 mouth 哥 ELDER BROTHER gē 218

ELDER BROTHER gē 哥

Ancient form

可 (open mouth singing) + 可 (singing) = elder brother

Catchphrase

When brothers are working hard in the fields, the ELDER BROTHER should sing encouraging words to support his younger brothers. ELDER BROTHER is 哥 gē.

Stroke order

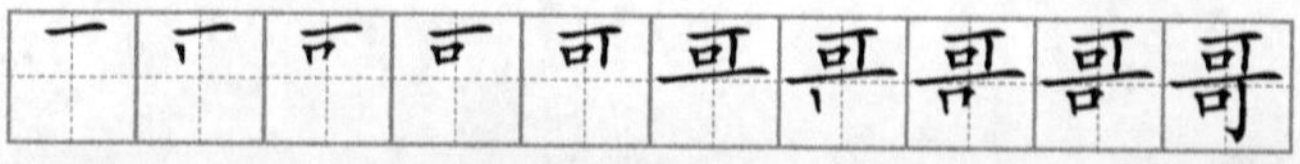

Radical/Component 欠 stretch 歌 SONG gē 219

SONG gē 歌

Ancient form

可 (open mouth singing) + 欠 (stretch) = song

Catchphrase

A good method for encouraging brothers to work harder is to stretch your body and sing SONGs for them to get energy. SONG is 歌 gē.

Stroke order

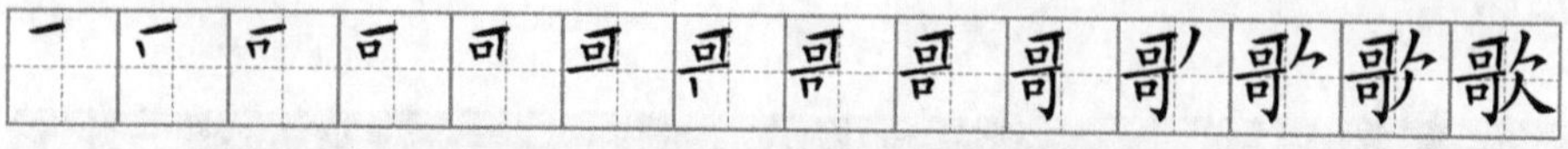

Radical/Component 纟 silk 给（給）GIVE gěi 220

GIVE gěi 给

Ancient form Traditional form 給

纟 (silk) + 合 (box) = to give

Catchphrase

When you GIVE someone a gift, you should tie the box with a silk ribbon. GIVE is 给 gěi.

Stroke order

Radical/Component 厶 private — 公 PUBLIC gōng 221

PUBLIC gōng 公

Ancient form [ancient form]

[two hands] 八 (two hands) + [private] 厶 (private) = public

Catchphrase

To share your treasure is PUBLIC-spirited. PUBLIC is 公 gōng.

Stroke order

丿 八 公 公

Radical/Component 一 the first stroke — 共 COMMON gòng 222

COMMON gòng 共

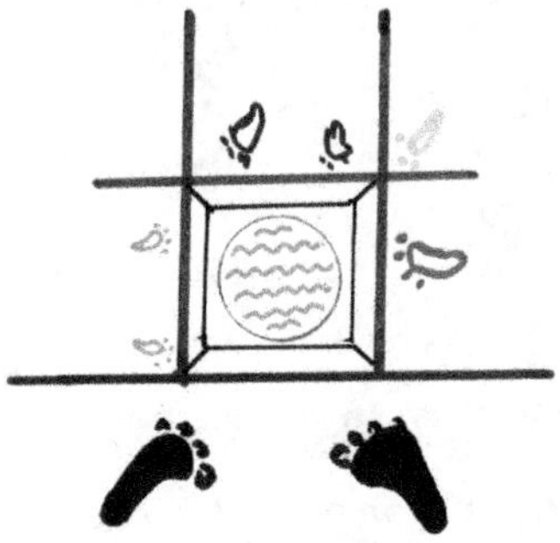

Ancient form [ancient form]

[resources] (resources) + [hands] (hands) = common

Catchphrase

It is COMMON sense for all the people around the well to share the water resource. COMMON is 共 gòng.

Stroke order

一 十 廾 丗 共 共

Radical/Component 瓜 melon — 瓜 MELON guā 223

MELON guā 瓜

Ancient form [ancient form]

[plant] (plant) + [fruit] (fruit) = melon

Catchphrase

This character looks like a huge MELON hanging on a wooden stick. MELON is 瓜 guā.

Stroke order

丆 厂 爪 瓜 瓜

Radical/Component 贝 money 贵（貴）EXPENSIVE guì 224

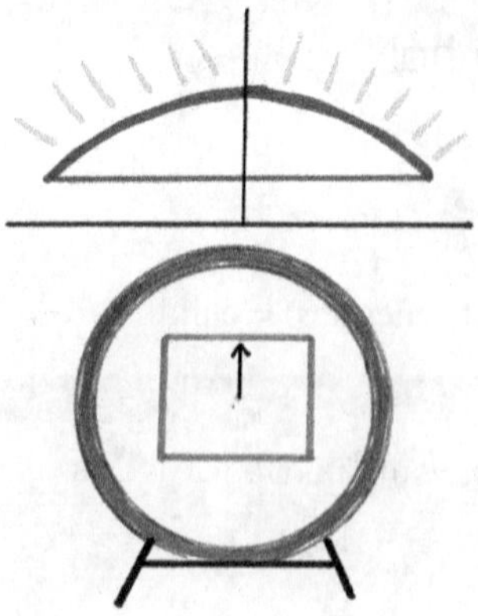

EXPENSIVE guì 贵

Ancient form Traditional form 貴

(two people exchange) + (中 + 贝) (the money value in the middle of day) = expensive

Catchphrase

It's best to go to the local market in the morning as things are more EXPENSIVE in the middle of the day. EXPENSIVE is 贵 guì.

Stroke order

丶	冖	口	中	虫	串	冑	贵	贵

Radical/Component 辶 walk/road 过（過）CROSS/PASS guò 225

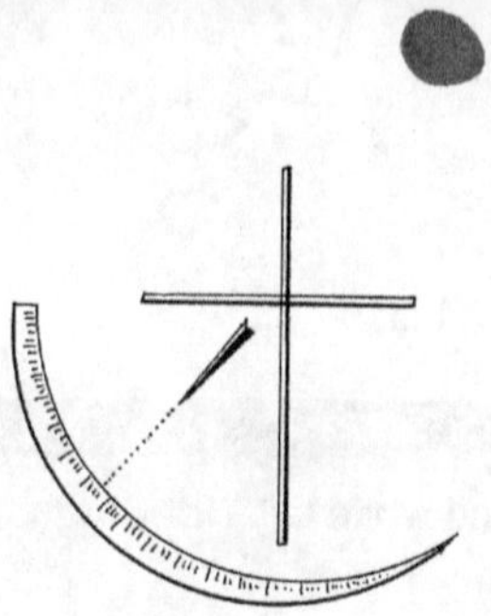

CROSS/PASS guò 过

Ancient form Traditional form 過

寸 (measure by hand) + 辶 (walk/access) = cross/pass

Catchphrase

If you measure the sun's position as it CROSSes the sky, you can tell how much time has PASSed. CROSS/PASS is 过 guò.

Stroke order

一	十	寸	寸	讨	过

Radical/Component 辶 walk/road 还（還）STILL/ALSO/EVEN hái; RETURN huán 226

STILL/ALSO/EVEN hái; **RETURN** huán 还

Ancient form Traditional form 還

不 (do not) + 辶 (walk/access) = still

Catchphrase

Do not lose concentration, you STILL have one more hole to play to win the golf competition. STILL/ALSO/EVEN is 还 hái.
还 has another meaning RETURN, pronounced huán.

Stroke order

一	ア	不	不	不	怀	还

Radical/Component 子 son 孩 CHILD hái 227

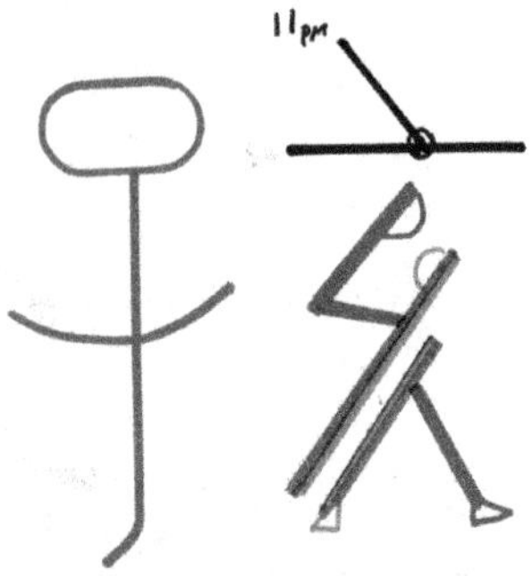

CHILD hái 孩

Ancient form

子 (child) + 亥 (two opposite energies) = child

Catchphrase

A CHILD begins life when a man and a woman unite. CHILD is 孩 hái.

Stroke order

㇇	了	子	孑	孑	孒	孩	孩	孩

Radical/Component 灬 fire 黑 BLACK hēi 228

BLACK hēi 黑

Ancient form

(blacked face) + (fire) = black

Catchphrase

The cat is all BLACK, except for her black and white tail. BLACK is 黑 hēi.

Stroke order

丨	冂	冂	冋	四	甲	甲	里	里	黑	黑	黑

Radical/Component 纟 silk 红（紅）RED hóng 229

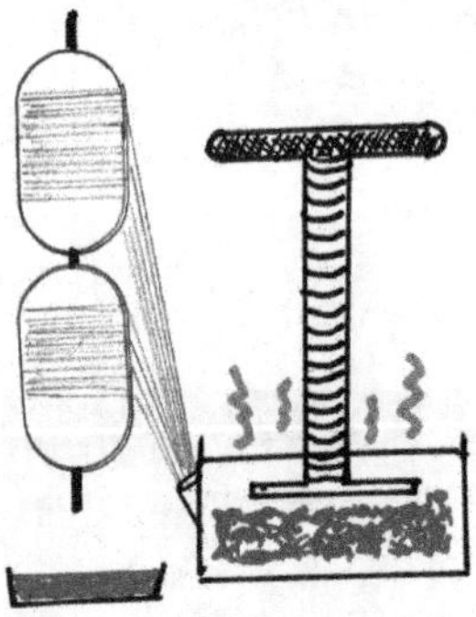

RED hóng 红

Ancient form Traditional form 紅

纟 (silk) + 工 (work) = red

Catchphrase

It takes a lot of work to turn natural silk into RED silk. RED is 红 hóng.

Stroke order

𠃋	纟	纟	纡	红	红

Radical/Component 鸟 bird 鸡（雞）CHICKEN jī 230

CHICKEN jī 鸡

Ancient form Traditional form 雞

又 (win/hand) + 鸟 (bird) = chicken

Catchphrase

This red-crested CHICKEN wants to fly. CHICKEN is 鸡 jī.

Stroke order

フ	又	又'	对	对	鸡	鸡

Radical/Component 门 door/gate 间（間）MW for room jiān 231

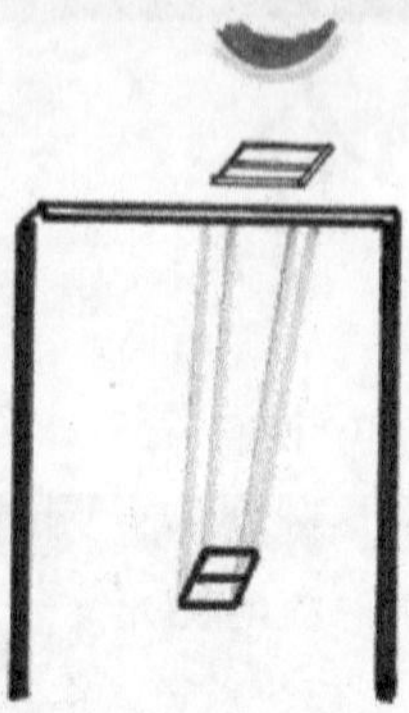

MW for room jiān 间

Ancient form Traditional form 間

门 (door) + 日 (sun) = MW for room

Catchphrase

Sunlight streams into the ROOM through the gap. MW for room is 间 jiān.

Stroke order

丶	门	门	门	间	间	间

Radical/Component 亻 mankind 件 MW for clothes jiàn 232

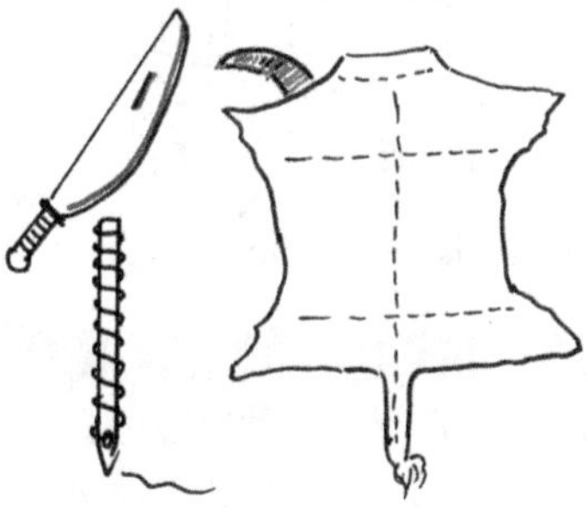

MW for clothes jiàn 件

Ancient form

亻 (man) + 牛 (cow) = measure word for clothes

Catchphrase

In ancient times, people's CLOTHES were made from cowhide. They used this measure word 件 jiàn (MW) to count them. MW for clothes is 件 jiàn.

Stroke order

ノ	亻	亻	仁	仁	件

Radical/Component 攵 tools 教 TEACH jiāo; EDUCATE jiào 233

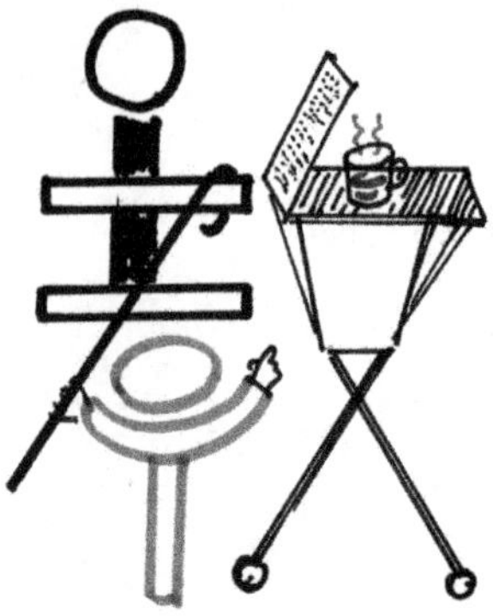

TEACH jiāo; **EDUCATE** jiào 教

Ancient form

(knowledge) + (children) + (tool) = teach/educate

Catchphrase

If you TEACH children with the right tools they will receive the best form of EDUCATION. TEACH is 教 jiāo. EDUCATE is 教 jiào.

Stroke order

一	十	土	耂	耂	考	孝	孝	孝	教	教

Radical/Component 人 person 介 INTRODUCE jiè 234

INTRODUCE jiè 介

Ancient form

个 (one person) + 个 (other person) = introduce

Catchphrase

Two people who have never met are being INTRODUCEd in a reception room. INTRODUCE is 介 jiè.

Stroke order

丿	人	介	介

Radical/Component 辶 walk 进（進）WALK FORWARD/ENTER jìn 235

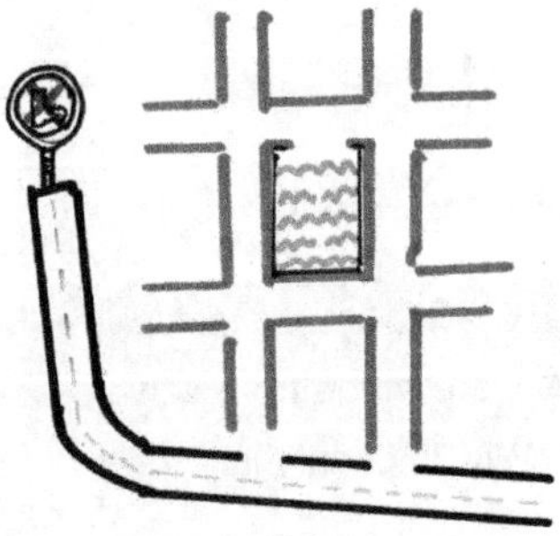

WALK FORWARD/ENTER jìn 进

Ancient form Traditional form 進

辶 (walk) + 井 (well) = walk forward/enter

Catchphrase

If you want to get water from the well, WALK FORWARD along the path and find the right place to ENTER. WALK FORWARD/ENTER is 进 jìn.

Stroke order

一	二	井	井	井	讲	进

Radical/Component 辶 walk 近 SHORTCUT/CLOSE jìn 236

SHORTCUT/CLOSE jìn 近

Ancient form

辶 (walk) + 斤 (axe) = close/shortcut

Catchphrase

Cut down the trees that are CLOSE to the road with an axe. That way, we can make a SHORTCUT. CLOSE/SHORTCUT is 近 jìn.

Stroke order

Radical/Component 纟 silk 经（經）PASS THROUGH jīng 237

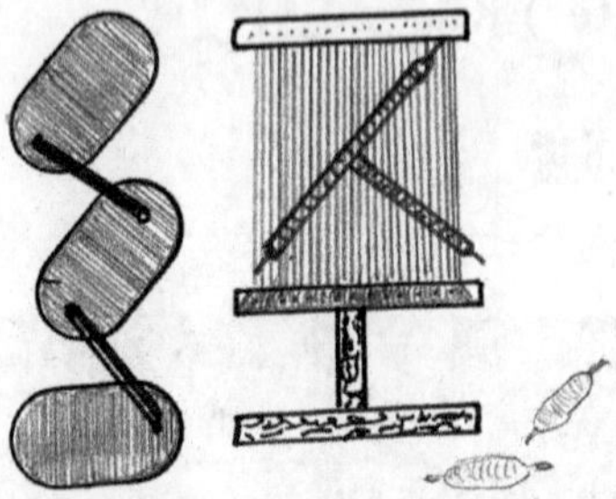

PASS THROUGH jīng 经

Ancient form Traditional form 經

纟 (silk) + 坙 (warps of a piece of fabric) = through

Catchphrase

The method of producing silk is to let the warp PASS THROUGH the weft. PASS THROUGH is 经 jīng.

Stroke order

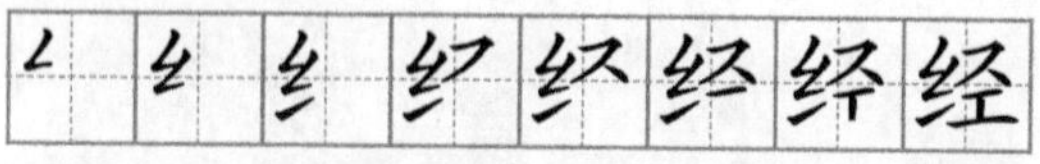

Radical/Component 目 eyes 睛 EYEBALL jīng 238

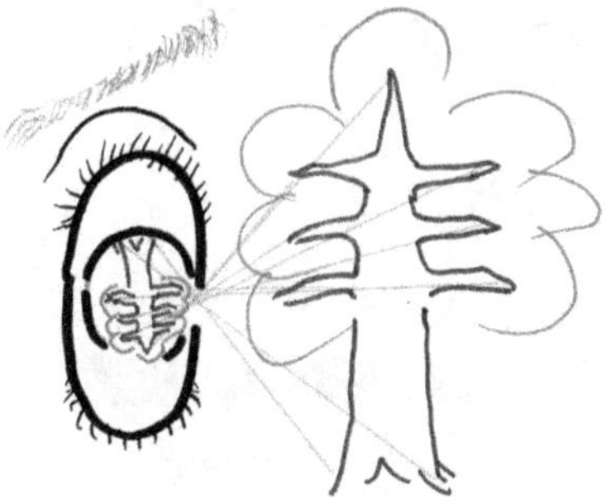

EYEBALL jīng 睛

Ancient form

目 (eye) + 青 (energy) = eyeball

Catchphrase

The EYEBALL reflects the image of a green tree upside down. EYEBALL is 睛 jīng.

Stroke order

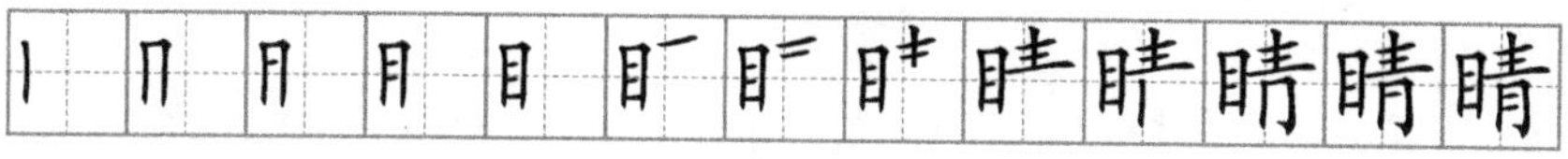

Radical/Component 尢 unusual 就 JUST/AS SOON AS jiù 239

JUST/AS SOON AS jiù 就

Ancient form

京 (tall building) + 尤 (special) = just/as soon as

Catchphrase

AS SOON AS they put a crane JUST next to the tall three-legged pavilion they were able to put a roof on it. Mission accomplished! JUST/AS SOON AS is 就 jiù.

Stroke order

丶	亠	亠	亠	亡	亨	亨	京	京	京	就	就

Radical/Component 口 (mouth) 咖 COFFEE (first character) kā 240

COFFEE (first character) kā 咖

Ancient form

口 (mouth) + 加 (strength+mouth) = coffee

Catchphrase

Strong COFFEE is so good that when you've had one mouthful you have to have another! COFFEE (first character) is 咖 kā.

Stroke order

丨	口	口	叨	叻	叻	咖	咖

Radical/Component 耂 / 考 old 考 TEST kǎo 241

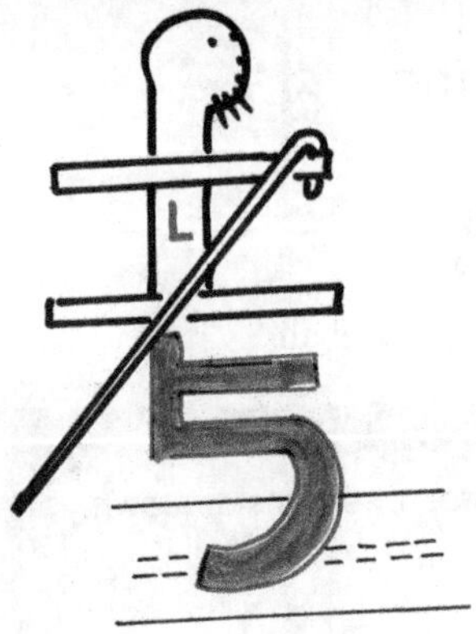

TEST kǎo 考

Ancient form

(bearded old man) + 丂 (test) = test

Catchphrase

This bearded old man has to pass a TEST before he can drive his wheelchair! TEST is 考 kǎo.

Stroke order

一	十	土	耂	耂	考

Radical/Component 口 mouth 可 BE ABLE TO kě 242

BE ABLE TO kě 可

Ancient form

shape + 口 (mouth) = be able to

Catchphrase

Open your mouth, otherwise you won't BE ABLE TO taste this delicious candy! BE ABLE TO is 可 kě.

Stroke order

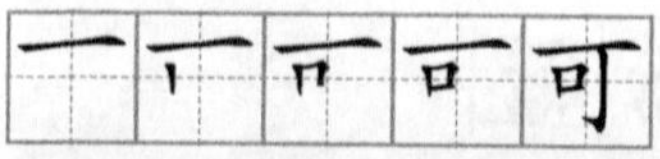

Radical/Component 讠 language 课（課）LESSON kè 243

LESSON kè 课

Ancient form Traditional form 課

讠 (language) + 果 (fruit) = lesson

Catchphrase

In ancient times, children were taught how to find food by giving them LESSONs in fruit tree recognition. LESSON is 课 kè.

Stroke order

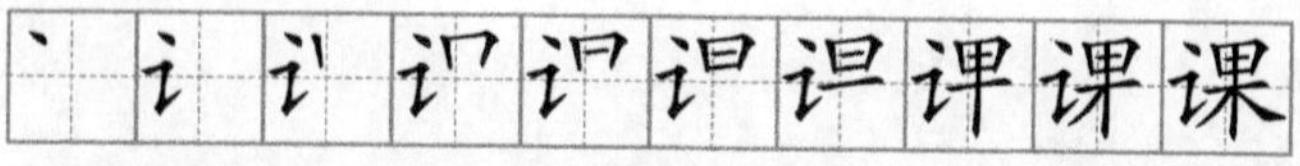

Radical/Component 忄 heart 快 FAST kuài 244

FAST kuài 快

Ancient form

忄 (heart) + (break) = fast

Catchphrase

Fundraising for the British Heart Foundation, this competitor ran so FAST that he broke the record! FAST is 快 kuài.

Stroke order

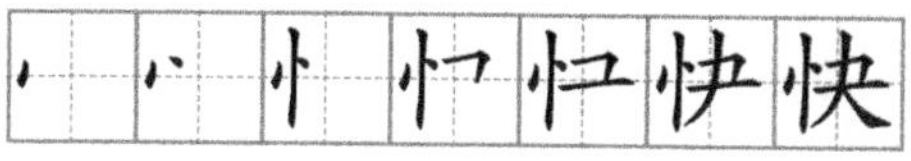

Radical/Component ⺮ bamboo 篮（籃）BASKET lán 245

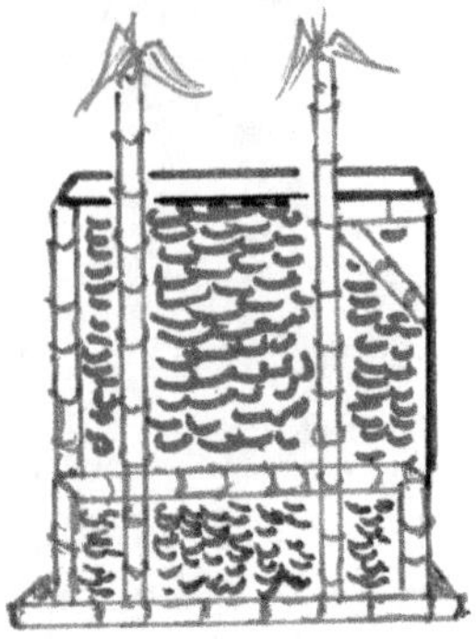

BASKET lán 篮

Ancient form Traditional form 籃

⺮ (bamboo) + 监 (hold/control/monitor) = basket

Catchphrase

In prison, the inmates have to make bamboo BASKETs. BASKET is 篮 lán.

Stroke order

ノ	⺊	⺮	⺮	⺮	⺮	𥫗	笁	笇	笓	笜	笩	筕	篮	篮	篮

Radical/Component 丿 downward stroke 乐（樂）HAPPY lè; MUSIC yuè 246

HAPPY lè; **MUSIC** yuè 乐

Ancient form Traditional form 樂

(drums) + (wooden rack) = music/happy

Catchphrase

Confucius said MUSIC is the real reason for happiness. HAPPY is 乐 lè ; MUSIC is 乐 yuè.

Stroke order

一	匚	乐	乐	乐

Radical/Component 田 farmland 累 TIRED lèi; PILE UP/ACCUMULATE lěi 247

TIRED lèi; **PILE UP/ACCUMULATE** lěi 累

Ancient form

田 (farmland) + 系 (spin silk) = tired

Catchphrase

Gathering food in the fields and spinning silk all day makes me TIRED! TIRED is 累 lèi; PILE UP/ACCUMULATE is 累 lěi.

Stroke order

丨	冂	冂	田	田	田	罒	罒	累	累	累

Radical/Component 亠 lid 离（離）LEAVE/AWAY FROM lí | 248

LEAVE/AWAY FROM lí 离

Ancient form Traditional form 離

(lid/roof) + (bird trap) = leave/away from

Catchphrase

LEAVE the building as soon as you can. It has a dangerous crack! LEAVE/AWAY FROM is 离 lí.

Stroke order

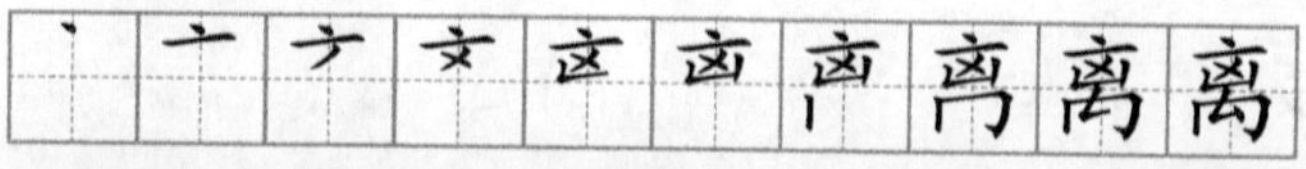

Radical/Component 一 one 两（兩）TWO liǎng | 249

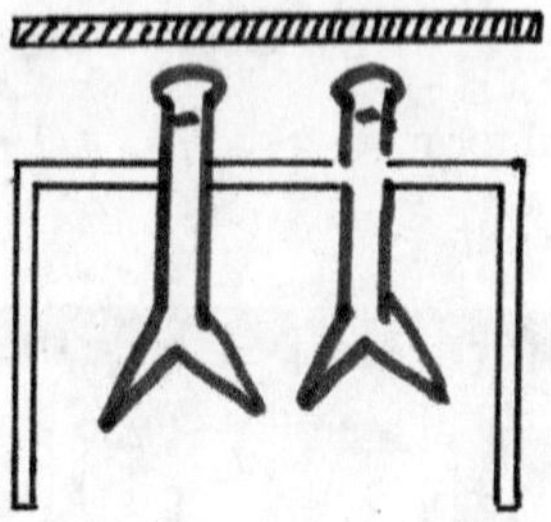

TWO liǎng 两

Ancient form Traditional form 兩

(divided room) + 从 (two people) = two

Catchphrase

The room has been divided in half so that TWO people can use it. TWO is 两 liǎng.

Stroke order

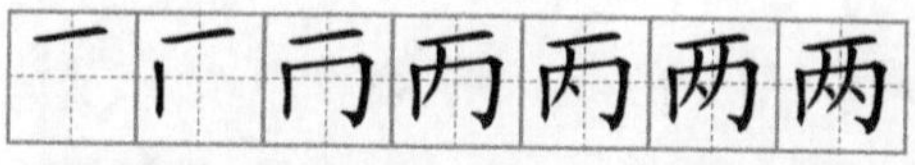

Radical/Component 足 foot 路 ROAD/PATH lù | 250

ROAD/PATH lù 路

Ancient form

足 (foot) + 各 (each) = road/path

Catchphrase

Each and every ROAD round here has a foot path so you can cross it. ROAD/PATH is 路 lù.

Stroke order

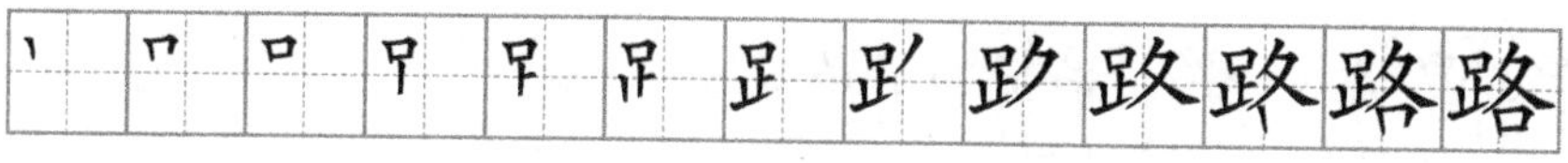

Radical/Component 方 square　旅 TRAVEL lǚ　251

TRAVEL lǚ 旅

Ancient form

(direction+flag) + (people) = travel

Catchphrase

Before you TRAVEL anywhere make sure you know which direction you need to go! TRAVEL is 旅 lǚ.

Stroke order

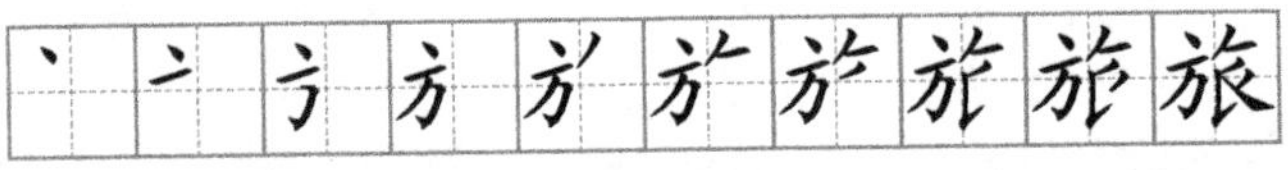

Radical/Component 十 ten　卖（賣）SELL mài　252

SELL mài 卖

Ancient form　Traditional form 賣

十 (ten) + 买 (buy) = sell

Catchphrase

You need a good head for business to SELL at a profit — try to earn at least 10%. SELL is 卖 mài.

Stroke order

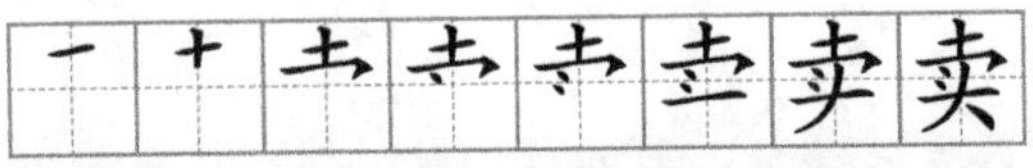

Radical/Component 忄 heart　慢 SLOW màn　253

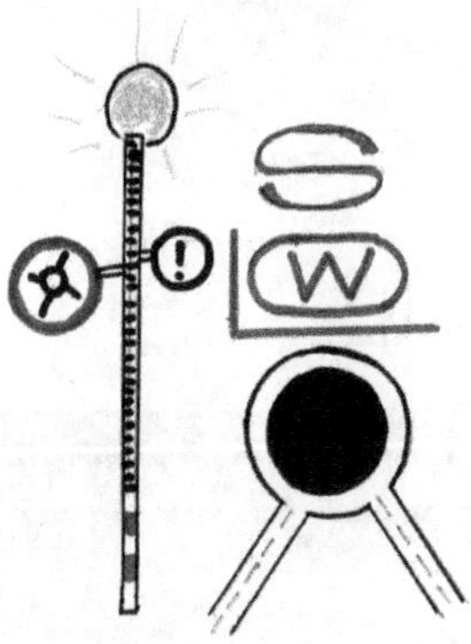

SLOW màn 慢

Ancient form

忄 (heart) + 曼 (creep/spread) = slow

Catchphrase

Is this a roundabout or a U-turn point? SLOW down first. SLOW is 慢 màn.

Stroke order

Radical/Component 忄 heart　忙 BUSY máng　254

BUSY máng 忙

Ancient form

(heart) + 亡 (death/escape) = busy

Catchphrase

Being too BUSY can lead to heart failure! BUSY is 忙 máng.

Stroke order

Radical/Component 母 mother　每 EACH měi　255

EACH měi 每

Ancient form

(hand) + 母 (breast/mother) = each

Catchphrase

The mother presses EACH of her two babies to her breasts to feed them. EACH is 每 měi.

Stroke order

Radical/Component 女 female　妹 YOUNGER SISTER mèi　256

YOUNGER SISTER mèi 妹

Ancient form

女 (female) + 未 (new branch/future) = younger sister

Catchphrase

A YOUNGER SISTER is like a new branch growing on the top of a family tree. YOUNGER SISTER is 妹 mèi.

Stroke order

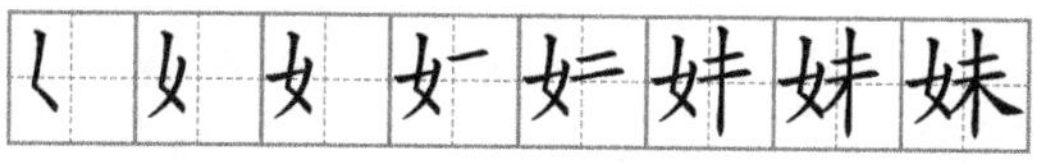

Radical/Component 门 gate　门（門）GATE/DOOR mén　257

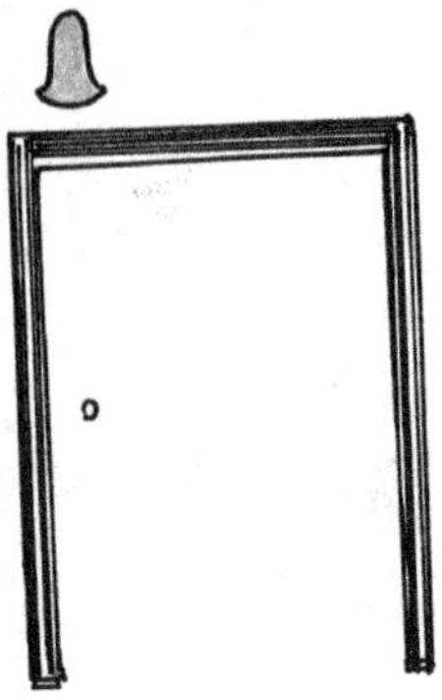

GATE/DOOR mén 门

Ancient form Traditional form 門

丶 (doorbell) + 冂 (door frame) = gate/door

Catchphrase

The DOOR is closed at the moment. If you want to come in, ring the bell. GATE/DOOR is 门 mén.

Stroke order

丶	丨	门

Radical/Component 女 female　奶 MILK/BREAST nǎi　258

MILK/BREAST nǎi 奶

Ancient form

女 (female) + 乃 (breasts) = milk/breast

Catchphrase

The right side of this character shows the shape of a woman's BREASTs, where MILK is produced. MILK is 奶 nǎi.

Stroke order

𡿨	女	女	奶	奶

Radical/Component 田 farmland　男 MAN nán　259

MAN nán 男

Ancient form

田 (farmland) + 力 (force) = man

Catchphrase

A strong MAN is working in the rice field. MAN is 男 nán.

Stroke order

丨	冂	日	田	田	男	男

Radical/Component 心 heart 您 YOU (respectful) nín 260

YOU (respectful) nín 您

Ancient form

你 (you) + 心 (heart) = you

Catchphrase

The young officer respectfully introduces YOU to his colleagues with heartfelt sincerity. YOU is 您 nín.

Stroke order

丿 亻 亻 亻 你 你 你 你 您 您 您

Radical/Component 牛 ox 牛 OX/COW niú 261

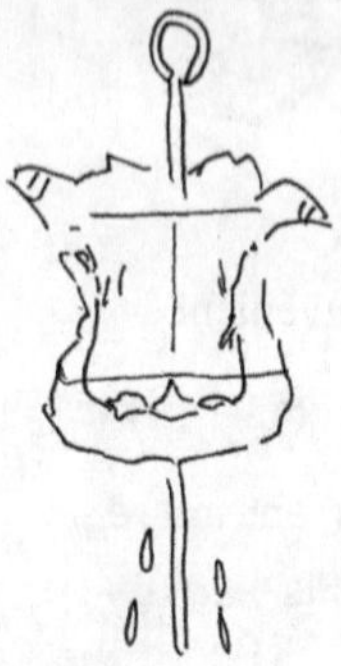

OX/COW niú 牛

Ancient form

Catchphrase

The head of a OX/COW is placed on a skewer to prepare it for cooking. OX/COW is 牛 niú.

Stroke order

丿 𠂉 𠂒 牛

Radical/Component 方 square 旁 SIDE páng 262

SIDE páng 旁

Ancient form

冂 (city gate) + 屮方 (chained criminal) = side

Catchphrase

In ancient times, criminals being led into the city could only get in through the SIDE gate! SIDE is 旁 páng.

Stroke order

丶 亠 亠 亠 产 产 产 产 旁 旁

Radical/Component 足 foot 跑 RUN pǎo 263

RUN pǎo 跑

Ancient form

足 (foot) + 包 (an unborn baby/energy inside) = run

Catchphrase

To RUN fast, our legs have to be propelled by a massive amount of energy. RUN is 跑 pǎo.

Stroke order

Radical/Component 亻 person 便 CHEAP pián; CONVENIENT biàn 264

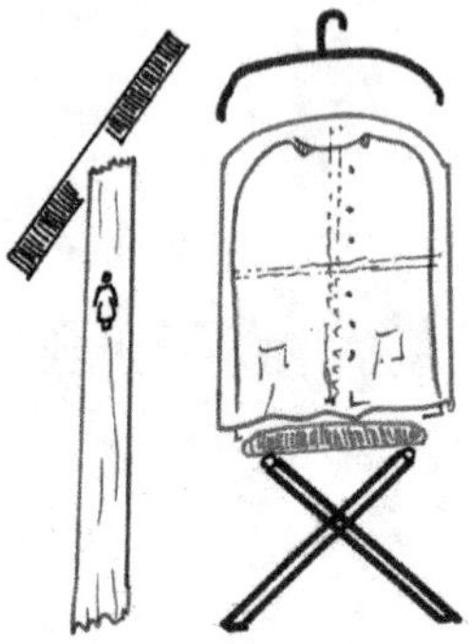

CHEAP pián; **CONVENIENT** biàn 便

Ancient form

亻(human) + 更 (change cloth) = cheap/convenient

Catchphrase

Buying clothes from small shops is even CHEAPer and more CONVENIENT than going to the big stores. CHEAP is 便 pián. CONVENIENT is 便 biàn.

Stroke order

Radical/Component 示 show 票 TICKET/BALLOT piào 265

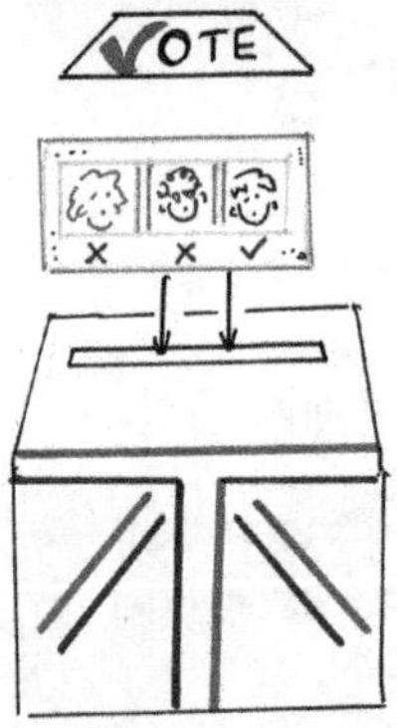

TICKET/BALLOT piào 票

Ancient form

西 (west) + 示 (show) = ticket/ballot

Catchphrase

In Western countries you must show your ID before you may cast a BALLOT. TICKET/BALLOT is 票 piào.

Stroke order

Radical/Component 女 female 妻 WIFE qī 266

WIFE qī 妻

Ancient form

(domestic tool) + 女 (female) = wife

Catchphrase

In most families, it is the WIFE who takes charge of the domestic tools. WIFE is 妻 qī.

Stroke order

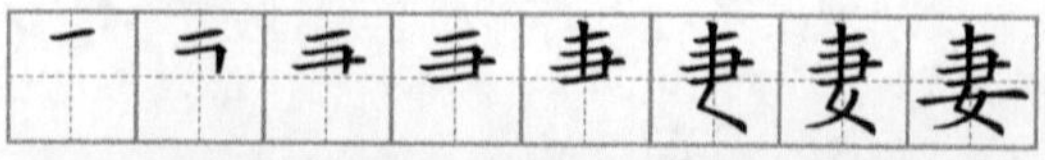

Radical/Component 氵 water 汽 VAPOUR/STEAM qì 267

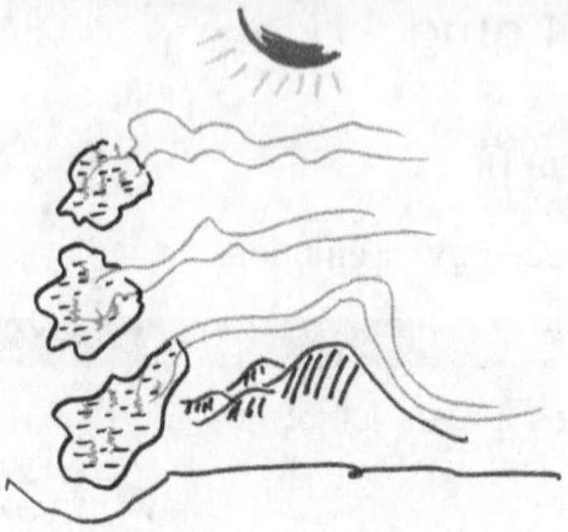

VAPOUR/STEAM qì 汽

Ancient form

氵 (water) + 气 (air) = vapour/steam

Catchphrase

When air absorbs water from lakes and seas, it becomes VAPOUR. VAPOUR/STEAM is 汽 qì.

Stroke order

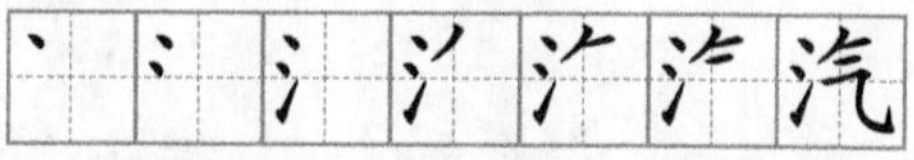

Radical/Component 十 ten 千 THOUSAND qiān 268

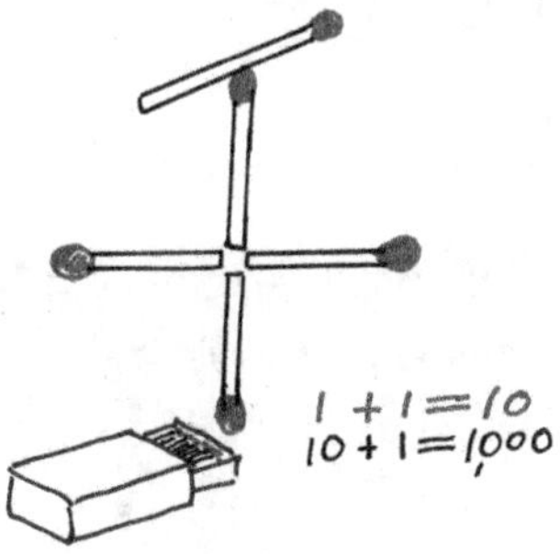

THOUSAND qiān 千

Ancient form

丿 + 十 (ten) = thousand

Catchphrase

Make ten into a THOUSAND just by adding a left-falling stroke on top. THOUSAND is 千 qiān.

Stroke order

Radical/Component 钅 metal 铅（鉛）LEAD qiān 269

LEAD qiān 铅

Ancient form Ttradition form 鉛

钅 (metal) + 㕣 (mountain cave) = lead

Catchphrase

LEAD is a metal which is often mined from mountain caves. LEAD is 铅 qiān.

Stroke order

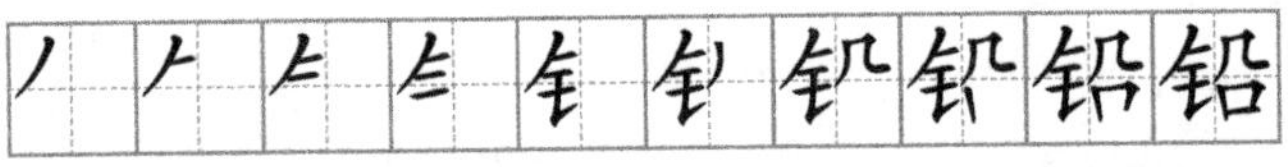

Radical/Component 忄 heart 情 EMOTION qíng 270

EMOTION qíng 情

Ancient form

忄 (heart) + 青 (green/energy) = emotion

Catchphrase

If your heart is still green, sometimes it feels full of EMOTION. EMOTION is 情 qíng.

Stroke order

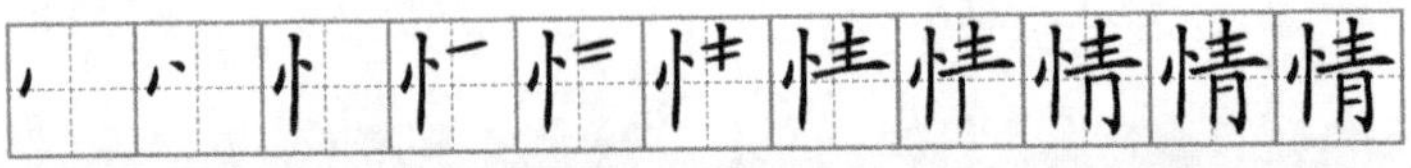

Radical/Component 日 sun 晴 CLEAR (weather) qíng 271

CLEAR (weather) qíng 晴

日 (sun) + 青 (green/energy) = sunny day

Catchphrase

If the weather is CLEAR, you can look out through your window and see the sun shining, giving energy to the trees and crops and turning them green. CLEAR (weather) is 晴 qíng.

Stroke order

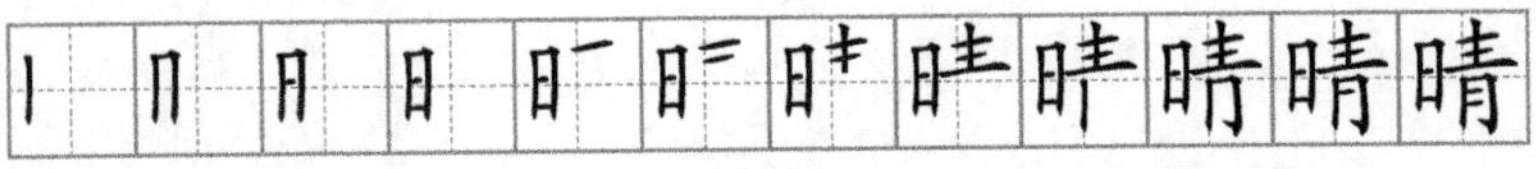

Radical/Component 王 jade 球 BALL qiú 272

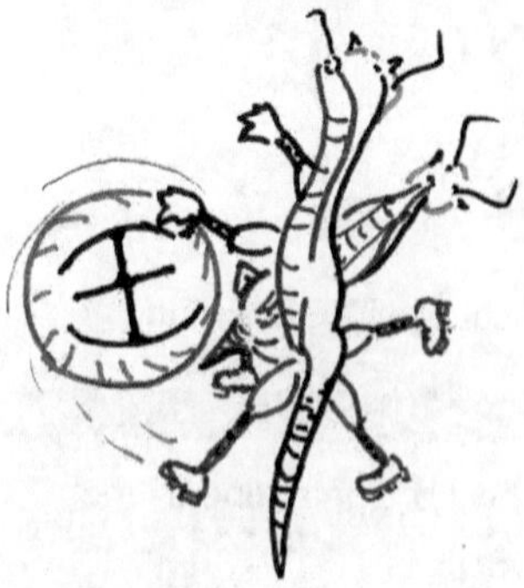

BALL qiú 球

Ancient form 球

玉 (jade) + 求 (catch) = ball

Catchphrase

The first Chinese ball game required the players to catch a BALL made of jade wrapped in leather. BALL is 球 qiú.

Stroke order

一	二	干	王	王一	玎	玎	玎	玤	球	球

Radical/Component 灬 fire 然 RIGHT rán 273

RIGHT rán 然

Ancient form 然

(barbecue) + 犬 (dog) + 灬 (fire) = right

Catchphrase

Get some meat on the barbecue, but be careful to cook it just RIGHT (and don't let the dog eat it!). RIGHT is 然 rán.

Stroke order

ノ	ク	夕	夕	夕一	夘	夶	肰	肰	然	然	然

Radical/Component 辶 walk/road 让（讓）GIVE WAY/ALLOW ràng 274

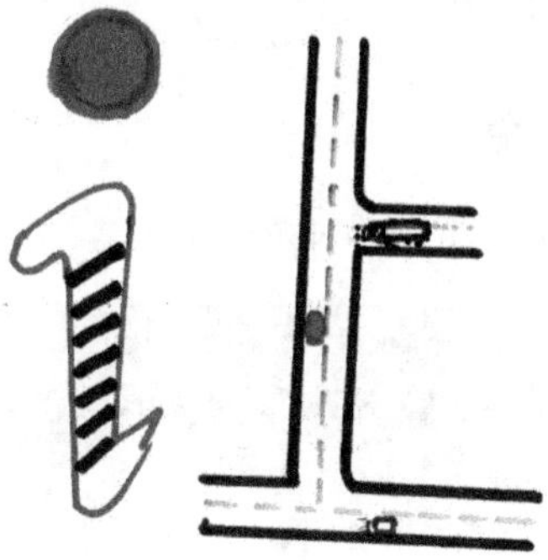

GIVE WAY/ALLOW ràng 让

Ancient form 讓 Traditional form 讓

讠(language) + 上 (above) = give way/allow

Catchphrase

This traffic signal instructs drivers to GIVE WAY. GIVE WAY/ALLOW is 让 ràng.

Stroke order

丶	讠	订	计	让

Radical/Component 日 sun 日 SUN rì 275

SUN rì 日

Ancient form

(the shape of sun) + (the indicator of HOT) = sun

Catchphrase

This character looks like the sun and the horizontal line in the middle indicates very high temperature. SUN is 日 rì.

Stroke order

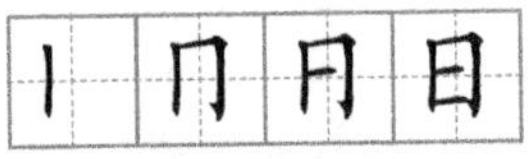

Radical/Component 肉 meat 肉 FLESH/MEAT ròu 276

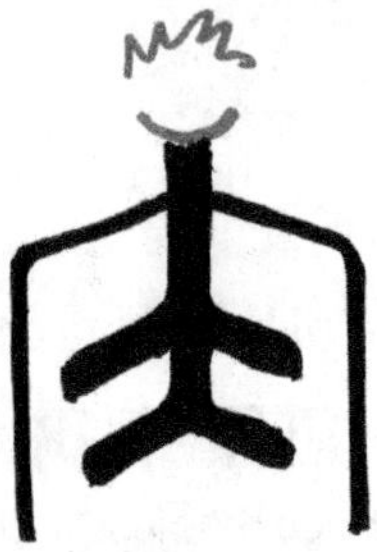

FLESH/MEAT ròu 肉

Ancient form

Catchphrase

In an X-ray, the body's FLESH is invisible and you can see the ribs. FLESH/MEAT is 肉 ròu.

Stroke order

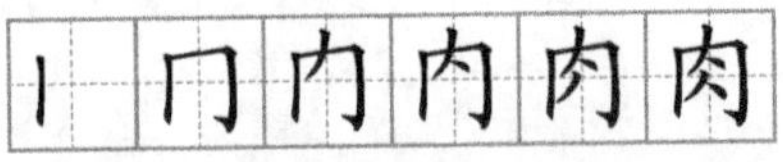

Radical/Component 色 colour 色 COLOUR sè 277

COLOUR sè 色

Ancient form

(person) + 巴 (snake's attraction) = sex/colour

Catchphrase

This lady has painted herself with different COLOURs to attract the opposite sex. COLOUR is 色 sè.

Stroke order

Radical/Component 纟 silk 绍（紹）CONTINUE/CARRY ON shào 278

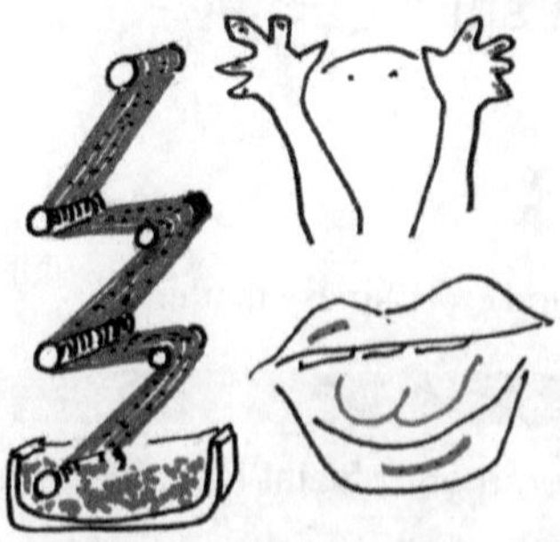

CONTINUE/CARRY ON shào 绍

Ancient form 紹 Traditional form 紹

纟 (silk) + 召 (call/beckon) = continue/carry on

Catchphrase

This man is making colourful silks and waving his arms to beckon you to CONTINUE or CARRY ON his business. CONTINUE/CARRY ON is 绍 shào.

Stroke order

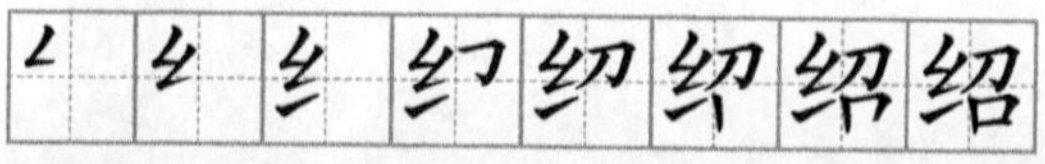

Radical/Component 身 body 身 BODY/PREGNANT shēn 279

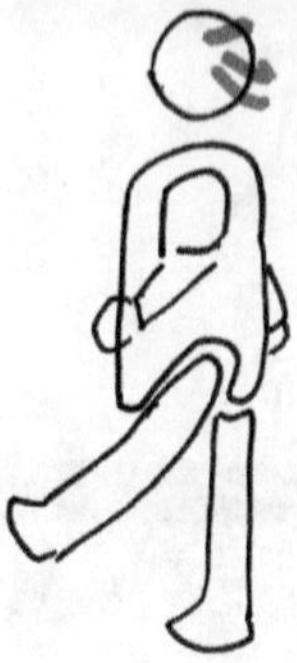

BODY/PREGNANT shēn 身

Ancient form

(pregnant) + (unborn baby) = body/pregnant

Catchphrase

When you're PREGNANT, you should keep your BODY straight, and walk every day. BODY/PREGNANT is 身 shēn.

Stroke order

Radical/Component 女 female 始 START shǐ 280

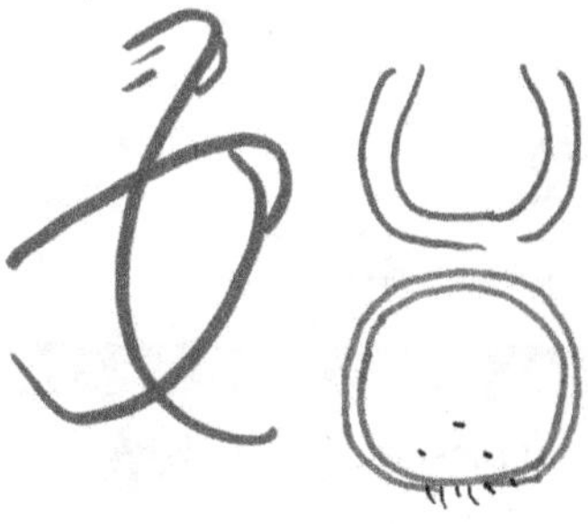

START shǐ 始

Ancient form

女 (woman) + 台 (platform/private and baby) = start

Catchphrase

A mother has just given birth to a baby, and a new life STARTs. START is 始 shǐ.

Stroke order

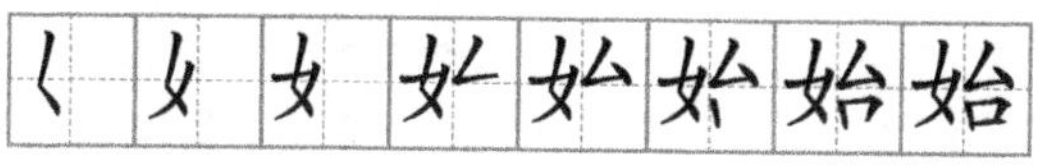

Radical/Component 亅 hook 事 BUSINESS/MATTER shì 281

BUSINESS/MATTER shì 事

Ancient form

口 (mouth) + (stand) + (hand) = business/matter

Catchphrase

The day-to-day BUSINESS of a government official includes processing a lot of documents by hand. BUSINESS/MATTER is 事 shì.

Stroke order

Radical/Component 讠 language 试（試）TEST/EXAM shì 282

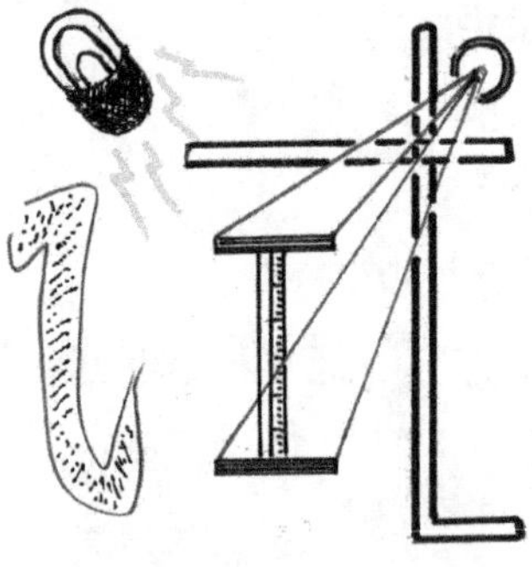

TEST/EXAM shì 试

Ancient form Traditional form 試

讠(speech) + 式 (form/model) = test/exam

Catchphrase

Spoken form is the best way to TEST this model. TEST/EXAM is 试 shì.

Stroke order

Radical/Component 宀 roof 室 ROOM shì 283

ROOM shì 室

Ancient form

宀 (roof) + 至 (bird reaching nest/arrive) = room

Catchphrase

There is ROOM for birds on the roof and inside. ROOM is 室 shì.

Stroke order

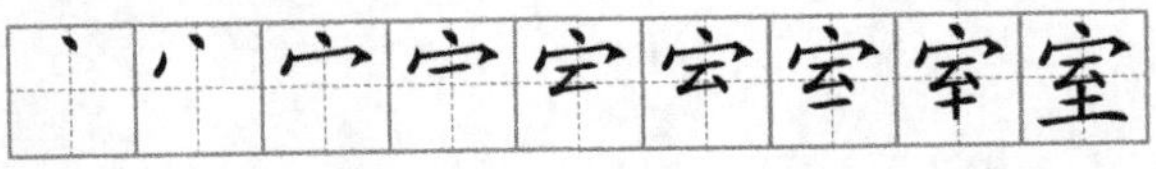

Radical/Component 手 / 扌 hand　手 HAND shǒu　284

HAND shǒu 手

Ancient form

Catchphrase

There are five fingers on each HAND. HAND is 手 shǒu.

Stroke order

一	二	三	手

Radical/Component 口 mouth　司 TAKE CHARGE OF sī　285

TAKE CHARGE OF sī 司

Ancient form

(support) + (mouth) = take charge of

Catchphrase

I'll TAKE CHARGE OF the cooking – the best way is to hang the pot from a horizontal pole. TAKE CHARGE OF is 司 sī.

Stroke order

𠃌	𠃌	司	司	司

Radical/Component 心 heart　思 THINK sī　286

THINK sī 思

Ancient form

囟 / 田 (brain) + 心 (heart) = think

Catchphrase

When THINKing, people often use both their brain and heart. THINK is 思 sī.

Stroke order

丨	冂	冃	用	田	田	思	思	思

Radical/Component 辶 walk 送 SEE OFF/GIVE sòng 287

SEE OFF/GIVE sòng 送

Ancient form

辶 (walk) + 关 (use both hands to close) = see off/give

Catchphrase

When you SEE OFF a visitor, close the door safely before you leave. SEE OFF/GIVE is 送 sòng.

Stroke order

丶	丷	䒑	兰	关	关	关	送	送

Radical/Component 讠 language 诉（訴）TELL/ACCUSE sù 288

TELL/ACCUSE sù 诉

Ancient form Traditional form 訴

讠(speech) + 斥 (condemn) = tell/accuse

Catchphrase

In court, when a prosecutor TELLs the jury about the case, he must use strong words to condemn the ACCUSEd. TELL/ACCUSE is 诉 sù.

Stroke order

丶	讠	讠	订	䜣	䜣	诉

Radical/Component 虫 insect 虽（雖）ALTHOUGH suī 289

ALTHOUGH suī 虽

Ancient form Traditional form 雖

(insect/reptile) + = although

Catchphrase

ALTHOUGH I am a spider, I am also a caring mother. ALTHOUGH is 虽 suī.

Stroke order

丨	冂	口	口	吕	吕	吊	虽	虽

Radical/Component 戶 / 户 door 所 HUT/MW suǒ 290

HUT/MW suǒ 所

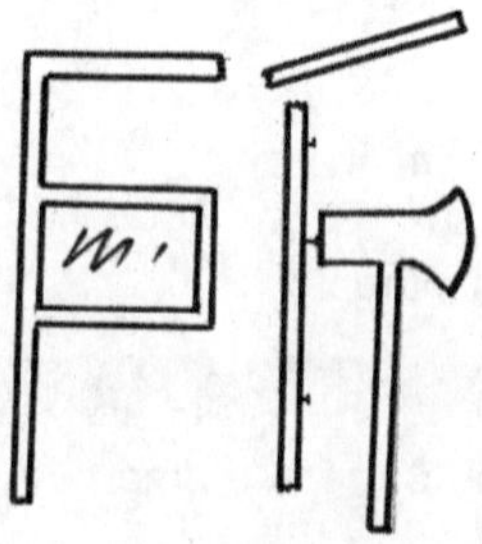

Ancient form

户 (door) + 斤 (axe) = hut/MW (for building)

Catchphrase

Although there is only one window of the HUT, it was built with a single axe. HUT/MW (for building) is 所 suǒ.

Stroke order

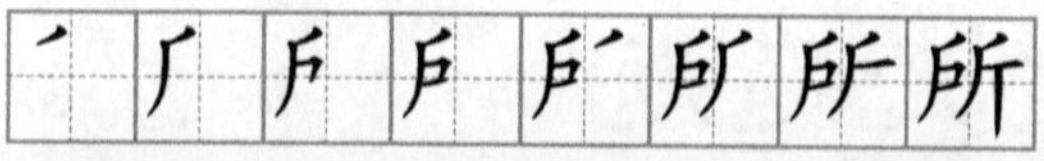

Radical/Component 宀 roof 它 IT tā 291

IT tā 它

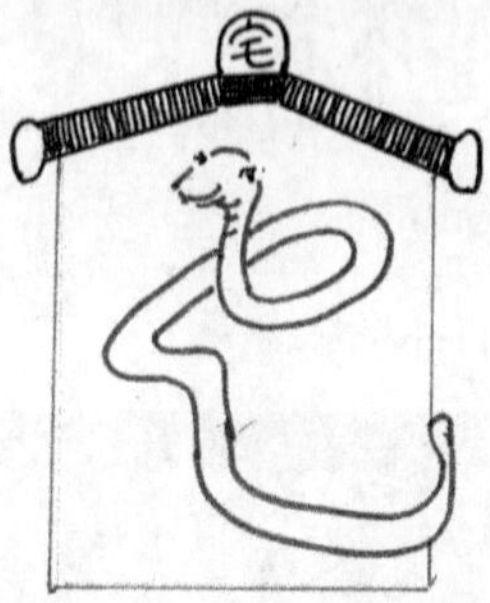

Ancient form

宀 (roof) + 匕 (knife/snake) = it

Catchphrase

Look, IT's a nice property. I am a snake, and the house owner. IT is 它 tā.

Stroke order

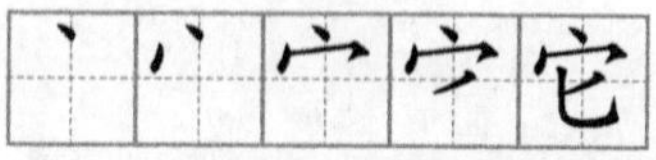

Radical/Component 足 foot 踢 KICK tī 292

KICK tī 踢

Ancient form

足 (foot) + 易 (exchange) = kick

Catchphrase

Switch the ball to your right foot and KICK it through the goal. KICK is 踢 tī.

Stroke order

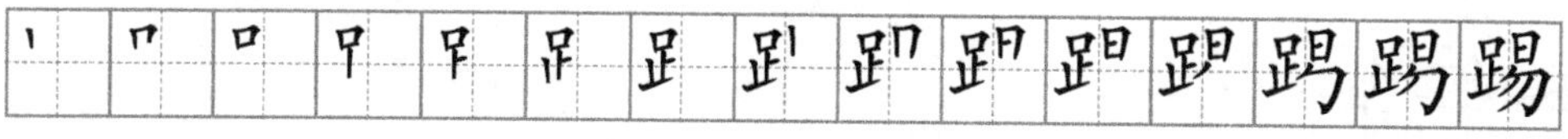

Radical/Component 页 page/head 题（題）SUBJECT/TOPIC tí 293

SUBJECT/TOPIC tí 题

Ancient form Traditional form 題

是 (to be) + 页 (head) = subject/topic

Catchphrase

"To be or not to be" is a tricky SUBJECT that needs a smart head to ponder. SUBJECT/TOPIC is 题 tí.

Stroke order

丨	冂	日	日	旦	早	早	是	是	是	是	是	题	题	题

Radical/Component 亻 person 体（體）BODY tǐ 294

BODY tǐ 体

Ancient form Traditional form 體

亻 (person) + 本 (base/root) = body

Catchphrase

The most basic need for a person is a healthy BODY. BODY is 体 tǐ.

Stroke order

丿	亻	仁	什	什	休	体

Radical/Component 木 wood 条（條）TWIG/MW tiáo 295

TWIG/MW tiáo 条

Ancient form Traditional form 條

攵 (tool) + 木 (tree) = twig/MW

Catchphrase

When some branches of a tree are sick, cut them off and weave the TWIGs into baskets. TWIG/MW (long thin items) is 条 tiáo.

Stroke order

丿	夕	夂	冬	夅	条	条

Radical/Component 足 foot 跳 JUMP/DANCE tiào 296

JUMP/DANCE tiào 跳

Ancient form

足 (foot) + 兆 (omen) = jump/dance

Catchphrase

The special DANCE instructor says, "Are you ready? JUMP!" JUMP/DANCE is 跳 tiào.

Stroke order

丨	㇆	口	早	早	𧾷	足	𧾷	𧾷	𧾷	跳	跳	跳

Radical/Component 夕 evening 外 OUTSIDE wài 297

OUTSIDE wài 外

Ancient form

夕 (evening) + 卜 (pray) = outside

Catchphrase

In rural communities, evening prayers take place OUTSIDE amidst nature. OUTSIDE is 外 wài.

Stroke order

ノ	ク	夕	外	外

Radical/Component 宀 roof 完 COMPLETE/FINISH wán 298

COMPLETE/FINISH wán 完

Ancient form

宀 (roof) + 二 (male & female) + 儿 (children) = complete/finish

Catchphrase

A loving couple who have children and live in a nice house enjoy a COMPLETE lifestyle. COMPLETE/FINISH is 完 wán.

Stroke order

丶	丶丶	宀	宀	宇	宇	完

Radical/Component 王 jade 玩 PLAY wán 299

PLAY wán 玩

Ancient form

王 (jade) + 元 (unit/element/currency) = play

Catchphrase

The jade mahjong pieces are used as four players PLAY for money. PLAY is 玩 wán.

Stroke order

Radical/Component 日 sun 晚 EVENING/LATE wǎn 300

EVENING/LATE wǎn 晚

Ancient form

日 (sun) + 免 (free/without) = evening/late

Catchphrase

Raise your hat to say goodbye to the sun and welcome the EVENING. EVENING/LATE is 晚 wǎn.

Stroke order

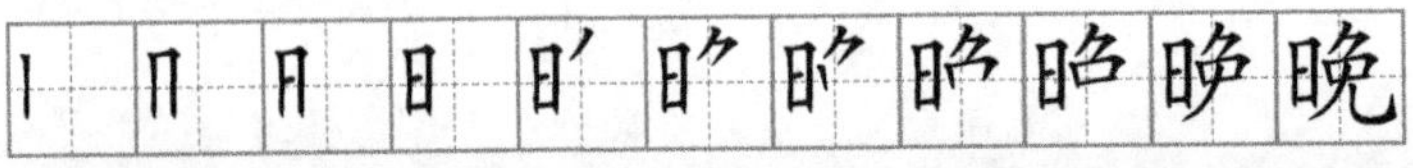

Radical/Component 彳 step 往 TOWARDS wǎng 301

TOWARDS wǎng 往

Ancient form

彳 (road) + 主 (king/master) = towards

Catchphrase

All the roads in the city lead TOWARDS the king's palace. TOWARDS is 往 wǎng.

Stroke order

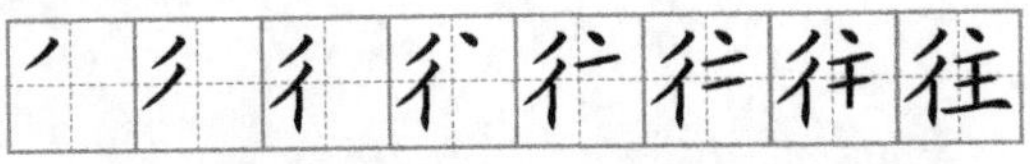

Radical/Component 王 jade 望 LOOK AT wàng 302

LOOK AT wàng 望

Ancient form

(person looks at the moon) + (hill) = look at

Catchphrase

In ancient China, it was said that anyone who found themselves far from their hometown could simply LOOK AT the moon to feel they are in touch with their family. LOOK AT is 望 wàng.

Stroke order

Radical/Component 丶 dot 为（為）FOR wèi; ACT AS/BECAUSE OF wéi 303

FOR wèi; ACT AS/BECAUSE OF wéi 为

Ancient form Traditional form 為

Catchphrase

This strongman holds one stone ball on to his shoulder and holds the other in the crook of his arm. But what FOR? FOR is 为 wèi; ACT AS/BECAUSE OF is 为 wéi.

Stroke order

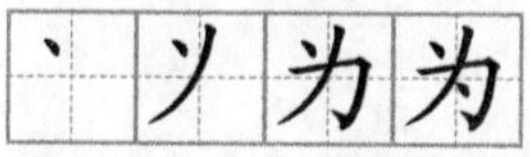

Radical/Component 口 mouth 问（問）ASK wèn 304

ASK wèn 问

Ancient form Traditional form 問

门 (door) + 口 (mouth) = ask/question

Catchphrase

Knock on the door first, if you want to ASK the house owner a question. ASK is 问 wèn.

Stroke order

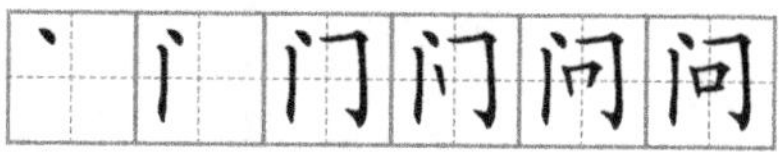

Radical/Component 舛 opposing foot　舞 DANCE wǔ　305

DANCE wǔ 舞

Ancient form

(dancing bodies) + (opposing foot) = dance

Catchphrase

A line of performers link hands and DANCE opposite their partners. DANCE is 舞 wǔ.

Stroke order

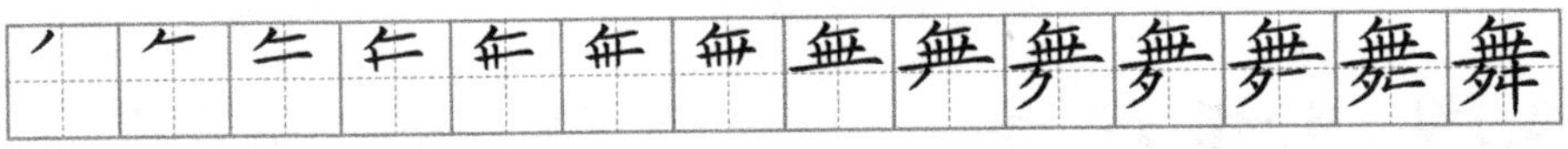

Radical/Component 力 force　务（務）MATTER/TASK wù　306

MATTER/TASK wù 务

Ancient form　Traditional form 務

文 (tools) + 力 (force/energy) = matter/task

Catchphrase

When travelling on an official MATTER you should take all the tools you need in a strong case. MATTER/TASK is 务 wù.

Stroke order

Radical/Component 巾 cloth/scarf　希 HOPE xī　307

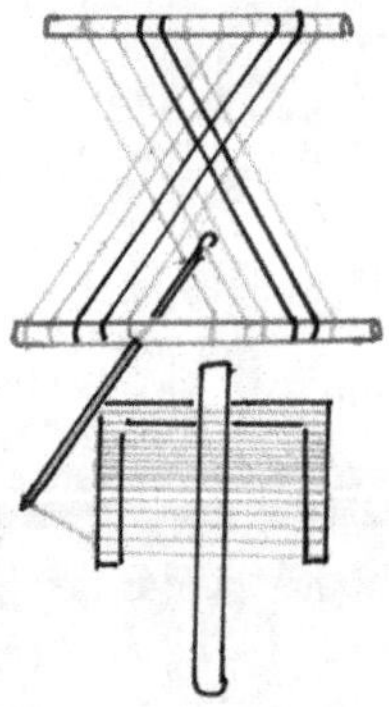

HOPE xī 希

Ancient form

(loom) + 布 (cloth) = hope

Catchphrase

All weavers HOPE the clothes they make on their simple loom will sell well. HOPE is 希 xī.

Stroke order

Radical/Component 心 heart 息 REST xī 308

REST xī 息

Ancient form

自 (oneself) + 心 (heart) = rest

Catchphrase

You can only REST easy when you have self-mastery over your own heart. REST is 息 xī.

Stroke order

丿 亻 冂 白 白 自 自 息 息 息

Radical/Component 氵 water 洗 WASH xǐ 309

WASH xǐ 洗

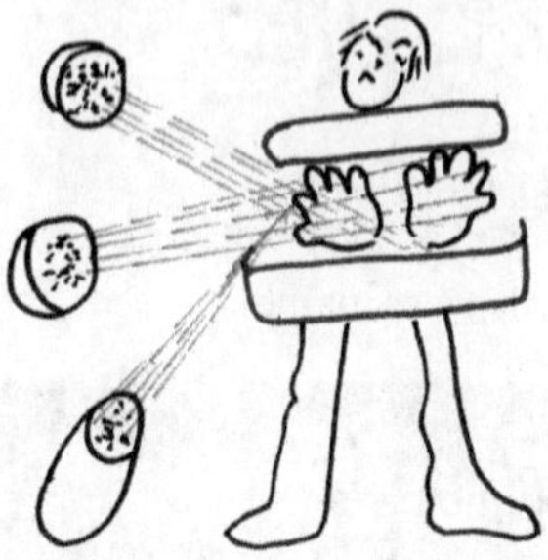

Ancient form

氵 (water) + 先 (first/before) = wash

Catchphrase

The first thing you must do before eating is to WASH your hands. WASH is 洗 xǐ.

Stroke order

丶 冫 氵 氵 汁 汁 泩 涉 洗

Radical/Component ⺮ bamboo 笑 LAUGH xiào 310

LAUGH xiào 笑

Ancient form

⺮ (laughing eyes)+ 夭 (body posture) = laugh

Catchphrase

This character seems to LAUGH with its eyes and body. LAUGH is 笑 xiào.

Stroke order

丿 𠂉 𠂉 𠂉 ⺮ ⺮ 竺 竺 笑 笑

Radical/Component 斤 axe 新 NEW xīn 311

NEW xīn 新

Ancient form

立 (new leaves) + 木 (tree) + 斤 (axe) = new

Catchphrase

When NEW leaves sprout from a young tree, it is important to tend it very carefully. NEW is 新 xīn.

Stroke order

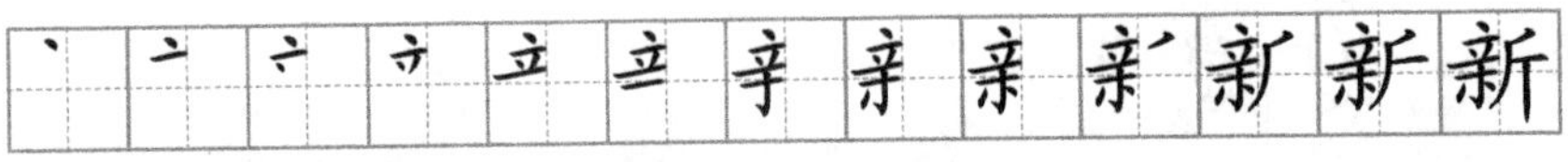

Radical/Component 女 woman 姓 SURNAME xìng 312

SURNAME xìng 姓

Ancient form

女 (woman) + 生 (give birth) = surname

Catchphrase

In ancient times, children were given their mother's SURNAME because she was the only parent they knew. SURNAME is 姓 xìng.

Stroke order

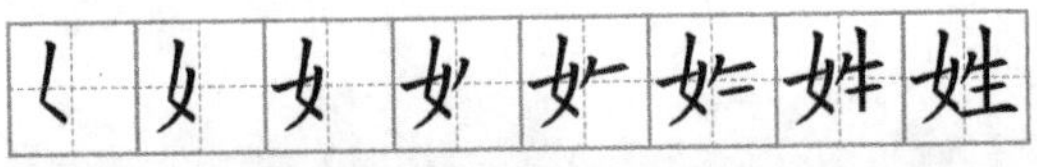

Radical/Component 亻 person 休 STOP/REST xiū 313

STOP/REST xiū 休

Ancient form

亻 (person) + 木 (tree) = stop/rest

Catchphrase

When a person feels tired, it's good to STOP what he is doing and REST against a shady tree. STOP/REST is 休 xiū.

Stroke order

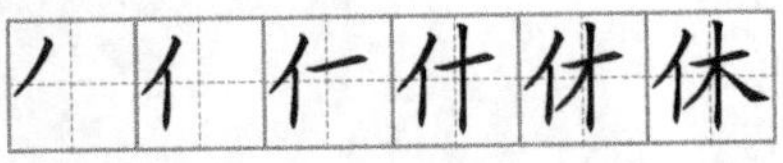

Radical/Component 雨 rain 雪 SNOW xuě 314

SNOW xuě 雪

Ancient form

雨 (cloudy sky/rain) + ⺕ (snowflakes & dustpan) = snow

Catchphrase

The SNOW may look very beautiful, but it is safer to sweep it away into the dustpan. SNOW is 雪 xuě.

Stroke order

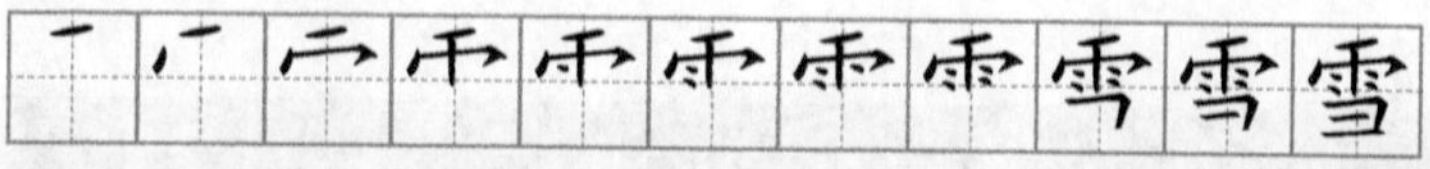

Radical/Component 页 page 颜（顏）COLOUR/FACE yán 315

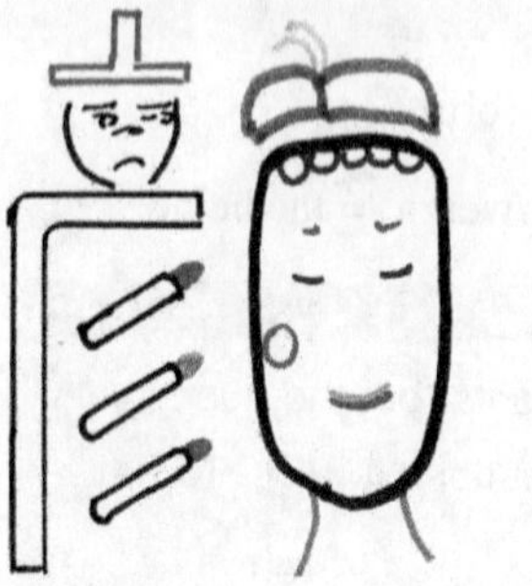

COLOUR/FACE yán 颜

Ancient form Traditional form 顏

彦 (morally good) + 页 (hair and face) = colour/face

Catchphrase

"Tell me," the young lady asks, "which of these three COLOURs make my FACE the prettiest?" COLOUR/FACE is 颜 yán.

Stroke order

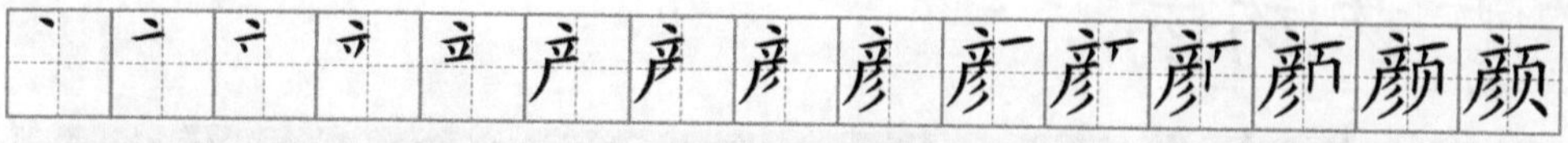

Radical/Component 目 eye 眼 EYE yǎn 316

EYE yǎn 眼

Ancient form

目 (eyeball) + 艮 (relative element) = eye

Catchphrase

The EYE on the left opens much wider than the eye on the right. EYE is 眼 yǎn.

Stroke order

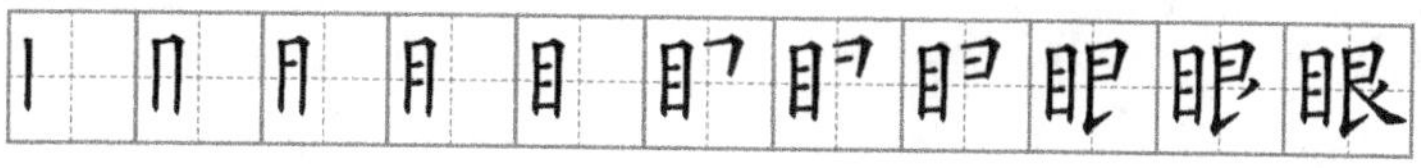

Radical/Component ⺷ sheep　羊 RAM/SHEEP yáng　317

RAM/SHEEP yáng　羊

Ancient form

Catchphrase

This character looks like the head of a smartly dressed RAM. RAM/SHEEP is 羊 yáng.

Stroke order

丶	丷	䒑	兰	兰	羊

Radical/Component ⺾ grass　药（藥）MEDICINE yào　318

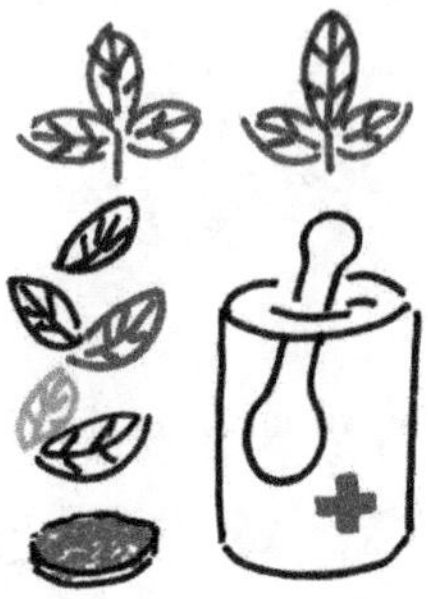

MEDICINE yào　药

Ancient form　Traditional form 藥

艹 (grass) + 纟 (silk)+ 勺 (spoon/weigh) = medicine

Catchphrase

Most Chinese MEDICINE is made from plants, but the quantity must be carefully weighed to get the correct dose. MEDICINE is 药 yào.

Stroke order

一	十	艹	艹	艺	艺	药	药	药

Radical/Component 西 west　要 WANT yào　319

WANT yào　要

Ancient form

西 (west; hands on waist) + 女 (standing woman) = want

Catchphrase

In the West, many young women WANT to become ballet dancers. WANT is 要 yào.

Stroke order

一	冂	冂	襾	襾	西	要	要	要

Radical/Component ⺃ second　也 ALSO yě　320

ALSO yě　也

Ancient form 

Catchphrase

I am a snake and I ALSO protect the environment. ALSO is 也 yě.

Stroke order

㇆	𠆢	也

Radical/Component 宀 roof　宜 SUITABLE yí　321

SUITABLE yí　宜

Ancient form 

宀 (house roof) + 且 (add something) = suitable

Catchphrase

This fridge has three compartments, so it is SUITABLE for all households. SUITABLE is 宜 yí.

Stroke order

丶	丶丶	宀	宁	宂	宜	宜	宜

Radical/Component 已 oneself　已 ALREADY yǐ　322

ALREADY yǐ　已

Ancient form 

Catchphrase

There's no chance of catching me now because I've ALREADY reached the finish line. ALREADY is 已 yǐ.

Stroke order

㇆	コ	已

Radical/Component 人 person 以 USE/BY MEANS OF yǐ 323

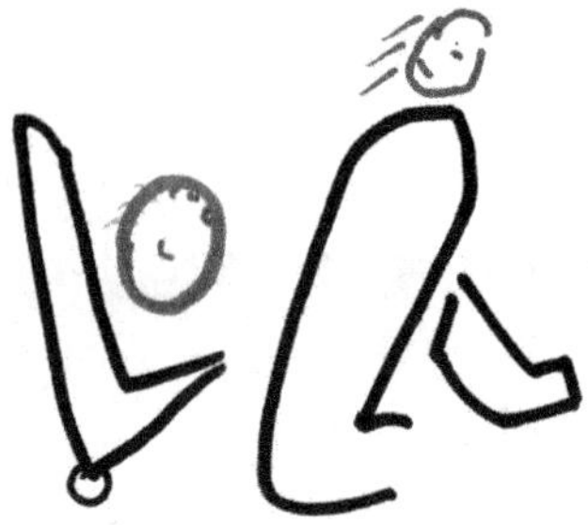

USE/BY MEANS OF yǐ 以

Ancient form

(basket/baby) + 人 (person) = use/by means of

Catchphrase

This person carries a baby about BY MEANS OF a small basket on their back. USE/BY MEANS OF is 以 yǐ.

Stroke order

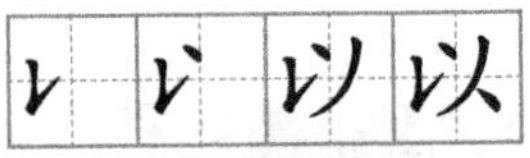

Radical/Component 心 heart 意 MEANING/IDEA yì 324

MEANING/IDEA yì 意

Ancient form

音 (sound) + 心 (heart/mind) = meaning/idea

Catchphrase

When you speak from your heart, you can use the sound of your voice to make your MEANING clear. MEANING/IDEA is 意 yì.

Stroke order

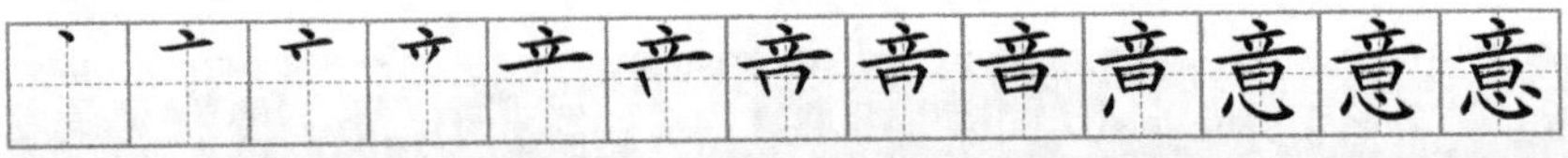

Radical/Component 囗 enclosure 因 REASON yīn 325

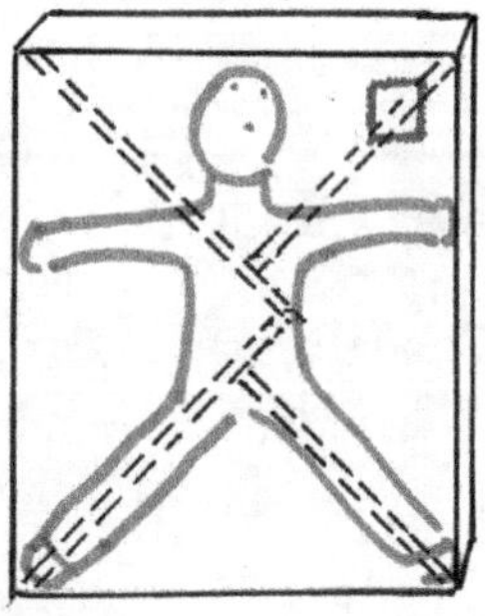

REASON yīn 因

Ancient form

口 (box) + 大 (adult) = reason

Catchphrase

What could be the REASON for enclosing this large person inside a box? REASON is 因 yīn.

Stroke order

Radical/Component 阝 cliff 阴（陰）NEGATIVE/CLOUDY yīn 326

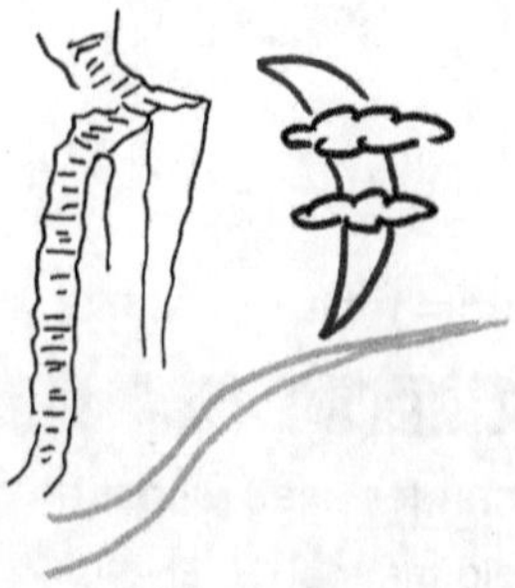

NEGATIVE/CLOUDY yīn 阴

Ancient form Traditional form 陰

阝 (cliff/step) + 月 (crescent) = negative/cloudy

Catchphrase

Clouds hide the moon, making it hard to see the cliff steps... it's enough to give anyone a NEGATIVE feeling! NEGATIVE/CLOUDY is 阴 yīn.

Stroke order

㇋	阝	阝丿	阴	阴	阴

Radical/Component 氵 water 泳 SWIM yǒng 327

SWIM yǒng 泳

Ancient form

氵 (river) + 永 (swim in river; ever) = swim

Catchphrase

Many lizards like water. This one SWIMs in a river. SWIM is 泳 yǒng.

Stroke order

丶	冫	氵	氵丶	氵㇇	氵永	泳	泳

Radical/Component 氵 water 游（遊）TRAVEL yóu 328

TRAVEL yóu 游

Ancient form Traditioual form 遊

氵 (river) + (traveller) = travel

Catchphrase

If you TRAVEL by river, it is easiest to go in the same direction as the water flows. TRAVEL is 游 yóu.

Stroke order

丶	冫	氵	氵丶	氵亠	汸	汸	浙	浙	游	游	游

Radical/Component 口 mouth 右 RIGHT yòu 329

RIGHT yòu 右

Ancient form

(arm & hand) + 口 (mouth) = right

Catchphrase

In general, the RIGHT hand is the commander even without eyes, and the left hand is an assistant to hold the tool. RIGHT is 右 yòu.

Stroke order

Radical/Component 鱼 fish 鱼（魚）FISH yú 330

FISH yú 鱼

Ancient form Traditional form 魚

Catchphrase

This FISH has just jumped out of the river. FISH is 鱼 yú.

Stroke order

Radical/Component 口 mouth 员（員）STAFF/MEMBER yuán 331

STAFF/MEMBER yuán 员

Ancient form Traditional form 員

口 (month) + 贝 (money) = staff/member

Catchphrase

Each individual MEMBER of STAFF should contribute his own skills to help the company make money. STAFF/MEMBER is 员 yuán.

Stroke order

Radical/Component 辶 walk 远（遠）FAR yuǎn 332

FAR yuǎn 远

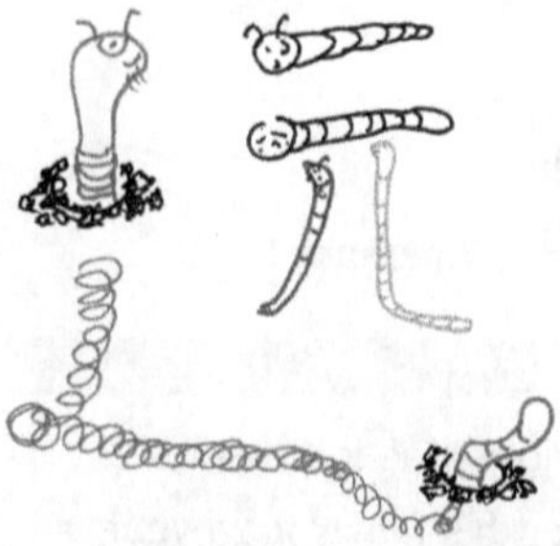

Ancient form Traditional form 遠

辶 (walk) + 元 (first/basic) = far

Catchphrase

Laozi, the founder of Daoism, said, "A thousand miles may seem too FAR to walk, but the longest journey begins with the first step." FAR is 远 yuǎn.

Stroke order

Radical/Component 辶 walk 运（運）MOVE/LUCK yùn 333

MOVE/LUCK yùn 运

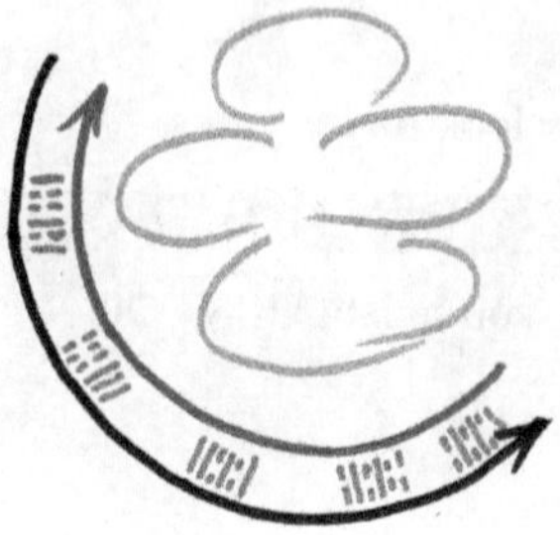

Ancient form Traditional form 運

辶 (walk) + 云 (cloud) = move/luck

Catchphrase

The MOVEment of clouds can predict the future — is good or bad LUCK coming your way? MOVE/LUCK is 运 yùn.

Stroke order

Radical/Component 日 sun 早 MORNING zǎo 334

MORNING zǎo 早

Ancient form

日 (sun) + 十 (grass) = morning

Catchphrase

When the sun rises above the horizon in the MORNING, it begins to warm this tiny grass. MORNING is 早 zǎo.

Stroke order

Radical/Component 一 one 丈 HUSBAND/MEASURE zhàng 335

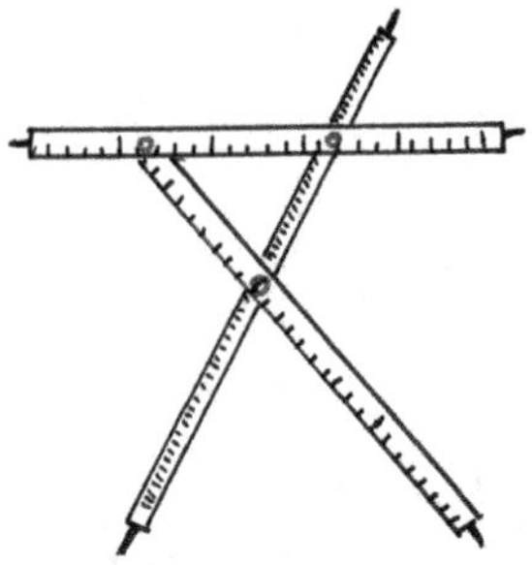

HUSBAND/MEASURE zhàng 丈

Ancient form 

 (stake) +  (hand) = husband/measure

Catchphrase

In ancient times, one of the HUSBAND's jobs was to MEASURE out a plot of farmland which would support his family for a year. HUSBAND/MEASURE is 丈 zhàng.

Stroke order

一 ナ 丈

Radical/Component 扌 hand 找 LOOK FOR zhǎo 336

LOOK FOR zhǎo 找

扌 (hand) + 戈 (weapon) = look for

Catchphrase

If you're empty-handed on the battlefield, you must LOOK FOR a weapon. LOOK FOR is 找 zhǎo.

Stroke order

一 十 扌 扌 扌 找 找

Radical/Component 目 eye 着（著）-ING (particle) zhe; Resultative Code zháo 337

–ING (particle) zhe; **Resultative Code** zháo 着

Ancient form  Traditioual form 著

 (eyebrow) +  (hand) +  目 (holding hand) = –ing (particle)

Catchphrase

How to catch a mosquito: whilst keepING your eye on it, grab it with your hand. The -ING (particle) is 着 zhe. It has another usage that is to play as a resultative code to a verb, such as (sleep) soundly, (light) up, (find) out etc., and its pronunciation is 着 zháo.

Stroke order

丶 丷 䒑 䒑 兰 羊 羊 着 着 着 着

Radical/Component 目 eye　真 REAL/TRUE zhēn　338

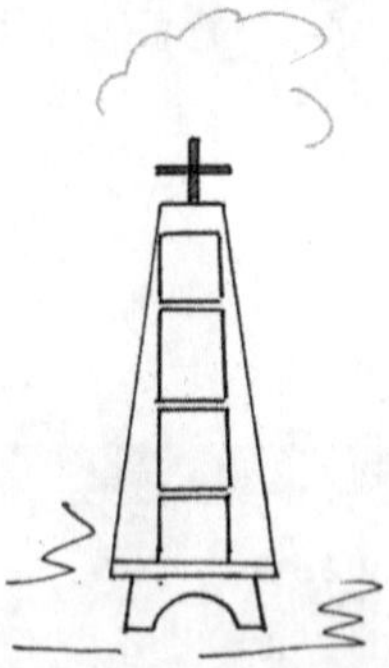

REAL/TRUE zhēn　真

Ancient form

十 (symbol) + 具 (tool) = real/true

Catchphrase

All the people in the four-storied church believe that the only TRUE teaching comes from Heaven. REAL/TRUE is 真 zhēn.

Stroke order

Radical/Component 止 stop　正 CORRECT zhèng　339

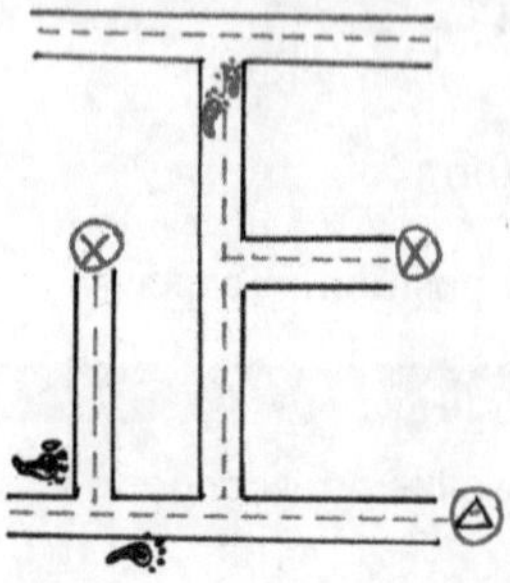

CORRECT zhèng　正

Ancient form

一 (line) + 止 (stop) = correct

Catchphrase

If you come across a road branching off from your route, you should stop to consider which might be the CORRECT path before proceeding. CORRECT is 正 zhèng.

Stroke order

Radical/Component 卜 heart　只 ONLY zhǐ; MW zhī　340

ONLY zhǐ; **MW** zhī　只

Ancient form

口 (box) + 八 (two legs) = only/MW

Catchphrase

This cupboard ONLY has two legs, best not to put anything in it! ONLY is 只 zhǐ; MEASURE WORD is 只 zhī.

Stroke order

Radical/Component 口 mouth 知 KNOW zhī 341

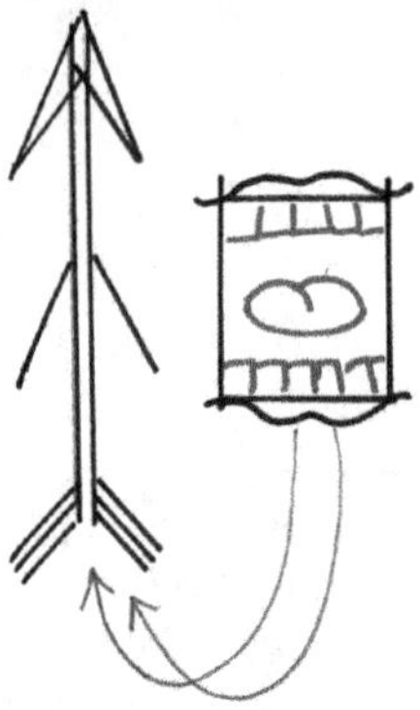

KNOW zhī 知

Ancient form

矢 (arrow) + 口 (mouth) = know

Catchphrase

If you speak with a tongue as quickly and sharply as an arrow, be sure you KNOW what you're talking about. KNOW is 知 zhī.

Stroke order

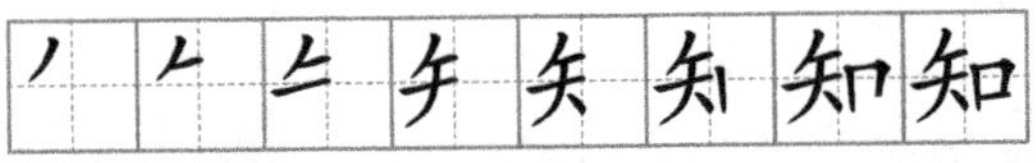

Radical/Component 纟 silk 纸（紙）PAPER zhǐ 342

PAPER zhǐ 纸

Ancient form Traditional form 紙

纟 (silkworm cocoon) + 氏 (lower position) = paper

Catchphrase

In ancient times, PAPER was made from silkworm cocoons mixed with tree bark. PAPER is 纸 zhǐ.

Stroke order

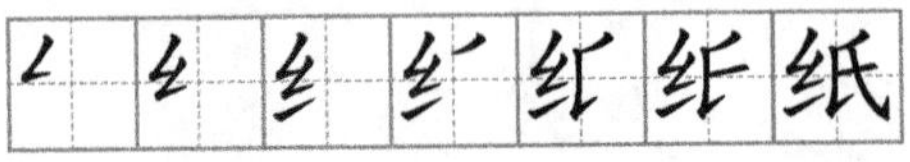

Radical/Component 力 force 助 HELP/ASSIST zhù 343

HELP/ASSIST zhù 助

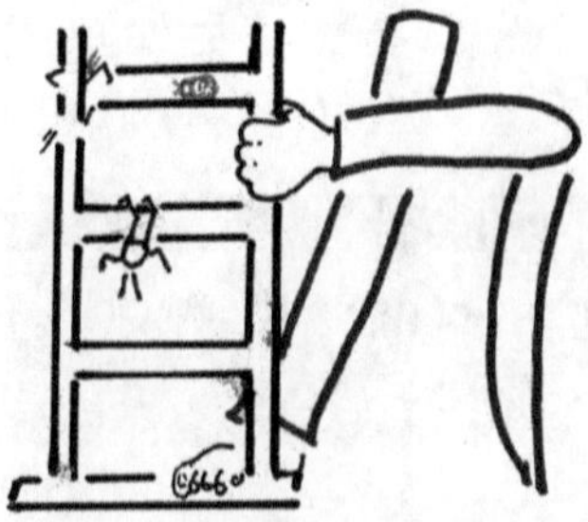

Ancient form

且 (add/ladder) + 力 (force) = help/assist

Catchphrase

I need your HELP please — can you hold this ladder with a strong grip while I climb it? HELP/ASSIST is 助 zhù.

Stroke order

丨	冂	月	月	且	助	助

Radical/Component 冫 ice 准（準）ACCURATE zhǔn 344

ACCURATE zhǔn 准

Ancient form Traditional form 準

冫 (two objects) + 隹 (bird) = accurate

Catchphrase

A hungry bird needs to make an ACCURATE strike if it wants to catch its prey. ACCURATE is 准 zhǔn.

Stroke order

丶	冫	丿	丬	氵	氵	汁	汻	淮	准

Radical/Component 走 walk 走 WALK/GO zǒu 345

WALK/GO zǒu 走

Ancient form

Catchphrase

When you WALK, swing your arms and take long strides to keep up a good pace. WALK/GO is 走 zǒu.

Stroke order

一	十	土	丰	丰	走	走

Radical/Component 足 foot 足 FOOT zú 346

FOOT zú 足

Ancient form

Catchphrase

Going to watch your FOOTball team in a cup game is enough excitement for anyone! FOOT is 足 zú.

Stroke order

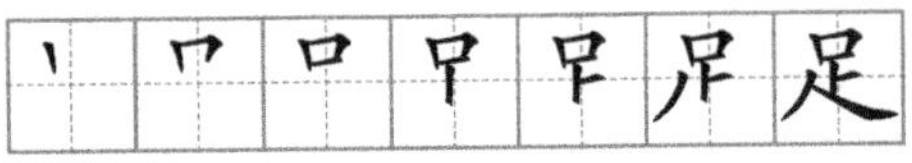

Radical/Component 曰 say 最 MOST zuì 347

MOST zuì 最

Ancient form

日 (hat) + 耳 (ear) + 又 (hand) = most

Catchphrase

People say the MOST cruel punishment in ancient times was cutting off your enemy's ear. MOST is 最 zuì.

Stroke order

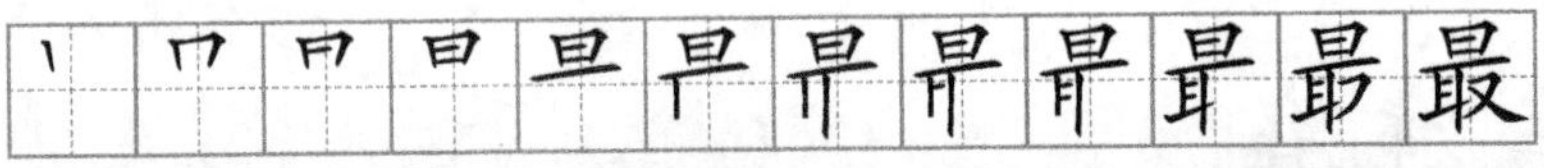

Radical/Component 工 job/work 左 LEFT zuǒ 348

LEFT zuǒ 左

Ancient form

(hand) + 工 (tool/work) = left

Catchphrase

When doing handiwork, most people hold their work steady with their LEFT hand. LEFT is 左 zuǒ.

Stroke order

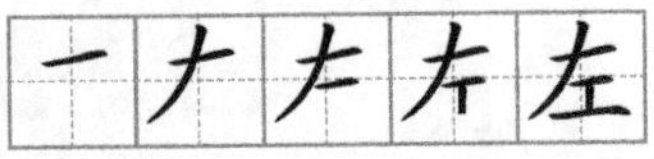

词句篇

As in the Book 1, it will be necessary to learn the grammatical functions of certain characters before understanding how they are used in the Example Sentences. These grammar structures involve the characters: 吧 ba (179), 比 bǐ (186), 别 bié (190), 得 de (207), 过 guò (225) , 也 yě (320) and 着 zhe (337).

B 179 吧 (suggestion particle) ba

吧 can be used with 好 to express approval or disapproval.

好吧，我们现在去吃午饭。	OK, now we can go to lunch.
不好吧，别人都在工作呢。	That won't do. Everyone else is working.

吧 can also be used at the end of a statement to indicate a request, guess or suggestion, in both positive and negative senses.

您是谢先生吧？	You are Mr. Xie, aren't you?
你不是北京人吧？	You are not from Beijing, I guess.

B 186 比 TO COMPARE bǐ

The principle of Natural Order grammar becomes particularly apparent when making comparisons. For instance, if you want to compare the temperature between Beijing and northeast China, in English you would say: Compared to northeast China, Beijing is hotter.

In Chinese the word order is:

北京—比—东北—热。	Beijing-compare-northeast China-hotter.

Two comparable types of question are:

北京—比—东北—热—吗？	Beijing-compare-northeast China-hotter-MA?
北京—比不比—东北—热？ （北京比东北热还是不比东北热）	Beijing-compare or not compare-northeast China-hotter? (Beijing compare northeast China hotter or not compare northeast China hotter)

Thus, in the natural order of things the speaker first of all compares the two places, and then comes to the conclusion that one is hotter than the other.

Notes:

The pattern of a comparative sentence is:

Comparison object A 比 Comparison object B + Description

别 DO NOT bié 190 B

别 (don't) is a negative command given to others; it is never used in a statement about oneself.

我去，你别去！	I'm going, but you're not.
我们下午有会，你别走！	We will have a meeting this afternoon. Don't leave!

得 (grammatical code) de 207 D

The grammatical code 得 is a verb qualifier usually placed between a verb and an adjective to comment on the performance of an action.

他们玩得很好。	They play very well.
他唱得不好。	He doesn't sing well.

得 also functions as an adjective modifier, in conjunction with 多 or 小 to indicate the degree of certain quality.

他比我高得多。	He is much taller than me.

过 (grammatical code) guò 225 G

过 is a verb modifier placed between a verb and a noun to denote past experience.

没有去过	has/have never been to
看过	has/have seen
我没有去过北京。	I have never been to Beijing.

Or:

他做过老师。	He used to be a teacher.

也 ALSO yě 320 Y

也 means also, too, still. It usually appears before a verb or a qualified adjective. If a time word is used, it is placed between 也 and the verb.

我很热，你呢？ 我也很热。	I'm hot. How about you? I'm also hot.
我不热，你呢？ 我也不热。	I'm not hot. How about you? I'm also not hot.
我去北京，你呢？ 我也去。	I am going to Beijing. How about you? I am going to Beijing too.
我明天去北京，你呢？	I will go to Beijing tomorrow. How about you?
我也明天去。	I will go (to Beijing) tomorrow too.

Z 337 着 (grammatical code) zhe

着 is a grammatical code that indicates the continuation of an action itself, or the action has been aborted, but the state it produces continues.

穿 + 着 → 穿着	to wear + (ongoing action particle) = is wearing
雨下着。	It's raining.
别站着。	Don't stand.
天还亮着。	It's still light.
走着去	go on foot
笑着说	say with a smile
忙着考试	busy with the exams

吧 (grammatical code) ba 179 B

Chinese	English	Character codes
好 + 吧 → 好吧	good + suggestion particle = OK; fine	039/179
去吧	Let's go.	102/179
吃吧	Let's eat.	011/179
你是姐姐吧?	You're the elder sister, aren't you?	089/118/057/057/179
快走吧	Please hurry up!	244/345/179
是这个吧?	It's this one, isn't it?	118/167/031/179

Example Sentences

1/179	好吧，我现在就打电话。 OK, I will make a phone call right now.
2/179	去吧，不 * 好，不去吧，也不 * 好。 Going is no good, but neither is not going.
3/179	我们快点儿 ** 吃吧。 Let's eat a bit quicker!
4/179	你就是本吧? You're Ben, aren't you?
5/179	你喝的茶，是这个吧? The tea you drink is this one, isn't it?

注释 Note

*The pattern 不 [adjective]... 也不 [contrasting adjective] = neither...nor...

** 快（一）点儿 = a bit quicker

B | 180 白 WHITE bái

Chinese	English	Character codes
明 + 白 → 明白	bright + white = clear; obvious; understand	083/180
白色	(the colour) white	180/277
白天	daytime	180/128
白纸	blank paper	180/342
白开水	plain boiled water	180/061/120
白雪	white snow	180/314

Example Sentences

1/180	我喜欢白色。 I like white colour.
2/180	她白天常常唱歌。 She often sings during the day.
3/180	请给我些白纸。 Please give me some blank paper.
4/180	中国人喜欢喝白开水。他们说白开水对身体好。 Chinese people like to drink hot water. They say hot water is good for (your) health.
5/180	你为什么不明白我的意思？ Why can't you understand what I mean?

百 HUNDRED bǎi 181 B

Chinese	English	Character codes
百 + 姓 → 百姓	one hundred + surname = common people	181/312
百年	a hundred years; century	181/090
一百	one hundred	152/181
《百家姓》	*Hundred Family Surnames*	181/053/312
百岁	one hundred years old	181/124
百分比	percentage	181/028/186

Example Sentences

1/181	你和我都是老百姓。 You and I are both ordinary people.
2/181	钱老师的房子有几百年了。 Teacher Qian's house is hundreds of years old.
3/181	小明考了一百分。 Xiaoming scored a 100%.
4/181	《百家姓》这本书里有五百零四个姓。 The book *Hundred Family Surnames* contains 504 Chinese surnames.
5/181	报纸上说 *，以前百岁老人不多，但现在每三千人中就有一个百岁老人。 It is said in the newspaper that there were not many centenarians in the past, but now there is one in every three thousand people.

注释 Note

*Reported speech: 报纸上说 / 听说 / 妈妈说 etc.

Chinese does not use a grammatical marker such as 'that' to introduce reported content. Instead, what was said is added directly after the verb (说 , 问 etc). In written Chinese, a comma is often added after 说 or 问 , but it can be omitted in short sentences.

B 182 班 CLASS/GROUP/WORK SHIFT/MW (scheduled transport) bān

Chinese	English	Character codes
上班	go to work	108/182
下班	leave work	139/182
班车	scheduled bus; shuttle bus	182/010
班次	scheduled transport (flights, trains, etc.)	182/200
班长	student leader; monitor	182/194
班机	scheduled flight	182/051
白班	day shift	180/182

Example Sentences

1/182	每天早上六点到十点有班车。 A shuttle bus service runs every morning between 6 and 10 am.
2/182	去北京的火车一天有四个班次。 There are four trains to Beijing each day.
3/182	我妈妈明天早上七点十分去上班。 My mother will go to work at ten past seven tomorrow morning.
4/182	小月常常坐公共汽车上下班，但是因为今天下雨，所以她就坐出租车了。 Xiaoyue often commutes to work by bus, but because it was raining today, she just took a taxi.
5/182	A: 喂，哥们儿，你知道下一班从北京来的飞机是几点吗？ B: 我也不知道。 A: Hi buddy, do you know what time the next flight from Beijing is? B: I don’t know either.

帮 HELP bāng 183 B

Chinese	English	Character codes
帮 + 助→帮助	help + assist = help	183/343
帮忙	give a hand	183/254
帮工	casual labourer	183/032
帮手	assistant	183/284
一帮子	team; squad; bunch	152/183/172
帮会	underworld gang	183/049

Example Sentences

1/183	我想请你帮个忙。 I'd like to ask for your help.
2/183	在英国，帮工不好 * 找。 In Britain, it is not easy to find casual labour.
3/183	钱老师说小明是她的好帮手。 Teacher Qian said Xiaoming is a great help.
4/183	你这次考得不好，让我帮助你好吗？ Your Chinese mark wasn't so good this time; would you like me to help you?
5/183	你为什么不学好，老是和一帮子学习不认真的男生在一起打篮球？ Why can't you be a good student instead of always playing basketball with a group of boys who don't take their studies seriously?

注释 Note

* 好 means 'good', but it can also be used to express that something is easy to do or good to do. The pattern is: 好 + verb = adjective.

E.g. 好吃 = delicious, 好玩儿 = fun, 不好找 = difficult to find

B | 184 报 REPORT/NEWSPAPER bào

Chinese	English	Character codes
报 + 纸 → 报纸	report + paper = newspaper	184/342
卖报	sell newspapers	252/184
电报	telegram	017/184
报馆	news agency	184/035
晚报	evening newspaper	300/184
看报	read a newspaper	062/184

Example Sentences

1/184	现在的中学生都不常看报了，对吗？ Nowadays middle school students don't often read newspapers, right?
2/184	我小的时候，每个小学生都会唱《卖报歌》。 When I was young, every elementary school student could sing the song “Selling Newspapers”.
3/184	这是我爸爸最喜欢看的报纸。 This is my father's favourite newspaper.
4/184	我要在大学学汉语，因为我以后想去报馆工作。 I'm going to study Chinese at university because I want to work in a newspaper office in the future.
5/184	A: 我上学的时候，我们一家都爱看报，你呢？ B: 我家也是。 A: When I was in school, our whole family loved reading newspapers. What about you? B: So did my family.

备 PREPARE bèi 185 B

Chinese	English	Character codes
准 + 备 → 准备	accurate + prepare = prepare; plan	344/185
备课	prepare lessons	185/243
备饭	prepare a meal	185/026
备件	spare part	185/232
后备	reserve	044/185
备有	be available; in stock	185/158

Example Sentences

1/185	这个新老师备了很长时间的课，所以他上课上得很好。 The new teacher spends a long time on lesson preparation; as a result his teaching is very good.
2/185	我准备星期六去看奶奶。 I plan to visit my grandmother on Saturday.
3/185	请问，你知道哪里能买汽车备件吗？ Excuse me, do you know where I can buy spare parts for cars?
4/185	午饭时间到了，您坐一会儿，我现在就去备饭。 It's lunchtime. Please take a seat for a moment, and I will get the meal ready.
5/185	A: 今天晚上的生日会都准备好了吗？ B: 都已经准备好了。我希望我的朋友都会来。 A: Is everything ready for the birthday party this evening? B: It's all done. I hope my friends will all come.

B 186 比 COMPARE/COMPETITION bǐ

Chinese	English	Character codes
二比一	two to one	025/186/152
比一比	compare	186/152/186
比不上	can't compare to; doesn't measure up to	186/007/108
比分	score	186/028
比试	have a competition	186/282

Example Sentences

1/186	A: 比分是多少？ B: 比分是二比一。 A: What's the score? B: The score is two-one.
2/186	来，我们比一比谁高。 Come on, let's see who is taller.
3/186	你是说我比不上她？ Are you are saying I don't measure up to her?
4/186	姐姐有点儿累了，所以她不想和我比试了。 My elder sister is a little tired, so she doesn't want to have a competition with me.
5/186	在中国，爸爸妈妈都给孩子吃最好的。所以我比 * 我爸爸高，我爸爸比他爸爸高。 In China, parents give their children the best food. As a result, I'm taller than my dad, and my dad is taller than his dad.

注释 Note

*To say that one thing is more [adjective] than another, the structure is:

Noun 1 + 比 + Noun 2 + Adjective.

笔 PEN/WRITING BRUSH bǐ 187 B

Chinese	English	Character codes
铅 + 笔 → 铅笔	lead + pen = pencil	269/187
铅笔字	handwriting	269/187/173
笔名	pen name	187/082
笔友	pen pal	187/157
笔试	writing test	187/282
红色的笔	red pen	229/277/015/187

Example Sentences

1/187	那些笔不是我的。 Those pens are not mine.
2/187	老师对小明说："你的铅笔字进步很大！" The teacher said to Xiaoming, 'Your handwriting has improved a lot!'
3/187	很多作家都有笔名。 Many writers have pen names.
4/187	我和我的笔友有一样的爱好*，我们都喜欢游泳。 I have the same hobby as my pen pal, we both like swimming.
5/187	A: 谁有红色的笔和白色的纸？ B: 我有很多，你要多少笔和纸？ A: Does anyone have a red pen and white paper? B: I have plenty. How many pens and how much paper do you want?

注释 Note

* 一样 (yíyàng) can be used to express that two things are the same, or share the same quality.

The structure is: Noun 1 + 跟 / 和 + Noun 2 + 一样 + Adjective.

B 188 边 EDGE/SIDE/BORDER biān

Chinese	English	Character codes
旁边	side; beside	262/188
前边	in front of	099/188
左边	left-hand side	348/188
右边	right-hand side	329/188
上边	above	108/188
边门	side door	188/257
一眼望不到边	as far as the eye can see	152/316/302/007/205/188

Example Sentences

1/188	我家旁边住着个老中医。 Next to my home lives an old Chinese medical doctor.
2/188	在北京火车站的左边，你能看到一个出租车站。 To the left of the Beijing Railway Station you can see a taxi stand.
3/188	电影院有一个边门，我在那儿等你。 The cinema has a side door. I'm waiting for you there.
4/188	这个机场大得不得了*，一眼望不到边。 This airport is so big that one can't take it all at once.
5/188	住在上边那几个男孩子天天在房间里踢足球，你说我怎么休息？ Those boys living upstairs play football in the room every day. How am I supposed to rest?

注释 Note

*The structure "adjective + 得不得了 (de bùdéliǎo)" is used to express that the level of something has gone to an extreme.

表 WATCH/SURFACE/APPEARANCE biǎo 189 B

Chinese	English	Character codes
手表	watch	284/189
新表	new watch	311/189
老表	antique watch	066/189
名表	famous watch	082/189
钟表店	watchmaker's shop	169/189/018

Example Sentences

1/189	谢先生送了他妻子一块手表。 Mr Xie gave his wife a watch as a present.
2/189	我的手表找不到了，您再帮我买一块新表吧！ I can't find my watch. Please help me buy a new one!
3/189	现在很多中国人都去国外买名表，因为比在中国买便宜 *。 Nowadays many Chinese people go abroad to buy famous brand watches because they're cheaper than those in China.
4/189	在我们同学中，小习过去在钟表店工作，我听说他现在去做生意了。 One of our classmates named Xiaoxi used to work in a watch shop. I hear that he's gone into business.
5/189	昨天是我的生日，妈妈给了我一块很好的表，但是我不喜欢。我想要苹果手表。 Yesterday was my birthday. My mum gave me a really good watch, but I don't like it. I want an Apple Watch.

注释 Note

* 便宜 piányi= cheap

B 190 别 (imperative) DON'T/STOP/TO LEAVE/OTHER bié

Chinese	English	Character codes
别笑	don't laugh	190/310
别吃	don't eat	190/011
别玩	don't play	190/299
别说	don't talk	190/122
别等	don't wait	190/208
别得意	don't be complacent	190/207/324

Example Sentences

1/190	别笑了！现在是上课时间。 Stop laughing! It's lesson time.
2/190	吃东西的时候，请别说话。 Please don't talk when you are eating.
3/190	别玩儿了，常常玩手机对 * 眼睛不好。 Please stop playing. Constantly playing on your mobile phone is not good for the eyes.
4/190	别等了，哥哥天天晚 ** 回家，也不打电话告诉我们。 Let's not wait. Elder brother comes home late every day and yet doesn't call to tell us.
5/190	别太得意了！虽然你汉语考得不错，但是你还有九门中学会考的考试没考呢！ Don't be complacent. Although your Chinese exam result is not bad, you still have nine more GCSEs to take!

注释 Note

* 对 duì = toward

** 晚 wǎn = late

宾 GUEST bīn 191 B

Chinese	English	Character codes
宾馆	hotel	191/035
来宾	guest	065/191
宾客	guest	191/063
贵宾	distinguished guest; VIP	224/191
我姓宾	my surname is Bin	132/312/191
宾朋	friends and guests	191/092

Example Sentences

1/191	颜先生和颜太太后天会住在我们宾馆。 Mr and Mrs Yan will stay in our hotel the day after tomorrow.
2/191	等来宾们都进场了，高医生就会开始做报告。 When the guests are all present, Doctor Gao will begin his speech.
3/191	对不起，这里是贵宾坐的，请你们坐那里。 Sorry, this seating is for VIPs. Please sit over there.
4/191	A: 我姓宾，就是宾馆的宾。请问您贵姓? B: 我姓高。 A: My surname is Bin, which is the 'bin' in 'binguan'. May I ask what your surname is? B: My surname is Gao.
5/191	我的一个同学过十八岁的生日，他请了三百位宾客。我很不喜欢他这样的做法，所以我那天就没去。 One of my classmates had his 18th birthday, and he invited 300 guests. I really don't like it when he does things like this, so I didn't go that day.

B 192 病 DISEASE/SICK bìng

Chinese	English	Character codes
生病	fall ill	112/192
病人	sick person; patient	192/104
病号	invalid; patient	192/040
病床	sickbed	192/199
病房	ward	192/213
病情	patient's condition	192/270
病友	fellow patient	192/157
病因	cause of disease	192/325

Example Sentences

1/192	米小姐病了，别叫她了。 Miss Mi is sick. Don't call her.
2/192	你看错了吧！医生在给病人喂饭，这不可能！ You must have got it wrong! The doctor is feeding the patient.That's impossible!
3/192	这个来买药的老病号是我以前的病友。 That old invalid who came to buy medicine was a fellow patient of mine.
4/192	医生说我身体没什么大病，病因就是运动得太少，所以从今天开始我要少吃多运动。 The doctor said that I have nothing seriously wrong with me. The reason I feel ill is too little exercise.So from today I'll start eating less and exercising more.
5/192	这个医院病人很多，病房少，所以病人为了 * 住院常常要等很长时间。 This hospital has a lot of patients, but not many wards, so patients often have to wait a long time before they are admitted.

注释 Note

* 为了 wèile = in order to, for the sake of

步 PACE/STEP bù 193 B

Chinese	English	Character codes
跑步	run; jog	263/193
进步	progress	235/193
步子	footstep	193/172
一步步	every step	152/193/193
一小步	one small step	152/143/193
大步	stride	014/193

Example Sentences

1/193	今天，这个老人走了几步，好多了。 This old man took a few steps today. He became much better.
2/193	同学们，你们知道这本书的名字《进步》是什么意思吗？ Students, do you know what this book's title *Progress* means?
3/193	虽然 * 哥哥走路的步子比弟弟的大，但是 * 弟弟比哥哥跑步跑得快多了。 Although the elder brother takes longer strides than his little brother, little brother runs much faster than him.
4/193	因为 ** 我觉得 *** 跑步会对身体有很多好处，所以 ** 现在我开始跑步了。我每个星期去公园跑三次。 Because I think running has a lot of benefits for the body, now I've started to run. I go to the park to run three times a week.
5/193	谢老先生九十九岁了，他虽然还能走，但每一步都走得很慢。 Mr Xie is ninety-nine years old. Although he can still walk, with every step he moves very slowly.

注释 Note

*Unlike in English, conjunctions are not normally needed when connecting clauses and sentences in Chinese. However, when using 虽然 (although), it must be coupled with a 'but', in the form 虽然……但是……

**The conjunctions 因为 and 所以 can be used either on their own or as a pair. 因为……所以…… (because…therefore…).

*** 觉得 juéde = feel

C 194 长* LONG cháng ; GROW zhǎng

Chinese	English	Character codes
长年	many years/all year round	194/090
长桌子	long table	194/171/172
长跑	long-distance running	194/263
长生不老	eternal youth/immortality	194/112/007/066
长远	long-term	194/332
长住	settle down (live)	194/170
长 ** 大	grow up	194/014
年长 **	older in age	090/194

Example Sentences

1/194	明明的爸爸长年都在北京工作。 Mingming's father has worked in Beijing for many years.
2/194	这不是你的咖啡，你的咖啡在那个长桌子上。 This is not your coffee.Your coffee is on that long table.
3/194	我的爱好是长跑。 My hobby is long-distance running.
4/194	从长远来看，我们希望儿子能上一个离家近的学校，能有多一点儿时间学习。 In the long term, we hope that our son can attend a school close to home and have a little more time to study.
5/194	我不想长生不老，我只 *** 希望每天都快乐。 I don't want to be immortal; I only wish to be happy every day.

注释 Note

* 长 is a polyphonic character: cháng = long, zhǎng = grow/increase

** 长 zhǎng = grow/increase (All other examples are pronounced as cháng.)

*** 只 zhǐ = only

常 COMMON/OFTEN cháng 195 C

Chinese	English	Character codes
非常	very; extremely	214/195
常常	often	195/195
常见病	common disease	195/054/192
常见问题	common problem; frequently asked questions	195/054/304/293
常客	regular visitor	195/063
常来常往	frequently see each other	195/065/195/301
常人	ordinary people	195/104
常识	general knowledge	195/116
常住	permanently reside	195/170

Example Sentences

1/195	我出生在中国东北，但现在常住西北。 I was born in northeast China, but now I permanently reside in northwest China.
2/195	我二十几岁的时候，常常下班以后玩儿到很晚。 When I was in my twenties, I often took a lot of pleasure after work.
3/195	你怎么这点儿常识都没有呢！ Why don't you have any common sense!
4/195	中学生太喜欢玩儿电脑，这是一个常见问题。 Middle school students like to play on computers too much.This is a common problem.
5/195	虽然他和我从小就认识，他爸妈和我爸妈也在同一家公司工作，但我们不常来往。 Although he and I have known each other since childhood, and his parents and my parents work in the same company, we don't often see each another.

C 196 场 FIELD/OPEN SPACE/MW chǎng

Chinese	English	Character codes
机场	airport	051/196
球场	(ballgame) field; pitch; court	272/196
场次	showing (of a film, play, etc.)	196/200
场面	scene (in drama, fiction, etc.); occasion	196/081
场子	venue	196/172
进场	enter an arena	235/196
出场	go on stage	012/196

Example Sentences

1/196	离我家不远 * 有一个机场。 There is an airport not far from my home.
2/196	今天下午四点零五分是中国运动员进场的时间。 The Chinese athletes will enter the stadium at five past four this afternoon.
3/196	今天是阴天，不热，我们去球场踢一场足球，好吗？ Today is a cloudy day; it's not hot. Let's go to the stadium to play football, OK?
4/196	小明今天唱歌的时候，一看见那么多的人，那么大的场面，他就说不出话来了。 When Xiaoming was singing today, as soon as he saw that so many people were watching on such a big occasion, he suddenly couldn't speak.
5/196	A: 听说下一个出场的歌手很有名，你认识吗？ B: 我觉得现在没有好听的歌，所以我一个歌星都不认识。 A: I hear that the next singer on stage is very famous. Do you know him? B: I reckon there are no good songs these days, and I don't know a single singer.

注释 Note

* 离 [……] 远 = far from [...]

** 觉得 juéde = feel

唱 SING chàng 197 C

Chinese	English	Character codes
唱歌	sing a song	197/219
唱国歌	sing the national anthem	197/036/219
说唱	rapping	122/197
欢唱	sing merrily	047/197
一唱一和 *	echo one another; sing a duet	152/197/152/042

Example Sentences

1/197	我儿子最喜欢唱歌。他每天从早唱到晚。 My son really enjoys singing. He sings from morning till night every day.
2/197	他们两个一唱一和 * 的，说着一些我们听不懂的话。 The two of them were singing the same tune, and saying things we couldn't understand.
3/197	我听到孩子们在院子里唱歌。 I heard children singing in the courtyard.
4/197	A: 现在电视上常常有老外 ** 出场唱中国歌，唱得真不错！ B: 是，昨晚电视上就有个老外 ** 唱歌，你看了没有？ A: Nowadays, you often see foreigners on TV singing Chinese songs, and they sing really well! B: Absolutely. There was a foreigner singing on TV last night. Did you see that?
5/197	我们小时候都希望长大后做老师、医生，去开飞机。现在好多孩子都学唱歌，他们想长大以后当歌星。 When we were young, we all wanted to be teachers, doctors, or pilots when we grew up. These days many children are learning to sing, and want to be pop stars when they grow up.

注释 Note

* 和 is polyphonic; hè = chime in with others (conversation, etc.)

** 老外 lǎowài = foreigner

C 198 穿 PENETRATE/WEAR chuān

Chinese	English	Character codes
穿衣服	wear clothes	198/153/029
穿帮	let something slip; see through a lie	198/183
穿好了吗?	Are you dressed yet?	198/039/067/073
穿过	pass through	198/225
说穿	speak bluntly	122/198
试穿	try on	282/198

Example Sentences

1/198	这个三岁的孩子已经会穿衣服了。 This three-year-old child can already dress himself.
2/198	很快就到你们上场了，怎么衣服还没有穿好! You're on soon! How come you're not dressed yet!
3/198	这个穿红颜色衣服的人是我妹妹的老师。 The person in red is my younger sister's teacher.
4/198	我的天，在商店里买衣服都可以先试穿的，这你都不知道? Good heavens, all the clothes you buy in the store can be tried on first. Didn't you know that?
5/198	A: 请问，学校电影院在哪儿? B: 穿过篮球场就是。 A: Excuse me, where is the school cinema? B: Just go through the basketball court and there's the cinema.

床 BED chuáng 199 C

Chinese	English	Character codes
起床	get up	097/199
大床	large-size bed	014/199
上床	go to bed	108/199
床边	bedside	199/188
病床	sick bed	192/199

Example Sentences

1/199	请问，你们旅店今晚还有没有大床的房间？ Excuse me, do you have a room in your hotel with a large-size bed for tonight?
2/199	我不喜欢住在学校，因为学校的床都太小。 I don't like to live at school, because the school beds are too small.
3/199	笑笑爱看书，所以她的床边常常有很多书。 Xiaoxiao loves to read, so she often has a lot of books by her bedside.
4/199	你今天一天看上去都很累。晚上就不要再 * 看电视了，早点儿上床休息，你明天还要很早起床呢。 You've been looking tired all day. Don't watch any more TV tonight and get an early night; you still have to get up very early tomorrow.
5/199	小孩子都喜欢在床上跳，因为他们觉得 ** 能跳得很高。 The children like to jump on their beds because they feel they can jump very high.

注释 Note

* 再 zài = again/any more/then

** 觉得 juéde = feel

C 200 次 TIME/NEXT/SECOND-RATE/MW cì

Chinese	English	Character codes
名次	position or rank in a competition	082/200
两次	twice	249/200
第一次	the first time	210/152/200
次日	next day	200/275
最后一次	the last (previous or final) time	347/044/152/200
次要	minor; secondary; less important	200/319
上一次	last (previous) time	108/152/200
这次	this time	167/200

Example Sentences

1/200	我上一次回国是二零一五年。 The last time I went back to my country was in 2015.
2/200	这可能是我们最后一次见面了。 This may be the last time we meet.
3/200	这次我请客，下次是小明请。 This time it's my treat; next time Xiaoming will take care of the bill.
4/200	A: 这次考试你在班上的名次是多少？ B: 妈，我考了第一名。 A: Where did you come in the class ranking for this exam? B: Mum, I got first place!
5/200	对一个学生来说，什么都是次要的，学习第一。 As far as a student is concerned, everything takes second place to learning.

从 FOLLOW/FROM cóng 201 C

Chinese	English	Character codes
从前	the past	201/099
从上到下	from top to bottom	201/108/205/139
从左到右	from left to right	201/348/205/329
从（来）不	never	201/(065)/007
从今往后	from now on	201/058/301/044
从小	since childhood	201/143

Example Sentences

1/201	我们的班长从不叫累。 Our class monitor is never tired.
2/201	她从小就很听话。 She has been obedient since she was a child.
3/201	从前卖水果的老高现在在开出租车。 That Mr Gao who used to sell fruit is driving a taxi now.
4/201	A: 请问，这边从左到右所有的商店都是卖衣服的吗？ B: 是，只有最右边的一家是卖小吃的。 A: Excuse me, do all the shops from left to right on this side sell clothes? B: Yes, apart from the one on the far right, which sells snacks.
5/201	我同事家的小孩儿从小到大都认真读书，你怎么不和他们学学？ My colleague's children have been studying hard since they were young. Why don't you behave like them?

C 202 错 WRONG/MISTAKE CUÒ

Chinese	English	Character codes
错过	miss (train, etc.)	202/225
错话	improper remarks	202/046
错字	incorrectly written character	202/173
认错	admit a fault	105/202
错事	mistake; error	202/281

Example Sentences

1/202	我早上起床晚了，错过了一班车。 I got up late this morning and missed the bus/train.
2/202	做了错事就要知道认错。 You ought to know that if you do something wrong, you should admit it.
3/202	这件事我做错了吗？我觉得 * 我没错！ Did I make a mistake with this? I think I'm right!
4/202	一开始学写字的时候都会写错字，多写就会进步了。 When you first start learning to write, you will likely get the words wrong; the more you write, the more you will improve.
5/202	A: 小雪为什么今天不和我说话了？ B: 谁让你昨天在会上说错话，他不高兴了。 A: Why was Xiaoxue not talking to me today? B: I don't know what made you come out with that inappropriate wording during the meeting yesterday, so he wasn't happy.

注释 Note

* 觉得 juéde = feel

但 BUT dàn 203 D

Chinese	English	Character codes
虽然……但是……	although…	289/273/203/118
不但	not only	007/203

Example Sentences

1/203	虽然这次考试我考得不错，但是，还不是最好。 Although I did well on the test this time, it was not my best.
2/203	虽然这个药非常贵，但是是我要的药，所以我还是买了。 Although this medicine is very expensive, it's the one I need, so I still bought it.
3/203	不但我做错了这个题，我们班的同学都做错了！ It wasn't only me that got the question wrong, the whole class did!
4/203	虽然下午要下大雨，但是我还是想和朋友们一起坐公共汽车去饭店跳舞。 Although it's going to rain heavily this afternoon, I still want to take the bus to the hotel and dance with my friends.
5/203	A: 她好像有不少钱，不然 * 怎么能天天穿不同的衣服来上班呢？ B: 你错了。她很会买东西，她的每件衣服不但 ** 漂亮，还 ** 非常便宜。 A: She looks like she has plenty of money, otherwise how could she wear different clothes to work every day? B: No, you're wrong. She's a very smart shopper. All of her clothes are not only beautiful, but also very inexpensive.

注释 Note

* 不然 = otherwise

** 不但……还…… = not only…but also…

D | 204 蛋 EGG dàn

Chinese	English	Character codes
鸡蛋	chicken egg	230/204
下蛋	lay an egg	139/204
蛋白	egg white	204/180
喜蛋 / 红蛋	red-painted egg	137/204/229/204
高蛋白	high protein	030/204/180

Example Sentences

1/204	听说每天吃一个鸡蛋对身体好，是吗？ I heard that eating an egg every day is good for one's health. Is that right?
2/204	现在不少商店里都卖有机的鸡蛋和菜。 Nowadays, organic eggs and vegetables are available in many stores.
3/204	白太太家的鸡每天都下蛋，所以她从来不买鸡蛋。 Mrs White's hen lays an egg every day, so she never needs to buy eggs.
4/204	A: 过去在中国，要是哪家生了儿子，就会送红蛋给大家。 B: 红蛋就是红色的鸡蛋，对吗？ A: 对。 A: In the old days of China, on the birth of a son, the family celebrated by giving red eggs to their friends and relatives. B: Red eggs are just red-coloured eggs, right? A: That's right.
5/204	多吃高蛋白的牛肉对身体好这是大家的共识。 It's common knowledge that eating more high-protein beef is good for health.

到 ARRIVE/REACH dào 205 D

Chinese	English	Character codes
到……去	go to...	205/102
来到	arrive/come	065/205
到家	arrive home	205/053
到会	be present at a meeting	205/049
到场	be present (at some event)	205/196
到点	it is time	205/016
到手	come into one's possession	205/284

Example Sentences

1/205	所有人都到了，我们开始开会吧。 Everyone is present, so let's start the meeting.
2/205	A: 还有谁没到？ B: 习大明。他去买水了，很快就回来。 A: Who else hasn't arrived yet? B: Xi Daming. He's gone to buy water, but he'll be back soon.
3/205	我妻子得到 * 了一个新工作，但是得到 ** 北京去。 My wife has got a new job, but she has to go to Beijing.
4/205	A: 晚饭已经做好了，你什么时候到家？ B: 我还在开会呢，今晚不回家吃饭了。 A: Dinner is ready. When are you going to be home? B: I am still in a meeting; I won't be home for dinner tonight.
5/205	A: 昨天电视上的《中国女生》你看到了吗？有一个歌手唱得很好！ B: 没看到，我回家太晚了。 A: Did you watch *Chinese Girls* on TV yesterday? One singer was really good! B: No, I didn't see it; I got home too late.

注释 Note

* 得到 dédào = get/obtain

** 得到 děi dào = have to go to

D | 206 道 ROAD/WAY/MORALS/SAY/MW dào

Chinese	English	Character codes
知道	know	341/206
近道	shortcut	236/206
下水道	sewer system	139/120/206
门道	access; social connections; knack	257/206
道家	Daoism	206/053
能说会道	silver-tongued; have the gift of the gab	088/122/049/206

Example Sentences

1/206	中国人吃饭是冷菜、热菜一起上；外国人吃饭，菜是一道一道上的。 When Chinese people have a meal, cold and hot dishes are served together; when foreigners eat, dishes are served as successive courses.
2/206	你的意思我知道了。 I know what you mean.
3/206	学习没有近道可以走。 There is no shortcut to knowledge.
4/206	那个高先生真是能说会道，客人们都很喜欢他。 That Mr Gao has a real way with words. All the customers like him.
5/206	A: 妈妈，这道题我不会做，你可以帮帮我吗？ B: 我也不会做，这是给小学生的问题吗？ A: Mum, I don't know how to answer this question. Can you help me? B: I don't know how to do it either. Is this a question for primary school students?

得 GET dé; Grammatical Code de; MUST/HAVE TO děi 207 D

Chinese	English	Character codes
觉得 *	to feel; to think	056/207
写得 * 很好	well-written	146/207/043/039
唱得 * 不好	sing badly	197/207/007/039
得 ** 分	to score	207/028
得 ** 到	get; obtain; gain	207/205
得 ** 出	reach (a conclusion); obtain (a result)	207/012
得 ** 意	complacent	207/324

注释 Note

* 得 de = grammatical code

** 得 dé = get

*** 得 děi = must; have to

Example Sentences

1/207	二四得 ** 八。 Two times four makes eight.
2/207	爸爸做了一个门，他很得 ** 意。 Dad made a door. He was very pleased with himself.
3/207	小红喜欢跑步，但是她跑得 * 不快。 Xiaohong likes running, but she doesn't run very fast.
4/207	A: 你怎么买这么多水果? B: 这些水果卖得 * 非常便宜，我得 *** 多买些给家里的老人和孩子吃。 A: How come you bought so much fruit? B: This fruit was on sale for a very good price, so I must buy some for my parents and the children as well.
5/207	我爱上汉语课，因为我觉得 * 我的汉语老师很好，她给我们的作业比别的课少。 I love going to Chinese class because I think my Chinese teacher is really nice. She gives us less homework than we get for other subjects.

D | 208 等 WAIT děng

Chinese	English	Character codes
等火车	wait for a train	208/050/010
等一会儿	wait a moment	208/152/049/024
等一等	wait	208/152/208
在火车站等	wait at the train station	164/050/010/166/208
等等	etc.; and so on; wait for a minute	208/208

Example Sentences

1/208	别跑，我等你。 Don't run, I'll wait for you.
2/208	因为这一班去北京的火车没有准时到，所以有很多人在火车站等着。 Because the train to Beijing didn't arrive on time, there are many people waiting at the station.
3/208	我喜欢的东西很多，看书、写字、唱歌、跳舞和踢球等等。 I like many things: reading, writing, singing, dancing, playing football, etc.
4/208	钱小姐，高先生说他星期三下午五点在北京饭店等您。 Miss Qian, Mr Gao said that he'll be waiting for you at the Beijing Hotel at 5 pm this Wednesday.
5/208	A: 那么多人在宾馆门前等谁呢？ B: 听说是北京来的一个作家住在这家宾馆。有些人已经等了五六个小时了。 A: Why are so many people waiting at the gate of the hotel? B: I heard a famous Beijing writer is staying in this hotel. Some people have been waiting for five or six hours.

弟 YOUNGER BROTHER dì 209 D

Chinese	English	Character codes
弟弟	younger brother	209/209
弟子	follower; disciple	209/172
弟妹	younger brother's wife	209/256
表弟	younger male cousin	189/209
老弟	(form of address for younger male) man	66/209

Example Sentences

1/209	他是道家弟子。 He is a Daoist disciple.
2/209	我虽然没有弟弟妹妹，但是有一个哥哥。 Although I don't have any younger brothers or sisters, I do have an elder brother.
3/209	老弟，你听我说，上一个有汉语课的大学，以后可以去中国工作。 Listen to me, man. If you go to a university that teaches Chinese, you'll be able to get a job in China.
4/209	A: 喂，表弟，是我，大明。明天是我的生日，想请你和你太太 * 一起来吃饭。 B: 好的，那我们明天见，还是在那个"北京饭馆"吧？ A: Hello, Cousin, it's me, Daming. Tomorrow is my birthday and I'd like to invite you and your wife for dinner. B: OK, we will see you tomorrow, still at the Beijing Restaurant?
5/209	虽然我弟弟不喜欢吃西瓜，但因为他爱人 ** 喜欢吃，所以热天的时候，他每天都会给她买一个。 Although my younger brother doesn't like watermelon, his wife does, so when the weather's hot, he buys one for her every day.

注释 Note

* 太太 = wife

** 爱人 = spouse (husband or wife)

D 210 第 (ordinal number prefix) dì

Chinese	English	Character codes
第一	first	210/152
第一手	first-hand	210/152/284
门第	family status	257/210
第一次	the first time	210/152/200
第一道菜	first course (of a meal)	210/152/206/008
第一班车	the first bus	210/152/182/010

Example Sentences

1/210	听说你们已经在北京开了第五家店了，怎么样，生意好不好？ I heard that you've already opened the fifth store in Beijing. How's business?
2/210	今天我们晚饭的第二道菜是鱼，你觉得可以吗？ The second course for dinner today is fish. Are you okay with that?
3/210	我第一次去北京是在我九岁的时候。 I went to Beijing for the first time when I was nine years old.
4/210	A: 钱医生明天要去的医院很远，所以他希望坐早上第一班车走。你能帮他买票吗？ B: 好的，没问题！ A: The hospital that Dr Qian wants to go to tomorrow is quite far, so he's hoping to take the first train in the morning. Can you help him buy a ticket? B: Okay, no problem!
5/210	在大学读书的时候，我最喜欢汉语，考试常常是第一、二名。但是现在我工作太忙，不常写汉字了，汉字都快不会写了。 When I was at university, my favourite subject was Chinese, and I often came first or second in the exam. But now that I'm busy with work and rarely write in Chinese, I've almost forgotten how to write Chinese characters.

懂 UNDERSTAND dǒng 211 D

Chinese	English	Character codes
懂得	understand	211/207
懂事	sensible	211/281
看懂	understand what one is reading or watching	062/211
听不懂	not understand what was heard	129/007/211
懂汉语	understand Chinese	211/038/160
不懂就问	if you don't understand, just ask	007/211/239/304

Example Sentences

1/211	懂得最多的人，常常说得最少。 The man who knows the most, often says the least.
2/211	说真的，你昨天会上说的什么我没听懂。 To tell the truth, I didn't understand what you said at the meeting yesterday.
3/211	要是他懂汉语多好！ It would be great if only he could understand Chinese!
4/211	A: 小雨，你在学校学习的时候不懂就问老师，知道吗？ B: 但是老师说上课的时候，小朋友们不可以说话。 A: Xiaoyu, when you're in class, you know you should ask the teacher if you don't understand, right? B: But the teacher said that the children mustn't talk during the lesson.
5/211	我学汉语的时候，能看得懂不少汉语小说，但是真的和中国朋友在一起的时候，很多东西说不出来。 When I was learning Chinese, I could read a lot of Chinese novels, but when I was with Chinese friends, I couldn't come up with much to say.

D 212 动 MOVEMENT/MAKE USE OF/TOUCH dòng

Chinese	English	Character codes
运动	sport	333/212
动笔	begin writing	211/187
动不动	easily	212/007/212
动车	CRH train (high-speed rail in China)	212/010
动工	start construction	212/032
动手	set about (a task); touch; hit	212/284
动人	(emotionally) moving	212/104

Example Sentences

1/212	这个作家开始动笔写一本新书。 The writer has started working on a new book.
2/212	我姐姐喜欢运动。 My elder sister likes to play sports.
3/212	你是一个老师，怎么可以动手打学生呢？ You are a teacher. How can you strike a student?
4/212	这个火车站从动工到完工只要四个月。 It will only take four months to build the railway station from start to finish.
5/212	现在从上海到北京坐动车七个多小时就到了，但是我觉得车票不便宜。 It takes the CRH train just over seven hours from Shanghai to Beijing, but I think the train ticket is not cheap.

房 BUILDING fáng 213 | F

Chinese	English	Character codes
房间	room	213/231
房子	house	213/172
房车	caravan; motorhome	213/010
房东	landlord	213/019
房客	tenant	213/063
客房	guest room	063/213
房钱	house rental	213/100
书房	study (room)	119/213
病房	(hospital) ward	192/213

Example Sentences

1/213	我奶奶家的房子很小，老老小小五个人住在一个房间里。 My grandmother's house is very small; five people of all ages live in one room.
2/213	我爸爸妈妈觉得住宾馆太贵，所以我们一家常常开房车旅游。 My parents think that staying in hotels is too expensive, so our family often travels in a motorhome.
3/213	我的房东姓钱，今年五十多岁，他非常喜欢运动。 My landlord's surname is Qian. He's in his fifties, and he really enjoys playing sports.
4/213	左老师病了，他不让学生们去医院的病房看他，但是我们还是想去。 Teacher Zuo is sick. Although he told the students not to go to the hospital to see him, we still want to go.
5/213	现在我们在北京的房子比以前的大多了，有五个房间，还有一间书房和一间客房。 Our current house in Beijing is much larger than any we've had before. There are five rooms, plus a study and a guest room.

D 214 非 NOT BE/WRONG/NON-/MUST fēi

Chinese	English	Character codes
非常	very; exceptionally	214/195
非但	not only	214/203
非人	inhuman	214/104
非同小可	not a trivial matter	214/130/143/242
是非	right and wrong	118/214
不明是非	be unable to know right from wrong	007/083/118/214
非……不可	bound to; must	214/007/242

Example Sentences

1/214	她的汉语说得非常好。 She speaks Chinese extraordinarily well.
2/214	他不懂得是非黑白。 He doesn't know the difference between right and wrong.
3/214	他非但不认真学习，现在还有时不来学校上课。 Not only does he not study hard, now he sometimes doesn't even come to school.
4/214	A: 老冷只来了我们学校三年，他怎么这么快就做校长了？ B: 老冷的本事非同小可，他懂九门外语呢！ A: Mr Leng has only been at our school for three years. How come he's been made the principal so soon? B: Mr Leng is a person with many skills. He even knows nine foreign languages!
5/214	我的汉语老师说，要想说好汉语，非得去中国，最好去北京。 My Chinese teacher said that if I want to speak Chinese well, I must go to China, and the best place to go is Beijing.

啡 COFFEE (2nd character) fēi 215 F

Chinese	English	Character codes
咖啡	coffee	240/215
咖啡店	coffee shop/café	240/215/018
咖啡馆儿	coffee shop/café	240/215/35/024
咖啡色	coffee-coloured/brown	240/215/277
咖啡因	caffeine	240/215/325
咖啡室	coffee room	240/215/283
咖啡机	coffee machine/coffee maker	240/215/051

Example Sentences

1/215	我喜欢一边 * 喝咖啡，一边 * 看书。 I like to drink coffee while reading a book.
2/215	今天他准备先出去跑步，回来以后再喝咖啡。 Today he plans to go out for a run first, and then have a coffee when he comes back.
3/215	这家咖啡馆儿我常去，虽然离我公司有点儿远，但是它的咖啡是北京最好的。 I often go to this café. Although it's a bit far from my office, the coffee is the best in Beijing.
4/215	咖啡里有咖啡因，茶里也有咖啡因，喝太多了都对身体不好。 Coffee contains caffeine, and there is caffeine in tea as well, so drinking them too much is not good for your health.
5/215	这次妈妈的生日，我想送她一个咖啡机。我去商店看过了，一个咖啡机要三千多块。 I want to get my mother a coffee machine for her birthday this year, so I went to the store and had a look. A coffee machine costs more than 3,000 yuan.

注释 Note

*The structure 一边 [activity 1] 一边 [activity 2] expresses that some action is carried out while doing something else.

D 216 夫 HUSBAND/MAN fū

Chinese	English	Character codes
丈 + 夫 → 丈夫	husband + man = husband	335/216
夫妻	husband and wife	216/266
夫人	wife (formal)	216/104
夫子	master	216/172
大 * 夫	doctor/physician	014/216
工夫	period of time	032/216
姐夫 / 妹夫	elder sister's husband/younger sister's husband	057/216/256/216

注释 Note

* 大 is a polyphone; here it is pronounced as dài.

Example Sentences

1/216	小明的外公是一个有名的中医大夫。 Xiaoming's grandfather is a famous doctor of traditional Chinese Medicine.
2/216	高老师的丈夫和她在同一个学校上班。 Teacher Gao and her husband both work at the same school.
3/216	我姐姐手真快，一会儿的工夫，她已经给我做好了羊肉饭。 My elder sister is really fast; in just a short time, she had cooked me mutton rice.
4/216	这个星期有一个新电影，里面有我妹夫，我们星期六一起去看吧！ There's a new movie out this week, and my younger sister's husband is in it. Let's go and see it together on Saturday!
5/216	钱老先生很有学问，什么都懂，大家有什么问题都去找他帮忙，我们都叫他老夫子。 Mr Qian is very learned and understands everything. Anyone with questions goes to him for help. We all call him "the old master".

告 INFORM/TELL/ANNOUNCE gào 217 G

Chinese	English	Character codes
告诉	tell/inform	217/288
告别	say goodbye to	217/190
告知	inform	217/341
报告	report	184/217
不可告人	not be divulged	007/242/217/104

Example Sentences

1/217	这件事是谁告诉你的？ Who told you of this matter?
2/217	他这个星期要写完这个报告。 He must complete the report this week.
3/217	我明天要去北京了，我是来和你告别的。 I'm going to Beijing tomorrow, so I've come to say goodbye to you.
4/217	A: 医生为什么上午到病房来了？ B: 他是来告诉我爸爸，他的病好了，下星期可以出院了。 A: Why did the doctor come to the ward this morning? B: He came to tell my dad that he's well enough to be discharged next week.
5/217	A: 我高中的时候就开始喜欢你了。 B: 真的？可是你从来没有告诉过我。 A: I began to like you when I was in high school. B: Really? But you never told me.

G | 218 哥 ELDER BROTHER gē

Chinese	English	Character codes
哥哥	elder brother	218/218
哥们儿	form of address between males	218/079/024
大哥	eldest brother	014/218
二哥	second eldest brother	025/218
老大哥	big brother	066/014/218
公子哥儿	dandy	221/172/218/024

Example Sentences

1/218	我哥哥在国外上大学，我以后也要去国外上大学。 My elder brother is studying abroad at a university, and I will also go to study abroad in the future.
2/218	我们天天在一起跑步，是哥们儿。 We run together every day. We're buddies.
3/218	我有三个哥哥，大哥是大夫，二哥是教师，三哥开出租车。我在宾馆工作。 I have three elder brothers; my eldest brother is a doctor, second brother is a teacher, and third brother drives a taxi. I work at a hotel.
4/218	A: 你怎么没有哥哥姐姐、弟弟妹妹呢？ B: 我是一九八二年生的，那时一对夫妻不可以生第二个孩子。 A: How come you don't have any brothers and sisters? B: I was born in 1982. At that time, married couples were not permitted to have a second child.
5/218	我们的同学乐乐是个公子哥儿，他每天玩到很晚，要睡到第二天下午起床，很少做作业，也不来考试。 Our classmate Lele is a dandy; he enjoys himself till late every night, then sleeps until the next afternoon. He rarely does any homework, and doesn't turn up to exams.

歌 SONG gē 219 G

Chinese	English	Character codes
歌唱	sing	219/197
唱歌	sing a song	197/219
歌唱家	singer	219/197/053
歌后	queen of song	219/044
歌手	singer	219/284
歌友会	fan club	219/157/049

Example Sentences

1/219	他天生就爱唱歌。 He loves to sing by nature.
2/219	他虽然从小喜欢唱歌，但是因为现在要高考，就没时间唱了。 Although he had liked to sing since he was a child, now that he has to study for the university entrance examination, he has no time for singing.
3/219	他外公是个歌唱家，他妈妈也是个歌唱家，他怎么没学唱歌呢？ His grandfather is a singer, his mother is also a singer, so why hasn't he learned to sing?
4/219	今天学生们去了老人院为老人们唱歌，还给老人们送了水果。 The students went to the nursing home today to sing for the old people and bring them some fruit.
5/219	小雪七月三十日的歌友会会开在北京。虽然那天会非常热，但是已经有三千多个歌友报名了。 Xiaoxue's fan club meeting will be held in Beijing on July 30. Although that day could be very hot, more than 3,000 fans have already signed up.

G | 220 给 GIVE/FOR/TO gěi

Chinese	English	Character codes
给我看病	(of a doctor) see me for an appointment	220/132/062/192
给面子	save face; do someone a favour	220/081/172
我给你	I give you	132/220/089
给不给	whether to give or not	220/007/220
给我看看	let me have a look	220/132/062/062
给他点颜色看看	teach him a lesson	220/125/016/315/277/062/062

Example Sentences

1/220	因为是中国新年，宾馆给了每个工作人员一个星期的假。 Because it's Chinese New Year, the hotel has given all of the staff a one-week vacation.
2/220	那个人打了我弟弟，我不去打他，但是我要给他点颜色看看。 That guy hit my younger brother. I'm not going to hit him back, but I want to teach him a lesson.
3/220	一个小生日，你送我这么好的书，真是太给面子了！ It's just an ordinary birthday, and you gave me such a nice book — you're really too good to me!
4/220	高先生在开会，现在请不要给他打电话。 Mr Gao is in a meeting, so please don't telephone him at the moment.
5/220	A: 这个水果篮是给谁的？ B: 是给钱老师的，因为大家知道钱老师病了。 A: Who is this fruit basket for? B: It's for Teacher Qian, because as everyone knows, Teacher Qian is ill.

公 PUBLIC/METRIC gōng 221 G

Chinese	English	Character codes
公共汽车	bus	221/222/267/010
公司	company	221/285
公道	justice	221/206
公房	public housing	221/213
公告	public notice	221/217
公里	kilometre	221/069
公开	publicly	221/061

Example Sentences

1/221	因为学校离我家有一百多公里，所以我住校。 Because the school is more than 100 kilometres away from my home, I am boarding.
2/221	哥哥每天都坐公共汽车去学校。 My elder brother goes to school by bus every day.
3/221	这事不可以公开。 This is not to be made public.
4/221	听说那个新来的服务员就要走了。说句公道话，他是一个很好的工作人员。 I hear that the new attendant is leaving. To be fair, he's a good employee.
5/221	国家给的房子就叫公房，就是公家房子的意思。但是现在很少有人住公房，大家都买房了。 Housing provided by the state is called *gongfang* (public housing), which is short for *gongjiafangzi*. However, very few people live in public housing nowadays; everyone buys their own housing.

G 222 共 COMMON/TO SHARE/TOGETHER gòng

Chinese	English	Character codes
公共汽车	bus	221/222/267/010
共同	common	222/130
共同点	common ground	222/130/016
共识	consensus	222/116
共有	altogether/in all	222/158
共和国	republic	222/042/036
共事	work together	222/281
一共	altogether/in total	152/222
公共场所	public place	221/222/196/290

Example Sentences

1/222	你我一起共事了多年，是真正的好朋友了。 You and I have been colleagues for many years, and we're really good friends.
2/222	我虽然比你大十五岁，可是我们有很多共同点。 Although I am 15 years older than you, we have a lot in common.
3/222	我们班共有十名女生。 Altogether there are ten girls in our class.
4/222	虽然你们国家的公共汽车票和火车票比中国的贵多了，但是吃和住这几年开始比中国便宜了。 Although your country's bus and train tickets are more expensive than they are in China, in recent years food and accommodation has been cheaper than in China.
5/222	A: 谢谢你介绍这家饭馆儿，今天的午饭真好吃，一共多少钱？ B: 没多少钱，今天是你第一天在我们公司上班，我请你。 A: Thank you for introducing me to this restaurant. Today's lunch was delicious. How much is it? B: It didn't cost much. Since today is your first day with the company, I'll treat you.

瓜 MELON guā 223 G

Chinese	English	Character codes
西瓜	watermelon	135/223
西瓜子	watermelon seeds	135/223/172
瓜子	melon seeds	223/172
瓜果	fruit	223/037
瓜分	divide up	223/028
北瓜	zucchini	005/223

Example Sentences

1/223	这两天天气很热，你去买个西瓜吃吧！ The weather has been very hot these past two days, go and buy a watermelon!
2/223	家里的客人要来了，准备些瓜果吧。 Our guests are coming, prepare some fruit.
3/223	A: 请问，西瓜怎么卖？ B: 每个卖 15 块 *，买两个送一个。 A: Excuse me, how much is the watermelon? B: Fifteen *kuai* each. Buy two and get another one free.
4/223	瓜子是中国人常吃的东西，以前在国外的店里很少买得到，但是现在很多店里都有了。 Melon seeds are something that Chinese people often eat. They used to be rarely sold in foreign stores, but now many stores have them.
5/223	这家饭店的北瓜做得非常好吃，但是我丈夫不喜欢吃。 The zucchini in this restaurant is really delicious, but my husband doesn't like it.

注释 Note

* 块 kuài = yuan, unit of money in China .

G 224 贵 EXPENSIVE/NOBLE/YOUR (honorific) guì

Chinese	English	Character codes
太贵了	too expensive	127/224/067
贵姓?	What is your surname? (respectful form)	224/312
贵客	distinguished guest	224/063
贵公司	your company (respectful form)	224/221/285
名贵	famous and valuable	082/224
可贵	valuable	242/224

Example Sentences

1/224	这个桌子太贵了，我买不起。 This table is too expensive. I can't afford it.
2/224	请问您贵姓? May I ask your surname?
3/224	爸爸说今天家里要来贵客，所以他要去车站等他。 Dad said we have an important guest visiting our home today, so he is going to the station to meet him.
4/224	A: 请问你们明天几点来我们公司开会? B: 我们明天下午两点会到贵公司。 A: What time will you come to our company for the meeting tomorrow? B: We will arrive at your company at 2 pm tomorrow.
5/224	真的好朋友很可贵，他们可以让我们开心，也能在学习和工作上帮助我们。 True friends are very valuable; they can make us happy, and can help us in our studies and our work.

过 CROSS/PASS/OVER- /(past experience marker) guò 225

Chinese	English	Character codes
开过	(of meeting etc.) have been held	061/225
来过	came; been (here)	065/225
没有去过	have never been to	078/158/102/225
吃过	have eaten (before)	011/225
看没看过?	have seen/read or not (question form)	062/078/062/225

Example Sentences

1/225	你来晚了，会已经开过了。 You're late. The meeting has already been held.
2/225	她早上来过，现在走了。 She was here this morning, but she has gone now.
3/225	我不是北京人，我也没有去过北京。 I'm not a Beijinger, and I've never been to Beijing.
4/225	我听我妈说钱奶奶年轻的时候很漂亮，还读过大学呢！ I heard my mum say that Granny Qian was beautiful when she was young, and she had even gone to university!
5/225	A: 我在看《情人》这本书，你看没看过？ B: 下个星期就要考试了，我没时间看小说。 A: I am reading the book *Lover*. Have you read it? B: There is an exam next week. I don't have time to read novels.

H 226 还 STILL/ALSO/EVEN hái; RETURN huán

Chinese	English	Character codes
还没来	has/have not come yet	226/078/065
还在工作	still working	226/164/032/176
还学	also study (some other subject)	226/150
还在	still be at/in	226/164
还好	not bad	226/039
还是	or; still; nevertheless; had better	226/118
还 * 书	return a book	226/119
还 * 车	return a car	226/010
还 * 给	return; give back	226/220

注释 Note

* 还 huán = return (All other examples are pronounced as hái.)

Example Sentences

1/226	现在两点了，他还没有来。 It's two o'clock now and he still hasn't come yet.
2/226	我妈已经七十九岁了，还在医院工作。 My mother is seventy-nine years old and still works in the hospital.
3/226	我们不但学汉语，还学日语。 We study not only Chinese but also Japanese.
4/226	还在上小学的时候，她就能看高中学生的课本了，她现在在大学教书呢。 When she was still in primary school, she could already read high school students' textbooks. She teaches at the university now.
5/226	A: 小红，你想吃米饭还是面条儿？ B: 学校的面条儿不好吃。我们还是去对面的饭馆儿吃吧。 A: Xiaohong, do you prefer rice or noodles? B: The noodles of our school aren't very good. Let's go to the restaurant across the road.

孩 CHILD hái 227 H

Chinese	English	Character codes
孩子	child	227/172
男孩儿	boy	259/227/024
女孩儿	girl	091/227/024
小孩儿	child	143/227/024
小孩子	child	143/227/172
孩子话	children's words	227/172/046
好孩子	good child	039/227/172

Example Sentences

1/227	我还是个孩子，不是很懂这些大人在想什么。 I am still a child; I don't really understand what these adults are thinking.
2/227	你看见那个男孩儿了吗？ Have you seen that boy yet?
3/227	我错了，我以后要做个好孩子。 I made a mistake. I will try to be a good kid in the future.
4/227	过去在中国大家都喜欢生男孩儿，但是现在生男生女都一样了。 In the past, Chinese people preferred to have boys, but nowadays there is no preference between boys and girls.
5/227	我们做大人的常常要孩子们听话，但是我们很少去听听孩子们想说什么。 As adults, we often want children to be obedient, but we rarely listen to what they want to say.

H | 228 黑 BLACK hēi

Chinese	English	Character codes
黑颜色	black (colour)	228/315/277
黑白	black and white	228/180
黑车	unlicensed vehicle	228/010
黑客	computer hacker	228/063
黑天白日	day and night	228/128/180/275
黑鱼	snakehead (fish)	228/330

Example Sentences

1/228	我上小学第二年的时候，我们家买了一个黑白电视机。 When I was in the second year of primary school, our family bought a black and white TV set.
2/228	因为下雨天在机场打不到车，所以人们有时候不得不打黑车回家。 On a rainy day it can be difficult to get hold of a taxi at the airport, so sometimes people have no choice but to take an unlicensed cab.
3/228	我不喜欢我们学校黑色的校服。 I don't like our school's black uniform.
4/228	这家饭店最便宜的房间也要 2000 块 *，比北京饭店还贵，太黑了！ The cheapest room in this hotel is 2,000 *kuai*, which is even more expensive than the Beijing Hotel. They're so greedy!
5/228	高先生工作起来没黑天白日的，吃也吃不好。这样下去他会生病的！ Mr Gao works all day and night, and he doesn't eat well. If he carries on like this, he's going to get ill!

注释 Note

* 块 kuài = yuan, unit of money in China

红 RED/POPULAR/PROSPEROUS hóng 229 H

Chinese	English	Character codes
红颜色	red (colour)	229/315/277
红茶	black tea	229/009
红火	flourishing; prosperous	229/050
红人	popular person	229/104
红十字会	Red Cross Society	229/114/173/049
走红	become popular	345/229

Example Sentences

1/229	很多中国人喜欢喝红茶。 Many Chinese people like to drink black tea.
2/229	中国人过新年的时候，喜欢穿红色的衣服。 Chinese people like to wear red during Chinese New Year.
3/229	学校对面的小吃店开得很红火。 The snack bar opposite the school is very popular.
5/229	钱老师是我们学校的红人，她上课上得很好，学生和家长都非常喜欢她。 Teacher Qian is very popular in our school; her lessons are really good, and both students and parents like her a lot.
5/229	虽然这位歌唱家在 1983 年就不走红了，但是他唱过的那些歌现在还很红。 Although the popularity of this singer has waned since 1983, those songs he sang are still very popular.

J | 230 鸡 CHICKEN jī

Chinese	English	Character codes
鸡蛋	chicken egg	230/204
公鸡	rooster	221/230
鸡飞蛋打	all is lost; a dead loss	230/027/204/013
鸡肉	chicken	230/276
小鸡	chick	143/230
鸡妈妈	mother hen	230/074/074
鸡叫	(rooster) crow	230/055

Example Sentences

1/230	这家店的鸡蛋为什么比那家店的贵那么多? Why are the eggs in this store so much more expensive than (the eggs) in that store?
2/230	每天早上公鸡一叫，爸爸就起床了。 Every morning, as soon as the rooster crows, Dad gets up.
3/230	晚饭你想吃牛肉还是鸡肉? What would you like, beef or chicken for dinner?
4/230	我们家有一只公鸡，还有鸡妈妈和四只小鸡。公鸡很漂亮，鸡妈妈每天都给我们下一个蛋。 We have a rooster at home, as well as a mother hen and four chicks. The rooster is very handsome, and the mother hen lays an egg for us every day.
5/230	他先是请老师教他踢足球，足球没踢好就去学唱歌，现在歌也不唱了，真是鸡飞蛋打。 First he found someone to teach him to play football, but he wasn't very good at it; so he tried learning to sing, but now he doesn't sing any more. He's a dead loss.

间 SPACE/TIME/BETWEEN/ROOM/MW (rooms) jiān 231 J

Chinese	English	Character codes
时间	time	115/231
房间	room	213/231
一个房间	one room	152/031/213/231
车间	workshop	010/231
人间	the human world	104/231
一时间	in a short time; very soon	152/115/231
午间	midday	134/231

Example Sentences

1/231	我没有时间天天睡大觉。 I don't have time to sleep a lot every day.
2/231	我的妻子已经不在人间了。 My wife is no longer in this world (i.e. she died).
3/231	老钱以前在这个车间工作过。 Mr Qian worked in this workshop before.
4/231	A: 你家好大啊，一共有几个房间? B: 四个房间，三个是睡觉的房间，还有一个是书房。 A: Your house is really big. How many rooms are there? B: Four, three bedrooms and a study room.
5/231	在我们学校，每个星期二和星期四学生们午间都有很长的休息时间。学生们可以运动或看书，但是不可以离开学校。 At our school on Tuesdays and Thursdays students have a long lunch break. Students can play sports or read books, but they can't leave the school.

J | 232 件 ITEM/MW (clothes, articles, events) jiàn

Chinese	English	Character codes
一件衣服	a piece of clothing	152/232/153/029
一件事	a matter	152/232/281
事件	event; happening; incident	281/232
快件	express delivery	244/232
机件	component (mechanics)	051/232
大件	bulk; large-sized object	014/232

Example Sentences

1/232	你还有很多件新衣服，不要再买了吧。 You already have a lot of new clothes, so don't buy any more.
2/232	那个四岁的小孩就会打人，这可不是一件小事。 It is no trivial matter that a four-year-old child hits people.
3/232	这个报告说的是两年前的事件，不是现在。 This report concerns the event happened in two years ago instead of current ones.
4/232	A: 小红，这是一个快件，明天早上十点以前要送到冷先生家。 B: 好的，我会叫个“京东快件”，今天晚上就可以送到。 A: Xiaohong, this is an express delivery. It needs to be sent to Mr Leng's house before ten o'clock tomorrow morning. B: OK. I'll call Jingdong Express and it will be delivered tonight.
5/232	A: 小天，要开学了，妈妈给你买几件新衣服吧。 B: 谢谢妈妈，不要了，一件都不要，因为在学校我们都穿校服。 A: Xiaotian, school will start soon. Shall I buy some new clothes for you? B: Thanks, Mum. But I don't need any as we'll all be wearing school uniform at school.

教 * TEACH jiāo; EDUCATE jiào 233 J

Chinese	English	Character codes
教 + 室 → 教室	teach + room = classroom	233/283
教师	teacher	233/113
教学	teaching	233/150
教工休息室	faculty room	233/032/313/308/283
家教	private tutor	053/233
教 ** 书	teaching	233/119
教 ** 书先生	school teacher	233/119/140/112

Example Sentences

1/233	我爸爸妈妈都是教 ** 书的。 My parents are both teachers.
2/233	我从小就想做一名教师。 I've wanted to be a teacher since I was a child.
3/233	我的老师虽然很有名，但是教学上很过时。 Although my teacher is well-known, his teaching is very outdated.
4/233	在中国的中小学，学生每天都在同一个教室里上课。但是我听说在国外，学生上不同的课要去不同的教室。 In China's primary and secondary schools, students stay in the same classroom all day. But I'm told that in foreign countries, students have to go to different classrooms for different classes.
5/233	钱老师，现在是课间休息时间，我们一起去教工休息室喝杯咖啡、吃点水果吧。 Teacher Qian, it's break time now. Let's go to the staff room to have a cup of coffee and some fruit.

注释 Note

* 教 is a polyphonic character. jiāo = teach; jiào = educatie.

** 教 jiāo = teach (All other examples are pronounced as jiào.)

J | 234 介 INTRODUCE/LIE BETWEEN jiè

Chinese	English	Character codes
介 + 绍 → 介绍	introduce+ continue = introduce; recommend	234/278
介绍人	referee	234/278/104
中介	act as intermediary; agency; agent	168/234
介意	care about; mind	234/324
别介意	never mind; take no notice	190/234/324

Example Sentences

1/234	我最近忙着找人帮我介绍工作呢！ Recently I've been busy looking for someone who can recommend me a job.
2/234	我在中介公司工作。要是你想在北京买卖房子，可以找我！ I work for an (real estate) agency. If you want to buy or sell a house in Beijing, come and find me!
3/234	妈，我给你介绍一下，这是我同学高大明。 Mum, let me introduce to you my classmate Gao Daming.
4/234	A: 请问，您介意我坐在您旁边吗？ B: 没关系，我一点儿也不介意，请坐。 A: Excuse me, do you mind if I sit next to you? B: That's all right. I don't mind at all. Please sit down.
5/234	高老师是我工作的介绍人，我的妻子也是他介绍的。 Teacher Gao was the referee for my job, and my wife was also introduced by him.

进 ENTER jìn 235 J

Chinese	English	Character codes
请进	please come in	101/235
进来	come in	235/065
进步	progress	235/193
进一步	go a step further	235/152/193
进场	enter the arena	235/196
进出	go in and out	235/012

Example Sentences

1/235	小明这几个月的学习有进步。 Xiaoming has made progress in his studies over the past few months.
2/235	快看电视，中国运动员正在进场。 Quick, have a look at the TV. The Chinese athletes are coming onto the field.
3/235	我们每个人都从这个门进出。 Each of us goes in and out through this door.
4/235	A: 谢先生，请进来，请给大家介绍一下你的工作好吗？ B: 大家好，我现在在医院工作，但是以前我是老师。 A: Mr Xie, please come in! Can you give us a little introduction to the work that you do? B: Hello, everyone. Currently I am working in a hospital, but I used to be a teacher.
5/235	学校大门是在北京路上，它的对面是一个叫"进步"的宾馆，学校门前有12路公共汽车，旁边还有一家咖啡馆儿。 The school entrance is on the Beijing Road, opposite the hotel Progress. The No. 12 bus runs past the main gate, and there is a cafe next door.

J 236 近 SHORTCUT/ClOSE jìn

Chinese	English	Character codes
近道	shortcut	236/206
近路	shortcut	236/250
近来	recently	236/065
最近	recently; soon	347/236
近日	the past few days; the next few days	236/275
走近	approach	345/236

Example Sentences

1/236	我常常走近道回家。 I often take a shortcut home.
2/236	你近来在做些什么呢？ What have you been doing lately?
3/236	我儿子最近会来北京。 My son will come to Beijing soon.
4/236	虽然我家离车站很近，但是我不喜欢坐车，所以我每天走两个小时的路上下班。 Although my home is very close to the (bus) station, I don't like to take the bus, so I spend two hours every day walking to and from work.
5/236	那个老太太常常穿着黑色的衣服，我从来没见她笑过。每次她走近孩子们的时候，孩子们都会叫起来。 That old lady often wears black, and I've never seen her laughing. Every time she approaches the children, they all scream.

经 PASS THROUGH/UNDERGO/CLASSIC WORKS jīng 237 J

Chinese	English	Character codes
已 + 经 → 已经	already + pass through = already	322/237
经过	passing; go through; undergo; after; process; course	237/225
经常	often	237/195
四书五经	Confucian classics	123/119/133/237
经手	handle; deal with	237/284
经书	scripture	237/119

Example Sentences

1/237	房明已经十八岁了，他今年六月就要考大学了。 Fang Ming is already eighteen years old. In June this year he'll be taking the college entrance exam.
2/237	北京的十月经常是晴天，天气不冷不热。 October in Beijing is often sunny, and the weather is neither hot nor cold.
3/237	我不是经手这件事的人。 I'm not the person who handles the matter.
4/237	A: 大哥，请问这里有电影院吗？ B: 有，往前走，经过那个书店就到了。 A: Excuse me, is there a cinema here? B: Yes, go straight ahead and it's right after passing the bookstore.
5/237	奶奶虽然不识字，也没有上过学，但是她每天早上五点就开始读经。 Although my grandmother was illiterate, and didn't attend school, every morning at 5 am she would begin to recite scripture.

J | 238 睛 EYE/EYEBALL jīng

Chinese	English	Character codes
眼睛	eye	316/238
点睛	dot in the eyes (add the finishing touch)	016/238
没长眼睛	are you blind	078/194/316/238

Example Sentences

1/238	小妹妹有两只大大的眼睛，真漂亮！ The little girl has a pair of big eyes. She is so beautiful!
2/238	我有两个弟弟，但是我二弟的一只眼睛看不见了。 I have two younger brothers, the second one has lost his sight in one eye.
3/238	你看，这个小男孩儿的眼睛看着他的爸爸，不知道他想要说什么。 Look, the little boy's eyes are fixed on his father. I wonder what he wants to say.
4/238	A: 医生，为什么我的眼睛最近老是红的？ B: 没关系，你是太累了，吃点药，多休息，很快会好的。 A: Doctor, why are my eyes always so red recently? B: Don't worry, it is because you're too tired. Take some medicine and get more rest; it will soon be better.
5/238	人们都说，眼睛亮是身体好，我同意这个看法；我的一些喜欢运动的朋友，眼睛都很明亮。 People say that bright eyes indicate good health. I agree with this view. Some of my sports-loving friends are very bright-eyed.

就 * AT ONCE/AS SOON AS/ONLY/THEN/JUST jiù 239 J

Chinese	English	Character codes
就是	exactly; just, only	239/118
一A就B	as soon as A, then B	152/239
就近	nearby	239/236
就学	go to school	239/150
就医	see a doctor	239/154
就要	about to	239/319

Example Sentences

1/239	我一吃完晚饭，就做作业。 I do my homework as soon as I finish dinner.
2/239	我每天一下课，就和同学一起在学校运动场上玩儿。 As soon as the lesson finishes every day, I go and play with my classmates on the school sports field.
3/239	我们飞到北京会很晚，还是就近找个旅馆先住一晚吧。 We shall land in Beijing until very late. We'd better stay in a hotel nearby for one night.
4/239	你早上开会为什么去晚了？你就是不说，我也知道是怎么回事。 Why were you late for the morning meeting? Even if you won't tell me, I know what it's about.
5/239	高明明很爱笑，家里的人都知道她一出生就爱笑，所以她的小名叫笑笑。 Gao Mingming loves to laugh. The whole family knows that she laughs more from the moment she was born, hence her nick name is Xiaoxiao.

注释 Note

* 就 is the most flexible character in Chinese, and it has at least a dozen usages. These include just, only, then, as soon as, even if, right away, in that case, approach, undertake, with regard to...

K 240 咖* COFFEE (first character) kā

Chinese	English	Character codes
咖啡	coffee	240/215
咖啡色	coffee-coloured; brown	240/215/277
咖啡馆	café	240/215/035
咖啡因	caffeine	240/215/325
咖啡店	coffee shop	240/215/018

Example Sentences

1/240	以前中国人都喝茶，现在中国人也开始喝咖啡了。 Chinese people used to drink tea, but now Chinese are also starting to drink coffee.
2/240	因为我不喜欢咖啡色，所以我一件咖啡色的衣服也没有。 Because I don't like the colour brown, I don't own a single item of brown-coloured clothing.
3/240	有人说，不但咖啡里有咖啡因，茶里也有咖啡因。 People say that it's not only coffee that contains caffeine, tea has caffeine in it as well.
4/240	A: 我们明天中午一起吃个饭好吗？ B: 好的，学校旁边新开了一家咖啡馆儿，想不想吃完饭后去那儿试一下？ A: Would you like to have lunch together tomorrow? B: OK. A new café has opened next to our school. Would you like to give it a try after lunch?
5/240	在北京路上有家咖啡馆儿，门面虽然不大，但是咖啡特别好喝。星期一和星期五的时候客人们还可以一边喝咖啡一边学做咖啡。 There is a coffee shop on the Beijing Road. Although the shop is quite modest, the coffee is especially good. On Mondays and Fridays, customers can also taste the coffee while learning how to make it.

注释 Note

* 咖 is also used as the first character of 咖喱 gālí (loanword for curry).

考 TEST/TAKE AN EXAM kǎo 241 K

Chinese	English	Character codes
考 + 试 → 考试	test + try = exam	241/282
考生	candidate	241/112
考场	exam room	241/196
考点	test centre	241/016
考分	test score	241/028
考题	exam question	241/293
高考	university entrance exam	030/241

Example Sentences

1/241	你的两个姐姐怎么一到考试就生病呢？ How come your two older sisters get sick whenever they are going to take the exam?
2/241	两个小时的考题那么多，很多考生都没做完。 There were too many exam questions to answer in two hours, and many candidates didn't finish it.
3/241	让我考一考你的汉语好吗？ Would you allow me to test your Chinese?
4/241	在中国，很多家长都认为高考是孩子人生中最大的一次考试。因为孩子考上了一个好大学，以后就可以找到一个好工作。 In China, many parents believe that the college entrance examination is the most important exam in their children's life. If a child can gain entrance to a good university, they will be able to find a good job in the future.
5/241	我知道你学习很认真，但是这次考试前你可能没有准备好，所以考分不高。不过没关系，下次还有机会。 I know that you're studying hard, but you might not be ready for this exam, and your marks were not good enough. But don't worry, there will be another chance next time.

K | 242 可 CAN/ABLE TO/APPROVE kě

Chinese	English	Character codes
可爱	lovely; cute	242/001
可以	can; possible	242/323
可不是	absolutely not	242/007/118
可贵	valuable	242/224
可能	possible; probable; perhaps	242/088
可见	it can be seen that…	242/054
可乐	cola	242/246

Example Sentences

1/242	这个女孩子很可爱，她做的饭菜也很好吃。 The girl is lovely. And the food she made is delicious.
2/242	请给我一大杯可乐。 Please give me a large cola.
3/242	明天的晚会，你可以去，也可以不去。 As for the party tomorrow evening, you may go or not.
4/242	我本来想出去走走，可是电视上说要下雨，所以我可能就在家看看书了。 I was hoping to go out for a walk, but they said on TV it was going to rain, so I'll probably just read at home.
5/242	A: 你下班后想做一点儿什么？ B: 我可能先去体育馆打一会儿篮球，再和女朋友一起去吃晚饭。你呢？ A: What do you plan to do after work? B: I might go to the gym to play basketball for a while, then go for dinner with my girlfriend. How about you?

课 CLASS/LESSON kè 243 K

Chinese	English	Character codes
上课	go to class	108/243
下课	finish class	139/243
课本	textbook	243/006
课间	class break	243/231
课时	class period	243/115
课外	extracurricular	243/297
课前	before class	243/099
课后	after class	243/044

Example Sentences

1/243	我每天早上九点上课。 I go to class at nine o'clock every morning.
2/243	同学们课间休息的时候常常一起踢足球。 Students often play football together during breaks.
3/243	现在的孩子每天课后都有很多作业，所以睡觉比我们小时候要晚。 Today's children have a lot of homework after class, so they get to bed later than we did when we were young.
4/243	A: 你每个星期上几次汉语课? B: 两次，我每星期三和五有汉语课。 A: How many Chinese lessons do you have a week? B: Two, every Wednesday and Friday.
5/243	因为房老师生病住院了，所以这个课不上了。等学院找到新老师以后，会让大家知道开课时间的。 As Teacher Fang is ill in hospital, this class is cancelled. When our college finds a new teacher, we'll let everyone know the time of the new class.

K 244 快 QUICK/FAST/SOON/SHARP/FORTHRIGHT kuài

Chinese	English	Character codes
快乐	happy	244/246
跑得快	run fast	263/207/244
进步很快	make rapid progress	235/193/043/244
快车	fast train	244/010
快车道	fast lane	244/010/206
快件	express delivery	244/232
快门	shutter	244/257
快人快语	straight talk from a straightforward person	244/104/244/160
快要	be about to	244/319

Example Sentences

1/244	大家都知道小雨跑得很快，没人比得过他。 Everyone knows that Xiaoyu runs very fast. No one can match him.
2/244	小明的学习最近进步很快！ Xiaoming has made rapid progress in his studies lately.
3/244	天快要下雨了，我们快回家吧。 It's about to rain. Let's go home soon.
4/244	A: 请问“京东”的快件几天能送到？ B: 那要看送到哪儿，可能一天，也可能两到三天。 A: Excuse me, how many days does it take for Jingdong Express to deliver express post? B: It depends on where it is sent; perhaps one day, or two or three days.
5/244	从这里去北京每小时有很多班快车，下一班快车十分钟后到，你准备上车吧。 There are quite a lot of express trains to Beijing per hour. The next one arrives in ten minutes. You should get ready to board.

篮 BASKET lán 245 L

Chinese	English	Character codes
菜篮	shopping basket	008/245
打＋篮球→打篮球	play + basketball = play basketball	131/245/272
篮球场	basketball court	245/272/196
篮子	basket	245/172
篮球衣	basketball jersey	245/272/153
篮球明星	basketball star	245/272/083/148

Example Sentences

1/245	我妈妈有一个很大的篮子，每天买的菜都在这个篮子里，你看，就在这儿。 My mother has a big basket. She puts all the vegetables she buys each day in it. Look, here it is!
2/245	每次下雨不能跑步的时候，我们都去篮球馆打篮球。 Whenever it rains, and we can't go out for a run, we will go to the basketball hall to play basketball.
3/245	我喜欢打篮球，以后想做一个篮球运动员。 I like playing basketball, and I want to be a basketball player in the future.
4/245	篮球是学生们很喜爱的一个运动。篮球场上不但有很多男生，也常常可以看到不少女生打球。 Basketball is a popular sport with students. You can often find many boys playing on the court, as well as girls.
5/245	妈妈，请你帮我买一件新的球衣吧！过几天是我的生日，我要和朋友们一起打篮球来过我二十岁的生日。 Mum, please buy me a new basketball jersey. It's my twentieth birthday in a few days, and I want to spend it with my friends playing basketball.

L 246 乐 HAPPY lè; MUSIC yuè

Chinese	English	Character codes
快乐	happy	244/246
以……为乐	take pleasure in	323/303/246
欢乐	happy; pleasure	047/246
乐天	carefree; optimistic	246/128
乐意	be willing	246/324
乐子	fun	246/172
西乐 *	Western music	135/246

Example Sentences

1/246	她就是这样一个快乐的、爱笑的人。 She is such a happy, cheerful person.
3/246	我们乐意帮忙，不过这个星期很忙，下星期吧！ We're happy to help, but this week we are very busy. We shall help you next week!
4/246	你都快五十岁了，不要天天想的都是工作，还是找点乐子吧。 You're almost fifty years old. Don't think about work every day and try to have some fun.
5/246	别人都觉得教书很累，可是钱老师在学校做了三十年，他一点儿都不觉得累。我觉得他是一个以 ** 教 *** 书为 ** 乐的人。 Other people may feel that teaching is very tiring, but Mr Qian has been in this school for thirty years and he doesn't consider it tiring at all. I think he's someone who takes delight in education.
2/246	他们不让我帮忙，我乐得 **** 在家看电视。 They didn't need my help, so I was only too happy to watch TV at home.

注释 Note

* 乐 yuè = music (All other examples are pronounced as lè.)

**The pattern 以 A 为 B means to regard A as B. In this instance, education is regarded as the source of happiness.

*** Polyphonic word 教 jiāo=teach; 教 jiào=educate

**** 得 dé=get, 乐得 = be too glad to

累 * TIRED lèi ; PILE UP/ACCUMULATE lěi 247 L

Chinese	English	Character codes
走累了	be tired from walking	345/247/067
累眼睛	tax the eyes	247/316/238
累了一天	get tired from a hard day	247/067/152/128
累得眼睛都红了	have bloodshot eyes due to tiredness	247/207/316/238/020/229/067
经年累 ** 月	for years	237/090/247/162

注释 Note

* 累 is a polyphonic character. lěi = pile up; accumulate; lèi = tired

** 累 lěi = accumulate (All other examples are pronounced as lèi.)

Example Sentences

1/247	医生说经常看小字会累眼睛。 Doctors say that reading small print can strain the eyes.
2/247	我累了一天，真想休息一会儿。 I've been working hard all day, and really fancy a bit of a rest.
3/247	看来你累了，进来坐坐，喝杯水吧。 You seem tired. Come in and sit down and have a glass of water.
4/247	A: 小天天，快睡吧，你累得眼睛都红了。 B: 妈，我的作业还没做完呢，您先去休息吧。 A: Little Tiantian, go to sleep. Your eyes are red from being tired. B: Mum, I haven't finished my homework yet. You go and have a rest first.
5/247	因为上有老下有小，人到中年以后常常会觉得很累。 Because they may have both old parents and young children to look after, middle-aged people often feel tired.

L | 248 离 LEAVE/PART FROM/BE AWAY FROM lí

Chinese	English	Character codes
离……近	near to	248/236
离……远	far from	248/332
离家出走	run away from home	248/053/012/345
离别	bid farewell	248/190
离开	leave	248/061
离题	digress from the topic	248/293

Example Sentences

1/248	他从小就离开家人，去国外上学了。 He left his family when he was still young, and went abroad to study.
2/248	你的话离题太远了。 Your comments are way off point.
3/248	我家离公司就一站路，所以有时间的话，我会走路上班。 My office is just one bus stop away from home, so if I have time I walk to work.
4/248	他十岁的时候离家出走过一次，后来再没有这么做了。他现在和爸爸妈妈的关系很好。 He ran away from home once when he was ten years old, but he never did it again. Now his relationship with his parents is very good.
5/248	A: 你离得这么远，老师说话你听得见吗？ B: 我听得见，再说，这几道题我已经知道怎么做了。 A: Are you going to be able to hear what the teacher's saying at such a distance? B: I can hear all right, besides, I already know how to answer these questions.

两 TWO/BOTH/SOME/A FEW liǎng 249 L

Chinese	English	Character codes
两个房间	two rooms	249/031/213/231
过两天	after a couple of days	225/249/128
两下子	a few tricks of the trade	249/139/172
两边	both sides	249/188
两点	two o'clock	249/016
两回事	two entirely different things	249/048/281

Example Sentences

1/249	我家有两个房间，我爸爸妈妈一间，我和姐姐一间。 My home has two rooms; mum and dad are in one room, and my sister and I are in the other.
2/249	这事过两天再说好吗？ Shall we put this matter aside for a couple of days?
3/249	你真有两下子！这么快就做好饭了。 You're really something! That meal was ready so quickly.
4/249	小习是我的好朋友。他第一天来公司上班，我就很喜欢他。后来我们两个去了不同的国家，但是我们两个还是好朋友。 Xiaoxi is my good friend. When he came to work on his first day, I liked him straight away. Later we went to different countries, but we're still good friends.
5/249	你想考第一名和你能考第一名是两回事。你天天玩儿手机，不认真学习，怎么可能在班里得第一呢！ Wanting to come first in the exam and being able to do it are two different things. You play on your phone every day rather than studying hard, so how are you going to become top of the class!

L 250 路 ROAD/ROUTE/PATH lù

Chinese	English	Character codes
问路	ask the way	304/250
路边	roadside	250/188
路过	pass by	250/225
路考	driving test	250/241
路西	on the west side of the road	250/135
路人	passer-by	250/104
路上	on the way	250/108
门路	(social) connections/way (to get job etc.)	257/250

Example Sentences

1/250	报纸上说女人比男人喜欢问路。 It said in the newspaper that women are more willing to ask for directions than men.
2/250	她每天都走路去学校。 She walks to school every day
3/250	每天回家的路上我都路过这家书店。 I pass this bookstore every day on my way home.
3/250	以前在这条路的两边，有很多人卖菜。后来有了菜场，路边卖菜的人就没有了。 There used to be many people selling vegetables on both sides of this road, but since the vegetable market opened, no one sells vegetables by the roadside.
5/250	我妈给我去北京的路上准备了好多好吃的东西，有鸡蛋、水果和咖啡。在送我去火车站的路上，她还给了我一些钱。 My mother prepared a lot of delicious food for me to eat on the way to Beijing; there were eggs, fruit and coffee. On the way to see me off at the train station she also gave me some money.

旅 TRAVEL lǚ 251 L

Chinese	English	Character codes
旅游	travel; tour	251/328
旅客	tourist	251/063
旅店	inn	251/018
旅馆	hotel	251/035
旅游车	sightseeing bus	251/328/010
旅游点	tourist spot	251/328/016

Example Sentences

1/251	现在每年都有很多中国游客去国外旅游。 Nowadays, many Chinese tourists travel abroad every year.
2/251	这次我们坐旅游车去北京，一路上会经过十几个旅游点，可以一路玩儿过去。 This time we will take a tourist coach to Beijing. On the way we will pass through more than ten tourist spots, so we'll be able to enjoy ourselves all the way there.
3/251	我想今年十月去中国旅游，因为听说那时的天气非常好。 I want to travel to China in October this year, as I've heard that the weather is particularly pleasant at that time.
4/251	这两年旅游红火了，工作机会也就多了。我们家也开了家小旅馆，生意一年比一年好。 In the past two years, tourism has been booming and there are more job opportunities. Our family has opened a small hotel, and business has been better every year.
5/251	我最喜欢这家旅馆的早饭，每天都有我最爱吃的西瓜、苹果和热牛奶。 I like the breakfast at this hotel the most; every day they have my favourite things: watermelon, apple and hot milk.

M | 252 卖 SELL mài

Chinese	English	Character codes
买卖	buy and sell; business	075/252
买卖人	businessman	075/252/104
卖唱	sing for a living; busk	252/197
卖出	sell	252/012
卖点	selling point	252/016
卖国	betray one's country	252/036
卖完	sold out	252/298
大卖场	hypermarket	014/252/196

Example Sentences

1/252	从我奶奶的奶奶的时候开始，我们家就是做买卖的。 Our family has been in business since my grandmother's grandmother's time.
2/252	这个卖唱的小女孩儿看上去不过七八岁。 That little girl who sings for a living looks to be no more than seven or eight years old.
3/252	不到一个小时，这些羊肉就都卖完了。 In less than an hour, the lamb had all sold out.
4/252	现在的大卖场里什么都有，从吃的、喝的到穿的，等等。再说，大卖场里卖的东西也比大商店里的东西便宜得多。 Hypermarkets sell everything now, from food and drink to clothes. What's more, the things in the hypermarket are much cheaper than they are in the big stores.
5/252	A: 我想卖了这只手机，你看看可以卖多少钱? B: 你这是苹果六，太老了，卖不出多少钱。 A: I want to sell this mobile phone. How much do you reckon I could get for it? B: This is an iPhone 6. It's too old, so you won't get much money for it.

慢 SLOW màn 253 M

Chinese	English	Character codes
慢班	normal class	253/182
慢车	slow train	253/010
慢车道	slow lane	253/010/206
慢动作	slow motion	253/212/176
慢火	low heat	253/050
慢跑	jogging	253/263
慢走	mind how you go/take care	253/345

Example Sentences

1/253	在我们这里，从小学第五年开始分快班和慢班。 In our area, classes are separated into gifted and normal starting from the fifth year of primary school.
2/253	我本来想坐早上九点的快车去北京，但是因为快车票比慢车票贵很多，所以我最后还是坐了慢车。 I initially thought about taking the express train to Beijing at 9 am, but because the express ticket was a lot more expensive than the slow train ticket, I ended up taking the slow train.
3/253	慢点儿走好吗？我有话和你说。 Wait a minute, please. I've got something to tell you.
4/253	在运动场上，有些人在踢足球，有些人在打篮球，有些人在快走，还有些人在慢跑。 On the sports field, some people are playing football, some are playing basketball, some are power walking, and others are jogging.
5/253	在中国，快车道在左边，慢车道在右边。你开车的时候，可别开错了道。 In China, the fast lane is on the left and the slow lane is on the right. When you're driving a car (in China), don't drive in the wrong lane.

M | 254 忙 BUSY/HURRY máng

Chinese	English	Character codes
正忙呢	being busy	339/254/087
帮忙	help	183/254
忙里忙外	bustle around	254/069/254/297
忙人	busy person	254/104
忙中出错	errors made in haste	254/168/012/202

Example Sentences

1/254	我现在正忙着呢。 I'm in a rush at the moment.
2/254	你可以帮我（一）点儿小忙吗？ Can you give me a bit of a hand?
3/254	高老师是个大忙人。 Teacher Gao is a very busy person.
4/254	A: 老同学，最近在忙什么呢？ B: 我最近去了家新公司上班，有很多新东西要学，所以很忙。 A: Old boy, what are you busy with recently? B: I just started to work at a new company. There's a lot of new things to learn, so I'm very busy.
5/254	在我家都是我妈忙里忙外，不过，我爸爸忙的东西不一样，他天天忙着写书。 At home, my mother is always bustling around doing all kinds of things, but my father's busy with something else; he's busy writing his book every day.

每 EVERY/EACH měi 255 M

Chinese	English	Character codes
每天	every day	255/128
每月	every month	255/162
每每	often	255/255
每次	every time	255/200
每个人	everybody	255/031/104
每小时	per hour	255/143/115

Example Sentences

1/255	我们公司每个月都要开一次大会。 Our company holds a meeting once a month.
2/255	每次我看见他的时候，都觉得他很快乐。 Every time I see him, I feel he's very happy.
3/255	钱医生是个大忙人，每天都不在家。 Doctor Qian is a very busy man; he's never at home every day.
4/255	从我们这里到北京的火车每小时有两班，一班是快车，一班是慢车，请问，你想买几点的火车票? There are two trains per hour from here to Beijing. One is an express and the other is a slow train. Excuse me, what time would you like to buy a ticket for?
5/255	做好事可以从小事做起，从我们每个人做起，从现在做起。 Doing good can start from small things, from every person, and from now.

M | 256 妹 YOUNGER SISTER mèi

Chinese	English	Character codes
妹妹	younger sister	256/256
小妹	youngest sister	143/256
妹夫	brother-in-law (younger sister's husband)	256/216
妹子	sister; girl	256/172
打工妹	female migrant worker	013/032/256
姐妹	sisters	057/256

Example Sentences

1/256	我有两个妹妹，小妹叫小雨，今年十一岁。 I have two younger sisters; the youngest is Xiaoyu and she is eleven this year.
2/256	我妹夫姓高，是开出租车的。虽然他每天的工作时间很长，但是身体还不错。 My brother-in-law's surname is Gao and he is a taxi driver. Although he works long hours every day, his health is pretty good.
3/256	妹妹，你要是不想上大学，姐姐给你介绍在饭店做一个服务员怎么样？ Sister, if you don't want to go to university, how about I recommend you for a job as a waitress in the restaurant?
4/256	这个打工妹人长 * 得漂亮，歌唱得好，舞跳得也不错。我希望她会有机会在新年晚会给大家唱歌。 This female migrant worker is very pretty, and she sings and dances well. I hope she will have the opportunity to sing for everyone at the New Year's party.
5/256	你我二人姐妹一场，没想到今天就要离别了。从今往后你住在东北，我住在西北，不能常常见面了。 You and I are such good sisters. I never thought the day would come when we would have to part. From now on, you'll be living in northeast China, and I'll be in northwest China. We won't be able to see each other very often.

注释 Note

* 长 zhǎng = grow, see 194 长 .

门 GATE/DOOR mén 257 M

Chinese	English	Character codes
关门	close the door	034/257
球门	goal (in ball game)	272/257
门道	knack	257/206
找门路	solicit help from social connections	336/257/250
门第	family status	257/210
门房	gatehouse; porter	257/213
热门儿	popular; in vogue	103/257/024

Example Sentences

1/257	有些事只要做起来就会知道门道是很多的。 With some things, it's only when you try to do them that you realise there's a knack to it.
2/257	那家衣服店的门前本来没有公共汽车站，现在有了。 Originally there was no bus stop at the front of the clothes shop, but there's one now.
3/257	我昨天在教室里见到一只红色的手表，后来我给了门房。 I found a red watch in the classroom yesterday; later I gave it to the gatekeeper.
4/257	说好是送客人到车站门口，都快一个小时了，姐姐怎么到现在还没回来呢？ My sister agreed to see the guests to the station entrance, but that was almost an hour ago. Why isn't she back yet?
5/257	我儿子明年就要读中学了，但是他的学习不太好，好的中学都很热门儿，所以他可能考不上好中学。 My son will start middle school next year. He's not very good at his study, and acceptance for good middle schools are very competitive, so he may not get a place at one of them.

N | 258 奶 MILK/BREAST nǎi

Chinese	English	Character codes
奶奶	grandmother (father's mother)	258/258
牛奶	milk	261/258
羊奶	goat's milk	317/258
吃奶	drink milk	011/258
奶白色	milky white	258/180/277
奶茶	tea with milk	258/009
奶名	childhood nickname	258/082
奶妈	wet nurse	258/074

Example Sentences

1/258	人们叫她"奶茶妹"，是因为她不但卖奶茶，还 * 长 ** 得很白很漂亮。 People call her 'bubble tea girl', not only because she sells bubble tea, but also because she is fair-skinned and pretty.
2/258	你还是个吃奶的孩子，怎么可以和你爸说话没大没小的！ You are still a milk-drinking child. How dare you talk to your father in such a cheeky manner!
3/258	奶奶给他起的奶名是狗子。 Grandma gave him his childhood nickname of Gouzi.
4/258	妈妈喜欢喝下午茶，也就是喝奶茶、吃一些小吃。下个月是她的生日，我想找一家饭店请她去喝下午茶。 Mum likes to have afternoon tea, i.e. milk tea and some snacks. It's her birthday next month, so I'm planning to invite her to a restaurant for afternoon tea.
5/258	以前一家有六七个小孩儿是常有的事。要是妈妈奶水没有了，家里就会请奶妈来。 In the past, it was common to have six or seven children in a family. If the mother had no more milk, the family would employ a wet nurse.

注释 Note

* 还 hái = also, see 226 还 .

** 长 zhǎng = grow, see 194 长 .

男 MAN nán 259 N

Chinese	English	Character codes
男人	man	259/104
好男儿	good man; hero	039/259/024
男孩儿	boy	259/227/024
男欢女爱	love between a man and a woman	259/047/091/001
男男女女	men and women	259/259/091/091
男朋友	boyfriend	259/092/157
男生	male student	259/112
男一号	male lead (actor)	259/152/040
男足	men's football	259/346

Example Sentences

1/259	他是我见过的最好的男人。 He's the nicest man I've ever met.
2/259	《好男儿》最近在电视上很火。 *Good Man* is a very popular programme on TV recently.
3/259	我们班有二十个男生，二十三个女生。 There are 20 boys and 23 girls in our class.
4/259	因为高大明是这个电影里的男一号，所以这个电影的票房非常好，他现在已经开始走红了。 Due to Gao Daming's performance as the male lead in this movie, it did very well at the box office, and he is starting to become much sought after.
5/259	A: 你说中国男足现在谁踢得最好？ B: 谁踢得好都和我没关系，我不喜欢看足球。 A: Who do you think is the best player of Chinese men's football at the moment? B: Who's playing well doesn't matter to me. I don't like watching football.

N | 260 您 YOU (respectful form) nín

Chinese	English	Character codes
您好	how do you do	260/039
您家	your home	260/053
您老	you	260/066
您早	good morning	260/334

Example Sentences

1/260	A: 老师，您早！ B: 同学们早！ A: Good morning, teacher! B: Good morning, class!
2/260	您老在我这家饭店吃好、喝好，我就高兴了。 It will be my pleasure that you can have a good meal in my restaurant.
3/260	奶奶，您怎么这么早就出来买菜呢？ Grandma, how come you're so early to do grocery shopping?
4/260	A: 您老今年已经九十多岁了，身体还很好！ B: 还好，还好。 A: You are already over ninety this year, and are still fit and healthy. B: Not so bad.
5/260	A: 老公公，听说您九十九岁了，是吗？ B: 你说什么，我听不见！我人老了，不但听不见，眼睛也看不见了。 A: Sir, I hear that you are ninety-nine years old. Is that right? B: What are you speaking? I can't hear you! I am old, and can neither hear nor see any more.

牛 OX/COW niú 261 N

Chinese	English	Character codes
奶牛	dairy cow	258/261
牛奶	milk	261/258
牛肉	beef	261/276
和牛	wagyu (Japanese) beef	042/261
公牛	bull	221/261
牛气	bullish; arrogant	261/098

Example Sentences

1/261	他可真牛气！ How arrogant he is!
2/261	我看到远远走来几只公牛和一些奶牛。 I've seen a few bulls and some cows coming from the distance.
3/261	最早的“和牛”是在日本，后来国外也有了。 Wagyu cattle originated in Japan and later appeared in other countries.
4/261	我们小时候吃的大多是白肉，因为红肉很贵。现在我想多给孩子吃点牛肉，我觉得牛肉对他们的身体比别的肉好。 Most of us ate white meat when we were young, because red meat was so expensive. Now I want to give my children more beef to eat, as it's better for their health than other meats.
5/261	冷太太现在常常买有机牛奶喝。天热的时候，她下班回家第一件事就是喝一杯冷的有机牛奶。 Mrs Leng often buys organic milk now. During hot weather, the first thing she does when she gets home after work is to drink a glass of cold organic milk.

P | 262 旁 SIDE/BESIDE/OTHER páng

Chinese	English	Character codes
旁边	side; beside	262/188
路旁	roadside	250/262
旁门	side door	262/257
旁门左道	unorthodox; heretical views	262/257/348/206
旁听	attend as an observer; sit in on	262/129
旁人	other people	262/104

Example Sentences

1/262	开会的时候，我可以坐在你旁边吗？ Can I sit next to you during the meeting?
2/262	他是从旁门进去的。 He entered via the side door.
3/262	这个人很喜欢钱，工作不好好做，老是想一些旁门左道。 That guy likes money very much, but he doesn't want to work hard for it; he's always trying to find some other way (of making money).
4/262	高老师，我是西大的老师，希望您不介意我来旁听您的课。听说您的汉语课上得非常好，我来学习学习，好吗？ Teacher Gao, I am a teacher from West University. I hope you won't mind if I sit in on your lesson. I've heard that your Chinese class is very good. Is it OK for me to come and learn something?
5/262	您是小谢的老师，不是旁人。那我就告诉您，他今年没有考大学，因为他想早点儿工作。 Since you're Xiao Xie's teacher, and not just an onlooker, I tell you that he didn't take the university entrance exam this year because he wants to find a job first.

跑 RUN pǎo 263 P

Chinese	English	Character codes
跑步	run; jog	263/193
慢跑	jog; jogging	253/263
长跑	long-distance run	194/263
跑道	runway	263/206
跑步机	treadmill	263/193/051
跑车	sports car	263/010
跑买卖	work as a commercial traveller	263/075/252

Example Sentences

1/263	老年人常常慢跑会对身体很好。 Jogging often is good for older people to stay healthy.
2/263	他是中国现在最好的长跑运动员。 He's the best long-distance runner in China at the moment.
3/263	你怎么能一吃完饭就跑步？ How can you begin to run straight after you've just finished eating?
4/263	我要买个跑步机。要是 * 下雨，我就 * 可以在家里跑步了。 I want to buy a treadmill. Then if it rains, I can run at home.
5/263	钱先生是跑买卖的，所以一个月没几天在家。钱太太不工作，因为她要在家看孩子。 Mr Qian works as a commercial traveller, so he's only at home a few days a month. Mrs Qian doesn't work because she needs to stay at home to look after the children.

注释 Note

* 要是 A 就 B = if [A] then [B]

P 264 便* CHEAP pián；CONVENIENT biàn

Chinese	English	Character codes
便+宜→便宜	convenient + suitable = cheap	264/321
小便宜	small gain	143/264/321
不便**	not convenient	007/264
便**道	shortcut; sidewalk	264/206
便**饭	a simple meal	264/026

Example Sentences

1/264	你家的饭桌很漂亮。便宜不便宜？ Your dining table is very nice. Is it cheap?
2/264	现在中国的东西不怎么便宜了。 These days things are not that cheap in China.
3/264	A: 这件衣服有点儿贵，可以便宜点儿吗？ B: 好吧，便宜三十块，怎么样？ A: This item of clothing is a bit expensive. Can you make it any cheaper? B: OK, 30 *kuai* cheaper. How about that?
4/264	最早的手机非常大，也很贵。现在的手机比那个时候的小多了，也便宜多了。 The earliest mobile phones were very big and very expensive. Mobiles nowadays are much smaller and much cheaper than they were then.
5/264	虽然坐火车快，但是坐公共汽车比坐火车便宜，所以我每天都坐公共汽车上班。 Although the train is quicker, taking the bus is cheaper; therefore I take the bus to work every day.

注释 Note

* 便 is a polyphonic character: pián = cheap; biàn = convenient.

** 便 biàn = convenient (All other examples are pronounced as pián.)

票 TICKET/BALLOT piào 265 P

Chinese	English	Character codes
火车 + 票→火车票	train + ticket = train ticket	050/010/265
快车票	express train ticket	244/010/265
慢车票	slow train ticket	253/010/265
飞机票	plane ticket	027/051/265
来回票	return ticket	065/048/265
月票	monthly ticket	162/265
年票	annual ticket	090/265
电影票	cinema ticket	017/156/265
票友	amateur performer (of Beijing opera etc.)	265/157
买票	buy tickets	075/265
出票	issue a ticket	012/265
门票	admission ticket	257/265
学生票	student ticket	150/112/265

Example Sentences

1/265	去你们学校的来回票多少钱？ How much is a return ticket to your school?
2/265	你的火车票买好了吗？ Have you bought your train ticket?
3/265	你要快车票还是慢车票？ Do you want a ticket for the express train or the slow train?
4/265	姐姐是大学生，她喜欢星期二晚上看电影，因为星期二晚上有学生票，可以便宜很多。 My elder sister is a university student. She likes to go see a film on Tuesday evenings because there are student tickets available then and it can be a lot cheaper.
5/265	要是七月去中国，什么时候买飞机票最便宜？六个月以前吗？ When is the cheapest time to buy air tickets to China for July? Six months in advance?

Q | 266 妻 WIFE qī

Chinese	English	Character codes
妻 + 子 → 妻子	wife + (noun suffix) = wife	266/172
妻儿老小	used for a married man's family (parents, wife and children)	266/024/066/143
夫妻	husband and wife; married couple	216/266
爱妻	beloved wife	001/266
前妻	ex-wife	099/266

Example Sentences

1/266	这对夫妻以前是大学时的同班同学。 That couple were university classmates before (they were married).
2/266	我朋友和他的前妻是同事。 My friend and his ex-wife are colleagues.
3/266	听说你的妻子是医生，她是中医吗？ I heard that your wife is a doctor. Is she a doctor of traditional Chinese medicine?
4/266	他出国工作的时候，妻儿老小都在北京。 When he went overseas to work, his entire family stayed in Beijing.
5/266	现在在中国，妻子可以不再姓丈夫的姓了。 Nowadays in China, a wife no longer takes the husband's surname.

汽 VAPOUR/STEAM qì 267 Q

Chinese	English	Character codes
公共 + 汽车 → 公共汽车	public + vehicle = bus	221/222/267/010
汽车	car; motor vehicle	267/010
公共汽车道	bus lane	221/222/267/010/206
汽车站	bus stop	267/010/166
汽车司机	bus driver	267/010/285/051
汽车票	bus ticket	267/010/265
汽水	soft drink	267/120
11 路公共汽车	Bus No. 11	250/221/222/267/010

Example Sentences

1/267	我爸爸做过公共汽车司机。 My dad used to work as a bus driver.
2/267	汽车票去年是一块 * 钱，今年一块 * 二了。 A bus ticket was one *kuai* last year, but this year it's one *kuai* twenty.
3/267	妈妈不让我喝汽水，她说喝汽水对身体不好，便宜也不能喝。 My mum doesn't let me have fizzy drinks. She says drinking fizzy drinks is not good for my health, no matter how cheap they are.
4/267	汽车站离我家不远。早上坐公共汽车上班比开车快。 The bus stop is not far from my house. In the morning, taking the bus to work is quicker than driving.
5/267	那是公共汽车道，从早上七点到晚上七点不能在那条道上开车。 That's a bus lane. Cars are not allowed to use it between 7 am and 7 pm.

注释 Note

* 块 kuài = yuan, unit of money in China .

Q 268 千 THOUSAND qiān

Chinese	English	Character codes
一千 + 米 → 一千米	one thousand + metre = 1 kilometre	152/268/080
一千里	500 km	152/268/069
一千公里	1000 km	152/268/221/069
千儿八百	a thousand or slightly less	268/024/002/181
一千左右	around one thousand	152/268/348/329

Example Sentences

1/268	我每天早上都跑五千米。 I run five kilometres every morning.
2/268	我们学校有几千名学生。 Our school has several thousand students.
3/268	中国从东到西是五千二百公里左右。 China is about 5,200 km across, from east to west.
4/268	现在的电视都不太贵，便宜的千儿八百块钱就可以买到。 These days TVs are not very expensive, you can buy a cheap one for about one thousand *kuai*.
5/268	想去那个公司工作的人太多了。要先考试，每年五千个人里只要五个。 So many people want to work for that company. You have to take an exam first, and only five people out of five thousand are successful each year.

铅 LEAD (metal) qiān 269 Q

Chinese	English	Character codes
铅 + 笔 → 铅笔	lead + pen = pencil	269/187
铅笔字	characters written in pencil	269/187/173
铅笔写	write in pencil	269/187/146
铅球	shot	269/272
铅字	type (printing term)	269/173

Example Sentences

1/269	他有红铅笔，也有黑铅笔。 He has red pencils, and also has black pencils.
2/269	哪个商店有铅笔卖？我得买铅笔了。 Which shop sells pencils? I need to buy pencils.
3/269	你能看见那些铅字吗？我看不见，读给我听好吗？ Can you read this (small) print? I can't make it out, can you read it to me?
4/269	那家早报上的铅太多，每次看完报纸我的手都很黑。 That morning newspaper uses too much lead (ink); every time I read the paper, my hands get black.
5/269	我最不喜欢的运动是铅球，因为铅球太大，我的手太小。 The shot put is my least favourite sport because the shot is too big for my hands.

Q | 270 情 FEELING/EMOTION/SITUATION qíng

Chinese	English	Character codes
事 + 情 → 事情	matter + situation = affair	281/270
情人	lover	270/104
情书	love letter	270/119
爱情	love	001/270
友情	friendship	157/270
热情	passion	103/270
同情	sympathy	130/270
情歌	love song	270/219
情报	information	270/184
情场	love affair	270/196
情面	sensibility	270/081

Example Sentences

1/270	我的中国同事都很热情。 All my Chinese colleagues are warm-hearted.
2/270	爸爸太忙了！他每天都得做很多事情。 Dad is so busy. He has many things to deal with every day.
3/270	这个情报准吗？你从哪儿知道的？ Is this information accurate? Where did you get it from?
4/270	我觉得中国的情歌很好听，你教我唱好吗？ I think Chinese love songs sound very beautiful. Will you teach me to sing?
5/270	这不是情面的问题。对的就是对的，错的就是错的。 This is not a question of saving face. Right is right, and wrong is wrong.

晴 FINE/CLEAR/SUNNY qíng 271 Q

Chinese	English	Character codes
晴 + 天 → 晴天	clear + day; sky = fine weather	271/128
大晴天	glorious sunny day	014/271/128
雨过天晴	sunshine after rain	159/225/128/271

Example Sentences

1/271	天这么晴，下午不会下雨吧？ The sky is so clear. It won't rain this afternoon, will it?
2/271	我喜欢这儿的天气，天天晴天，还不冷不热。 I like the weather here — it's sunny every day, and not too hot or too cold.
3/271	天气晴的时候，我的心情就会很好。 When the weather is bright and sunny, I will be in a good mood.
4/271	雨过天晴了，我们出去走走好吗？ The rain has stopped and the sky is clear, so shall we go out for a walk?
5/271	听说今天是晴天，我怎么看不出来呢？ I heard it was going to be fine today, so how come I don't see any fine weather?

Q | 272 球 BALL/GLOBE qiú

Chinese	English	Character codes
踢 + 足球 → 踢足球	kick + football = play football	292/346/272
打 + 篮球 → 打篮球	beat + basketball = play basketball	13/245/272
气球	balloon	098/272
打球	play ball sports (with hand, racquet etc.)	013/272
球门	goal	272/257
球场	ball sports ground/pitch/court	272/196
球星	ball sports star	272/148

Example Sentences

1/272	那个生日气球很漂亮。 That birthday balloon is very pretty.
2/272	这是这儿最好的篮球场。 This is the best basketball court here.
3/272	我踢足球踢得不错，但是不会打篮球。 I play football quite well, but I can't play basketball.
4/272	今天晚上踢完足球我们一起去吃饭吧？ Let's go eat together after playing football this evening.
5/272	你看过那个（篮球）球星打球吗？他真的打得很好吗？ Have you seen that basketball star play? Does he really play well?

然 RIGHT/THUS rán 273 R

Chinese	English	Character codes
不 + 然 → 不然	not + correct = otherwise	007/273
虽然……但是……	although…	289/273/203/118
先 A 然后 B	first A, then B	140/273/044
果然	sure enough; as expected	037/273
公然	openly; publicly	221/273
天然气	natural gas	128/273/098

Example Sentences

1/273	我们先去书店给弟弟买书，然后去菜店买鸡蛋吧！ Let's go to the bookstore to buy books for little brother first, and then go to the grocery store to buy eggs.
2/273	我们快回家吧！不然雨要下大了。 Quick, let's go home before the rain gets any heavier.
3/273	中国的公共汽车是电的还是天然气的？ Do Chinese buses use electricity or natural gas?
4/273	他说晚上不会下雨，果然没下。 He said it wouldn't rain in the evening, and sure enough it didn't.
5/273	虽然我听不懂汉语，但是我看得懂。 Although I can't understand spoken Chinese, I can read it.

R | 274 让 YIELD/LET/ALLOW/MAKE (somebody feel) ràng

Chinese	English	Character codes
出 + 让 → 出让	go out + yield = sell off (property or rights)	012/274
让路	make way	274/250
让步	concede; give in	274/193
让车	give way to a vehicle	274/010
让开	get out of the way; step aside	274/061

Example Sentences

1/274	来车了，快让开！ There's a car coming! Quick, move out of the way!
2/274	爸爸让我先去商店买牛奶再回家。 My dad asked me to go to the shop and buy milk first, and then go home.
3/274	第一医院旁边的宾馆在出让，我们明天去看看吧？ The hotel next to Number One Hospital has been put up for sale. Shall we go and have a look tomorrow?
4/274	我的儿子每天玩儿四个小时电脑，不喜欢学习，让我很生气。 My son plays on the computer for four hours every day and isn't keen on studying. It makes me very cross.
5/274	每次家里有客人的时候，妈妈都让我给客人上茶。 Every time when we have guests at home, my mum asks me to offer them tea.

日 DAY/DATE/SUN rì 275 R

Chinese	English	Character codes
生 + 日 → 生日	give birth to + day = birthday	112/275
日子	day	275/172
日期	date	275/096
星期日	Sunday	148/096/275
早日	soon	334/275

Example Sentences

1/275	你的生日是几月几号？ When is your birthday?
2/275	今天是什么日子，你为什么请我吃饭？ What's the occasion today? Why are you inviting me for dinner?
3/275	这个星期日我们去踢足球还是打篮球？ Shall we play football or basketball this Sunday?
4/275	我准备以后去中国工作，所以我希望能早日学好中国话。 I intend to work in China in the future, therefore I hope I can soon master Chinese.
5/275	你看一看牛奶上的日期，要是时间太长了，过期了，就不能喝了。 You have a look at the date on the milk carton — if it's been too long, it expires and becomes undrinkable.

R | 276 肉 FLESH/MEAT ròu

Chinese	English	Character codes
羊 + 肉 → 羊肉	sheep + meat = lamb; mutton	317/276
鸡肉	chicken	230/276
牛肉	beef	261/276
鱼肉	fish	330/276
肉球	meatball	276/272
肉店	butcher's shop	276/018
生肉	raw meat	112/276
果肉	flesh of fruit	037/276
肉眼	the naked eye	276/316

Example Sentences

1/276	你喜欢吃什么肉？ What meat do you prefer?
2/276	中国人不喜欢喝生水，也不喜欢吃生牛肉。 Chinese people don't like to drink tap water, and they don't like to eat raw beef.
3/276	字太小了！肉眼看不见。 The characters are so small that they're invisible to the naked eye!
4/276	家里的肉吃完了，我们去肉店再买一些鸡肉和羊肉吧！ We don't have any meat left at home. Let's go to a butcher's to buy some chicken and lamb.
5/276	多吃牛肉对身体好。 Eating plenty of beef is good for people's health.

色 COLOUR/LOOK sè 277 R

Chinese	English	Character codes
颜 + 色 → 颜色	colour + colour = colour	315/277
出色	outstanding; remarkable	012/277
白色	white	180/277
黑色	black	228/277
红色	red	229/277
茶色	dark brown (tea-coloured)	009/277
冷色	cold colour	068/277
气色	complexion	098/277
眼色	wink; signal with one's eyes	316/277
色情	pornographic	277/270

Example Sentences

1/277	我喜欢热天穿冷色的衣服。 I like to wear cold colours on hot days.
2/277	我看不出这两个颜色有什么不同。 I can't tell the difference between these two colours.
3/277	他是一个出色的歌手，会唱歌，也会写歌。 He's a remarkable singer. As well as singing, he writes songs.
4/277	病好了吗？你的气色看起来好多了。 Are you fully recovered? Your complexion seems much better.
5/277	这件红色的上衣不错，也不太贵。要不要试一试？ This red top is quite nice, and also not too expensive. Would you like to try it on?

S | 278 绍 CONTINUE/CARRY ON shào

Chinese	English	Character codes
介 + 绍 → 介绍	introduce+ continue = introduce; recommend	234/278
介绍人	introducer	234/278/104
做介绍	give an introduction	178/234/278
介绍一下	introduce briefly	234/278/152/139

Example Sentences

1/278	谁听说过中国新年？能不能介绍一下？ Who has heard of Chinese New Year? Can you give us a brief introduction?
2/278	你在这家公司工作吗？请介绍一下你们公司，好吗？ Do you work for this company? Could you please introduce your company?
3/278	你们可能不认识谢老师，我先做个介绍吧。 You probably don't know Teacher Xie, so let me make an introduction first.
4/278	我的爸爸妈妈是大学同学，他们是自己认识的，不是介绍人介绍的。 My parents were classmates at university. They got to know each other on their own; they weren't introduced by an introducer.
5/278	我知道你，我们的汉语老师介绍过你，说你的汉语说得非常好。 I know you. Our Chinese teacher has already mentioned you. She said you speak Chinese very well.

身 BODY/PREGNANT shēn 279 S

Chinese	English	Character codes
身 + 高 → 身高	body + tall = height	279/030
身体	body; health	279/294
身子	body	279/172
出身	family background	012/279
本身	itself	006/279
身上	on one's body	279/108
上身	upper part of the body	108/279
下身	lower part of the body	139/279
动身	go on a journey	212/279
一身	all over the body	152/279
身边	at one's side	279/188
身手	skill; talent	279/284
车身	body of a car	010/279

Example Sentences

1/279	你的身高是多少？你比你弟弟高吗？ How tall are you? Are you taller than your little brother?
2/279	你怎么了？为什么一身的水？ What happened? Why are you all wet?
3/279	我身边的朋友都会唱中国歌，跳中国舞。 All my close friends can sing Chinese songs and dance Chinese dances.
4/279	你准备什么时候动身去中国？我送你。 When are you preparing to leave for China? I'll see you off.
5/279	我身上一分钱都没有，不能买西瓜了。 I don't have a penny on me, and I can't buy a watermelon.

S 280 始 BEGIN/START shǐ

Chinese	English	Character codes
开 + 始 → 开始	open + start = start	061/280
从……开始	start from...	201/061/280
一开始	at the beginning	152/061/280
起始	originate	097/280

Example Sentences

1/280	你明天的考试几点开始？ When does your exam start tomorrow?
2/280	这件事的起始时间是什么时候？ When did this matter come up?
3/280	电影快开始了，你朋友怎么还没来？ The film will start soon. How come your friend isn't here yet?
4/280	你从哪儿开始写的？现在写到哪儿了？ Where did you start writing from? And where are you up to now?
5/280	我到中国的时候，一开始听不懂中国人说的话，觉得他们说话说得太快了，后来慢慢就能听懂了。 When I arrived in China, at first I couldn't understand what Chinese people said, and I felt they spoke too fast. But later I could understand.

事 THING/WORK/MATTER/BUSINESS shì 281 S

Chinese	English	Character codes
同 + 事 → 同事	same + business = colleague	130/281
事 + 情 → 事情	matter + situation = affair	281/270
事件	incident; event	281/232
时事	current affair	115/281
出事	have an accident	012/281
事前	in advance	281/099
事后	afterwards	281/044
事先	beforehand	281/140
人事	human affairs	104/281
从事	undertake; be engaged in	201/281
国家大事	state affairs	036/053/014/281
本事	skill; ability	006/281

Example Sentences

1/281	这是国家大事，每个人都知道。 This is a national issue. Everyone knows about it.
2/281	我每天早上都看电视，我最喜欢看时事。 I watch TV every morning. I especially like to watch current affairs.
3/281	我不希望你生气，所以事前没说这件事。 I didn't want you to get angry, so I didn't tell you about this matter beforehand.
4/281	外面出了什么事？为什么那里有很多车？ What happened outside? Why are there so many cars there?
5/281	我的好朋友是做人事工作的，他说我们公司新请了一个会说汉语的同事。 My good friend works as a HR professional, and he said that our company just recruited a Chinese-speaking colleague.

S 282 试 TRY/TEST/EXAM shì

Chinese	English	Character codes
考 + 试 → 考试	test + try = exam; take an exam	241/282
笔试	written exam	187/282
面试	interview	081/282
试想	just think; imagine	282/142
试试	have a try	282/282
试衣间	fitting room	282/153/231
试穿	try on (a garment, shoes, etc.)	282/198
试纸	test paper	282/342
比试	have a competition	186/282
试点	pilot scheme	282/016
试车	test drive	282/010

Example Sentences

1/282	我没开过出租车，不过我想试试。 I haven't driven a taxi, but I'd like to try.
2/282	学生没有考试真的好吗？试想一下吧！ It would be really good if students didn't have exams, wouldn't it? Just imagine it!
3/282	请问试衣间在哪儿？我想试穿一下这件衣服。 Excuse me, may I ask where the fitting room is? I'd like to try this item of clothing on.
4/282	我弟弟不觉得我跑得比他快，所以要和我比试一下。 My little brother doesn't think I can run faster than him, so he wants us to have a competition.
5/282	我找了一个新工作，笔试考过了，明天下午去面试。 I found a new job and have passed the written exam. The interview is tomorrow afternoon.

室 ROOM shì 283 S

Chinese	English	Character codes
教 + 室 → 教室	teach + room = classroom	233/283
休息室	lounge/lobby	313/308/283
工作室	studio; workshop	032/176/283
室外	outdoors	238/297
室外运动	outdoor sport	283/297/333/212
室友	roommate	283/157

Example Sentences

1/283	那个在休息室里读报纸的人是谁？ Who is that person reading a newspaper in the lounge?
2/283	你们学校一共有多少间教室？汉语教室大不大？ How many classrooms does your school have in total? Is the Chinese classroom big?
3/283	我们公司的对面有一个室外篮球场。 There is an outdoor basketball court opposite my company.
4/283	我的室友在机场旁边开了一间很漂亮的工作室。 My roommate has opened a beautiful studio next to the airport.
5/283	现在在中国的东北虽然室外非常冷，但是房间里很热。 Although it's currently extremely cold outside in northeast China, it's very hot inside.

S 284 手 HAND shǒu

Chinese	English	Character codes
手 + 机 → 手机	hand + machine = mobile phone	284/051
手表	watch	284/189
分手	(of a couple) break up	028/284
对手	opponent	022/284
手工	handiwork	284/032
二手	second hand	025/284
手球	handball	284/272
多面手	all-rounder	023/081/284
能手	expert	088/284
手边	on hand; at hand	284/188
手笔	one's own handwritten work	284/187
手气	luck at gambling	284/098
手纸	toilet paper	284/342
手足	brothers (hand & foot)	284/346
手语	sign language	284/159
手电	flashlight	284/017

Example Sentences

1/284	我在上课，不能打手机。 I'm in a lesson, and can't use the mobile phone.
2/284	每个国家的手语都一样吗？ Is every country's sign language the same?
3/284	现在几点了？我没有手表，手机也没在身上。 What time is it? I don't have a watch, and I don't have my phone on me.
4/284	这件上衣是手工做的，所以比别的贵很多。 This top is handmade, so it's much more expensive than the others.
5/284	中国的二手店多不多？中国人喜欢去二手店买东西还是去商店买新的东西？ Are there many second-hand shops in China? Do Chinese people like to shop in second-hand shops, or do they prefer to buy new things in stores?

司 TAKE CHARGE OF/DEPARTMENT sī 285 S

Chinese	English	Character codes
司 + 机 → 司机	take charge of + machine = driver	285/051
公司	company	221/285
分公司	branch office	028/221/285
子公司	subsidiary company	172/221/285
上司	boss; superior	108/285

Example Sentences

1/285	这家公司有两家子公司。 This company has two subsidiary companies.
2/285	是我的室友介绍我来这家公司工作的。 It was my roommate who recommended me for a job with this company.
3/285	从明年一月开始，我要去我们公司在北京的分公司工作。 I will start work at the Beijing branch of our company from the beginning of next January.
4/285	我上司的太太是中国人，所以他现在生病的时候也和太太一样喜欢看中医。 My boss's wife is Chinese, so when he gets sick, he, like his wife, prefers to see a traditional Chinese doctor.
5/285	我们公司的司机说做司机太累了，他不想做司机了，他想在别人买车的时候帮别人试车。 Our company driver said that driving is too tiring, and he doesn't want to carry on doing it. He wants to test drive cars for potential buyers.

S | 286 思 THINK/CONSIDER sī

Chinese	English	Character codes
思 + 想 → 思想	consider + think = thought/thinking	286/142
前思后想	weigh ideas carefully	099/286/044/142
意 + 思 → 意思	idea + think = meaning	324/286
有意思	interesting	158/324/286
没意思	boring	078/324/286
不好意思	feel embarrassed; embarrassing	007/039/324/286
小意思	(of a gift) mere trifle; small token	143/324/286
思路	train of thought; reasoning	286/250

Example Sentences

1/286	喜欢就去做，不要前思后想。 If you like it, then go and do it. Don't think about it over and over.
2/286	我不懂你的思路，给我说说好吗？ I don't understand your line of reasoning. Could you explain it to me?
3/286	你看过哪些有意思的书？给我介绍几本好吗？ What interesting books have you read? Can you recommend some to me?
4/286	我今天早上上课晚了，走进教室的时候觉得很不好意思。 I was late for the lesson this morning, so I felt very embarrassed when entering the classroom.
5/286	今天是你的生日，这是我的一点儿小意思，希望你喜欢。生日快乐！ Today is your birthday. This is just a little something. I hope you like it. Happy birthday!

送 SEND/DELIVER/GIVE (as present)/SEE OFF sòng 287 S

Chinese	English	Character codes
送 + 站 → 送站	see off + station = see someone off at a station	287/166
送别	see someone off	287/190
送上门	deliver to the door	287/108/257
送给	send; give as a present	287/220
运送	carry; transport	333/287
欢送	see off; send off	047/287
欢送会	farewell party	047/287/049
白送	give away free	180/287

Example Sentences

1/287	我每天都开车送孩子上学。 I drive my children to school every day.
2/287	这本汉语小说是我的汉语老师送给我的，非常有意思。 It was my Chinese teacher who gave me this Chinese novel; it's very interesting.
3/287	你明天的火车是几点的？在东站还是西站？我送你去车站吧！ What time is your train tomorrow? Is it going from East or West Station? Let me see you off there.
4/287	下个星期就是我爸爸的生日了，我还没想好送他什么呢。 It'll be at my dad's birthday next week. I haven't decided what to give him yet.
5/287	我的同事要去东北的分公司工作了，所以我们今天下午要给他开一个欢送会欢送欢送他。 My colleague is going to work at our northeast branch, so we're holding a farewell party for him this afternoon.

S | 288 诉 TELL/ACCUSE sù

Chinese	English	Character codes
告诉	tell; inform	217/288
诉说	tell; recount	288/122
上诉	appeal (a case)	108/288
起诉	sue; bring a lawsuit against	097/288
起诉书	indictment; list of charges	097/288/119
公诉	public prosecution	221/288
公诉人	public prosecutor	221/288/104

Example Sentences

1/288	那个小男孩儿在和妈妈诉说他为什么不高兴。 The little boy is telling his mum why he's not happy.
2/288	这件事他们已经上诉了。 They have already lodged an appeal regarding this matter.
3/288	他爸爸是有名的公诉人。 His father is a famous public prosecutor.
4/288	帮我看看我写的起诉书好吗？我写不好。 Could you do me a favour and take a look at the indictment that I've written? I'm not that good at writing them.
5/288	姐姐告诉我，离我家不远新开了一家咖啡馆儿。那儿的咖啡很好喝，可是有点儿贵。 My older sister told me that there's a new coffee shop not far from my home. Although the coffee is really good there, it's a bit expensive.

虽 ALTHOUGH suī 289 S

Chinese	English	Character codes
虽然……但是……	although…	289/273/203/118
虽说	though; although	289/122
虽是	even though; even if	289/118

Example Sentences

1/289	我虽说没有钱，但是一样很快乐，因为我的工作是我喜欢的。 Although I don't have much money, I'm happy as I am, because I'm doing a job that I like.
2/289	虽然我的车已经很老了，可是它一点儿问题都没有。 Although my car is very old, it doesn't have any problems at all.
3/289	虽然我非常爱吃肉，但是我不多吃，因为吃多了对身体不好。 Although I really like to eat meat, I don't eat that much of it, because too much meat is not good for your health.
4/289	我虽然在北京工作过两年，可是因为工作太忙，所以没学过汉语。 Although I worked in Beijing for two years, I didn't learn Chinese because I was too busy with work.
5/289	我虽然是住在中国的外国人，但不觉得自己是外国人，因为我已经在中国住了十几年了，觉得自己就是中国人了。 Although I'm a foreigner living in China, I don't feel I'm an outsider because I've lived here for more than ten years, and I feel like a Chinese person.

S 290 所 PLACE/HUT/MW (buildings, institutions) suǒ

Chinese	English	Character codes
因为……所以……	because... so; therefore	325/303/290/323
场所	place; location	196/290
公共场所	public place	221/222/196/290
住所	habitation; residence; dwelling place	170/290
所有	all; possess; own	290/158
所有人	owner	290/158/104
所在	location	290/164
所作所为	all one's actions	290/176/290/303

Example Sentences

1/290	我们学校所有的学生都是中国人。 All of the students at my school are Chinese.
2/290	因为我今天忙了一天，太累了，所以晚上不想做饭了。我们出去吃吧！ Because I was busy all day today, I'm really tired, and I don't want to cook this evening. Let's eat out.
3/290	我们去旅游的时候，看到了那个有名的作家生前的住所。 When we went sightseeing, we saw the place where that famous writer had lived.
4/290	你本来不明白，现在知道了吧？你的做法就是问题的所在。 You didn't understand at first, but you do now, do you? The way you're handling (the matter) is where the problem lies.
5/290	我从来没在公共场所唱过歌，因为我觉得不好意思。 I've never sung in public places, because I feel embarrassed.

它 IT tā 291 T

Chinese	English	Character codes
它+们→它们	it + (plural suffix) = they (animals, things)	291/079
它本身	itself	291/006/279

Example Sentences

1/291	我的狗太老了，它现在喜欢睡觉，不喜欢跑了。 My dog is so old. These days it likes sleeping, and doesn't like running any more.
2/291	那只黑色的小猫在喝牛奶呢。你看，你看，它喝得真快！ That black kitten is drinking milk. Look, how quickly it drinks!
3/291	我女儿说这些奶牛都很漂亮，因为它们的眼睛都很大、很黑，也很亮。 My daughter says these dairy cows are very pretty because their eyes are very big, very black and very bright.
4/291	我的猫看不见了已经两天了。你是在哪儿找到它的？谢谢你！ I haven't seen my cat for two days. Where did you find it? Thank you!
5/291	你们看见我的那只猫了吗？它两分钟以前还在桌子上跳呢，现在怎么没有了？ Have you seen my cat? It just jumped on to the table a couple of minutes ago. Where's it gone now?

T | 292 踢 KICK tī

Chinese	English	Character codes
踢 + 足球 → 踢足球	kick + football = play football	292/346/272
踢门	kick the door	292/257

Example Sentences

1/292	你弟弟会踢足球吗？ Can your little brother play football?
2/292	进球了！谁踢的？ It's a goal! Who's the scorer?
3/292	在你们班，谁踢球踢得最好，司明还是冷希雨？ Who's the best footballer in your class, Si Ming or Leng Xiyu?
4/292	哥哥会打篮球，但是不会踢足球，他也不喜欢踢足球。他说踢来踢去没意思。 My elder brother can play basketball, but he doesn't play football. In fact he doesn't like football; he says it's boring kicking a ball back and forth.
5/292	那个足球运动员现在不踢球了。他开了一个足球学校，教小孩子踢足球。 That footballer doesn't play anymore. He opened a football school and teaches children to play football.

题 TOPIC/SUBJECT/TITLE tí 293 T

Chinese	English	Character codes
问 + 题 → 问题	ask + topic = question; problem; issue	304/293
没问题	no problem	078/304/293
话题	subject; topic	046/293
题字	inscribe	293/173
题名	autograph	293/082
课题	task; problem; issue	243/293
考题	exam question	241/293
习题	(schoolwork) exercise	136/293
跑题	stray from the topic; digress	263/293
离题	stray from the topic; digress	248/293
小题大做	make a fuss over a minor issue	143/293/014/178

Example Sentences

1/293	请问谢老师在吗？我想问他一些问题。 Excuse me, could you tell me if Teacher Xie is here? I'd like to ask him some questions.
2/293	书后面的习题很多，我都做完了，你呢？ There are lots of exercises at the back of the book. I've done all of them. What about you?
3/293	昨天上课的时候我们做了几道前几年的考题。 We answered some questions from past exams in yesterday's lesson.
4/293	我想租的房子便宜是便宜，可是离车站太远了，上班坐车是个问题。 The house that I want to rent is cheap, but it's too far from the bus stop, so taking the bus to work would be a problem.
5/293	要是每天都工作很长时间，两三年下去，身体会出问题的。 If you work for long hours every day, in two or three years you may experience health issues.

T | 294 体 BODY/FORM/STYLE/SYSTEM tǐ

Chinese	English	Character codes
体 + 会 → 体会	body + able to = learn from experience	294/049
身体	body; health	279/294
个体	individual	031/294
体能	physical strength; stamina	294/088
体面	dignity	294/081
大体	in general; more or less	014/294
体现	embody	294/141
体热	body heat	294/103
体表	surface of the body	294/189
气体	gas	098/294
体校	sports school	294/144

Example Sentences

1/294	说一说你读这本书的体会好吗？ Can you tell me a bit about what you've learned from this book?
2/294	弟弟上过体校，长跑和游泳都不错。 My little brother went to a sports school. He's quite good at long-distance running and swimming.
3/294	我哥哥的体能很好，因为他从小就每天都跑步。 My older brother is very fit because he has run every day since he was little.
4/294	我小的时候，妈妈不让我在公共场所吃东西，她说不体面。 When I was little, my mum didn't allow me to eat in public places; she said it wasn't dignified.
5/294	我大体知道那家医院在哪儿，到了那儿以后我们可以再问问。 I know the general area where the hospital is; we can ask again when we get close there.

条 STRIP/MW (long thin items) tiáo 295 T

Chinese	English	Character codes
面 + 条 + 儿→ 面条儿	wheat flour + strip + suffix = noodle	081/295/024
字条	brief note	173/295
纸条	slip (of paper); note	342/295
条件	condition; circumstances; qualification	295/232
有条件	conditional	158/295/232
一条路	a road	152/295/250

Example Sentences

1/295	面条冷了，热一热再吃吧！ These noodles are cold, so heat them before eating.
2/295	我家门前的那条小路上有很多的小商店。 There are many little shops in the alley in front of my house.
3/295	我想试试那个工作，希望他们要的条件不太高。 I would like to try for that job. Hopefully their requirements are not too high.
4/295	现在上大学要花很多钱，不是所有人家的孩子都有条件上大学。 Going to university costs a lot of money nowadays, and not every child can afford to go to university.
5/295	我回家的时候，妈妈出去了，但是饭桌上有她给我写的字条，字条上告诉我面条做好了，让我先吃。 My mum was out when I got home, but she had left me a note on the dining table to tell me that the noodles had been cooked, and that I should eat first.

T | 296 跳 JUMP/DANCE tiào

Chinese	English	Character codes
跳 + 舞 → 跳舞	jump + dance = to dance	296/305
跳动	beat; pulse	296/212
跳水	dive; diving (sport)	296/120
跳远	long jump (athletics)	296/332
跳高	high jump (athletics)	296/030
跳出	jump out; appear suddenly	296/012

Example Sentences

1/296	中国有很多有名的跳水运动员。 China has many famous divers.
2/296	我的丈夫不很高，但是他喜欢跳高。有一次，他跳过了两米！ My husband is not very tall, but he likes the high jump. One day he jumped over two metres.
3/296	快下来，别在椅子上跳来跳去的！ Get down! Don't jump around on the chair!
4/296	我姐姐很喜欢跳舞，她什么舞都会跳，不过她中国舞跳得最好。 My older sister likes dancing. She can dance many different styles, but her Chinese dance is the best.
5/296	昨天晚上我在回家的路上，看到从路边跳出了一只小黑猫，它站在路的中间看着我，一动不动，非常可爱。 On my way home yesterday evening a little black cat jumped out from the roadside and stood still in the middle of the road looking at me — it was very cute.

外 OUTSIDE/EXTERIOR wài 297 W

Chinese	English	Character codes
外 + 面 → 外面	outside + side = outside	297/081
外国	foreign country	297/036
外国人	foreigner	297/036/104
国外	abroad; overseas; foreign	036/297
外语	foreign language	297/160
以外	apart from; beyond; outside	323/297
意外	unexpected; accident	324/297
外表	outward appearance; external; outside	297/189
外人	outsider	297/104
外公	mother's father; maternal grandfather	297/221
外星人	extra-terrestrial; alien	297/148/104
外号	nickname	297/040

Example Sentences

1/297	外面在下雨，进来坐坐吧。 It's raining outside. Come in and sit down.
2/297	近年来，来中国工作和上学的外国人比以前多多了。 In recent years the number of foreigners coming to China to work and study has greatly increased.
3/297	你会几门外语？都是在国外学的吗？ How many foreign languages do you know? Did you learn all of them abroad?
4/297	这个人的外表是很不错的，就是不知道他做起事来怎么样，希望和他的外表一样就好了。 That guy is good-looking, but we don't know what sort of an employee he is; hopefully he works as well as he looks.
5/297	外面出了意外，车都不能走了。我们走路去好不好？要去的那个商店离这儿不太远。 There's been an accident outside, and the traffic's not moving. Shall we go on foot? The shop we're going to is not too far from here.

W | 298 完 FINISH/COMPLETE/USE UP/WHOLE wán

Chinese characters / words	English	Character codes
完 + 人 → 完人	complete + person = perfect person / paragon	298/104
完工	finish work; complete a project	298/032
完好	intact; in good condition	298/039
完事儿	finish; get through; conclude	298/281/024
吃完	finish eating	011/298

Example Sentences

1/298	我吃完 * 早饭了，现在准备上学了。 I've finished my breakfast, and now I'm getting ready to go to school.
2/298	你今天的事情怎么这么多，做得完做不完？ You have so much to do today. Will you able to finish it all?
3/298	那条新开的路离我家很近，听说下个星期完工。 That new road is very close to my house. They say it'll be finished by next week.
4/298	没关系，我们都不是完人，都有做错的时候。 Don't worry. We're all imperfect, and we all make mistakes sometimes.
5/298	这本小说太长了，我这个星期看不完了。你要是想看，就等下个星期吧。 This novel is too long. I won't be able to finish it this week. If you want to read it, could you wait until next week?

注释 **Note**

*When this word 完 appears after the verb, the Natural Order calls it "yin-yang linkage". For example, 完 after drinking means from the start to the end of drinking. It is a continuous process called the journey from yin to yang. In English grammar it is called a complement.

玩 HAVE FUN/ENJOY/PLAY wán 299 W

Chinese	English	Character codes
玩儿 + 球 → 玩儿球	play + ball = play a ball game	299/024/272
玩笑	joke; jest	299/310
开玩笑	play a joke on; make fun of	061/299/310
好玩儿	fun; amusing; interesting	039/299/024
玩乐	play around; indulge in pleasure	299/246
玩儿火	play with fire	299/024/050
游玩	go on an outing; amuse oneself; have fun	328/299
玩儿手机	play on a mobile phone	299/024/284/051
玩儿电脑	play on a computer	299/024/017/086

Example Sentences

1/299	再见！有时间来我家玩儿。 Bye! You're welcome to come to my house whenever you're free.
2/299	现在看电视的人少了，但是玩儿电脑的人多了。 These days fewer people are watching TV, and more people are playing on computers.
3/299	你是在开玩笑还是认真的？ Are you joking or being serious?
4/299	你已经学了很长时间了！休息一下，去玩儿一会儿球吧。 You've been studying for quite a while. Take a break and go and play ball for a bit.
5/299	你为什么不学好，老是和一帮子学习不认真的男生在一起打篮球。 Why can't you be a good student, instead of always playing basketball with a group of boys who don't take their studies seriously?

W | 300 晚 EVENING/LATE wǎn

Chinese	English	Character codes
晚 + 点 → 晚点	late + o'clock = late; behind schedule	300/016
晚上	evening	300/108
晚间	evening; night	300/231
晚饭	dinner; supper	300/026
晚报	evening paper	300/184
晚会	evening party	300/049
晚年	old age; one's later years	300/090
晚期	late stage; terminal	300/096
今晚	this evening	058/300
昨晚	yesterday evening	175/300
明晚	tomorrow evening	083/300
一天到晚	all day long	152/128/205/300
早晚	morning and evening; sooner or later	334/300
为 * 时已晚	be too late	303/115/322/300

注释 Note

*see 303 为 wéi

Example Sentences

1/300	我们大学今晚七点到十二点开新年晚会。 Our university is holding a New Year's party this evening from 7 pm to 12 am.
2/300	我爸爸妈妈的晚年很快乐。他们已经去很多国家旅游过了。 My parents' life in their later years has been very happy. They have travelled to many different countries.
3/300	少吃点儿，晚饭吃得太多对身体不好。 Try to eat a bit less. Eating too much at dinner is not good for your health.
4/300	昨天一天我工作了十几个小时，睡得很晚，所以今天觉得非常累。 I worked for more than ten hours yesterday and didn't get to bed till very late, so I'm feeling really tired today.
5/300	妈妈生气了，打电话告诉爸爸说我的弟弟一天到晚不学习，只知道玩儿电脑。 My mum got angry. She told my dad on the phone that my little brother doesn't spend any of his time studying; the only thing he does is playing on the computer.

往 TOWARDS/GO (in a direction)/PAST (time) wǎng 301 W

Chinese	English	Character codes
往 + 事 → 往事	past + matter = past events	301/281
往日	in former days	301/275
往年	in former years	301/090
往常	as one used to do	301/195
往往	often; usually	301/301
以往	in the past; formerly	323/301
前往	leave for; proceed towards	099/301
往后	from now on; in future	301/044
往来	back and forth; dealings; contacts	301/065
来往	come and go; have dealings with	065/301
过往	in the past; come and go; on friendly terms with	225/301
来来往往	come and go	065/065/301/301
人来人往	bustling; busy with people coming and going	104/065/104/301

注释 Note

*This 往往 (often) is used for behaviour or habit, not for time.

**The original meaning of 往 is 'facing', so to describe an action that occurs in a particular direction it must be followed by a direction word and then a verb.

Example Sentences

1/301	爸爸妈妈往往 * 不知道、也不明白孩子想的是什么。 Parents often don't know and don't understand what their children think.
2/301	我们是中学同学，上了大学以后，就没有什么来往了。 We were classmates at secondary school. After going off to university we haven't been in touch with each other.
3/301	离开十年后再回到北京，让我想起了很多往事。 Returning to Beijing after being away for ten years has reminded me of lots of things.
4/301	你是不是要去那个大卖场？往 ** 前走三十米，再往西走，大卖场就在你的左手边。 Are you going to that hypermarket? Go straight on for 30 metres, then turn west; the hypermarket is on your left hand.
5/301	前往北京的飞机就要起飞了，请旅客们做好准备。 This flight to Beijing is about to take off. All passengers please prepare yourselves.

W | 302 望 EXPECT/HOPE/LOOK AT wàng

Chinese	English	Character codes
希 + 望 → 希望	hope + hope = hope; wish for	307/302
期望	hope, expectation	096/302
名望	renown; prestige	082/302
看望	call on someone	062/302
大喜过望	delighted with unexpected good news	014/137/225/302

Example Sentences

1/302	明天我要去看望我生病的奶奶。 I'm going to visit my sick grandma tomorrow.
2/302	那个老师教得很好，他的名望很高。 That teacher is very capable, and he has a good reputation.
3/302	我希望我们能坐上最后一班公共汽车。 I hope we can catch the last bus.
4/302	我听说中国的爸爸妈妈对孩子的期望比别的国家的爸爸妈妈高得多，这是真的吗？ I've heard that Chinese parents' expectations of their children are much higher than those of parents in other countries. Is that true?
5/302	我有几个大学的同班同学说，他们希望有一天能去中国做生意，因为中国很大，机会很多。他们还问我有没有什么认识的人和门路。 Several of my university classmates said that they hoped to be able to go into business in China one day because China is a big country, with many opportunities. They also asked me if I had any contacts I could give them.

为 ACT AS/BECAUSE OF wéi; FOR wèi 303 W

Chinese	English	Character codes
为 + 什么 → 为什么	for + what = why	303/111/077
因为……所以……	because... so	325/303/209/323
为了	for; in order to; for the sake of	303/067
为 * 生	make a living	303/112
为 * 人	behaviour; conduct	303/104
人为 *	man-made; artificial	104/303
为 * 期	to be done by (a certain date); lasting	303/096
为 * 时	in terms of time	303/115
认为 *	believe; think; consider; feel	105/303
以为 *	think (take something to be true)	323/303
作为 *	conduct; deeds; act as	176/303
一公里为 * 一千米	1 kilometre is equivalent to 1000 metres	152/221/069/303/152/268/080

注释 Note

* 为 wéi = act as; serve as; become; be

(All other examples are pronounced as wèi.)

Example Sentences

1/303	那家宾馆为什么关了？ Why was that hotel closed?
2/303	妈妈为了我们从去年起就不工作了。 My mum gave up work last year in order to look after us.
3/303	我认为 * 我们应该再给他一次机会。 I think we should give him one more chance.
4/303	爸爸妈妈老了的时候，作为 * 子女，我们得多去看看他们。 When parents are old, as children we should visit them more.
5/303	为什么不坐火车呢？这儿离火车站很近。别坐公共汽车了好不好？汽车太慢了！ Why don't you take the train? The train station is not far from here. Don't take the bus. It's too slow!

W | 304 问 ASK wèn

Chinese	English	Character codes
问 + 题 → 问题	ask + topic = question; problem; issue	304/293
问问题	ask a question	304/304/293
学问	learning; knowledge	150/304
问候	give one's regards; send a greeting	304/045
过问	show an interest in; get involved with	225/304
请问	Excuse me, may I ask...?	101/304
问好	send one's regards to	304/039
问号	question mark; unknown factor; open question	304/040

Example Sentences

1/304	请问二十五号房间在哪儿？ Excuse me, may I ask where Room 25 is?
2/304	这里为什么是问号？写错了吧？ Why is there a question mark here? Is it a mistake?
3/304	妈妈，我不喜欢这件衣服。你为什么不先问问我喜不喜欢，然后再买？ Mum, I don't like this item of clothing. Why didn't you ask me if I liked it before you bought it?
4/304	我上学的时候，爸爸从来不过问我的学习。我的妈妈是老师，很有学问，我有问题的时候常常问她。 When I was a student, my dad never took an interest in my studies. My mum is a teacher and very knowledgeable, so I often asked her if I had questions.
5/304	小明不在，我不知道他去哪儿了，可能去教室了。你再问问别人吧。 Xiaoming is not here. I don't know where he has gone to. He might be in the classroom. You can ask someone else.

舞 DANCE wǔ 305 W

Chinese	English	Character codes
跳 + 舞 → 跳舞	jump + dance = to dance	296/305
中国舞	Chinese dance	168/036/305
舞会	dance (social event); ball	305/049
歌舞	singing and dancing	219/305
飞舞	dance in the breeze; flutter	027/305

Example Sentences

1/305	你想看歌舞还是想看电影？ Would you like to go see a song-and-dance show or watch a movie?
2/305	我和我先生是在大学的舞会上认识的。 My husband and I got to know each other at a university ball.
3/305	看，天上飞舞的那些东西是什么？是报纸还是什么？ Look, what are those things fluttering in the sky? Is it newspaper or what?
4/305	听说你中国舞跳得很好。我们都还没看过中国舞，给我们跳一个好吗？ I hear you're very good at Chinese dancing. We've never seen Chinese dancing. Would you dance for us?
5/305	你跳的舞真好看！好学吗？不知道我能不能学会。新年快到了，我想跳给我妈妈看。 Your dancing is lovely to watch. Is it easy to learn? I don't know if I can master it. New Year is coming and I'd like to dance for my mum.

W | 306 务 BUSINESS/MATTER/TASK wù

Chinese	English	Character codes
服务 + 员 → 服务员	service + employee = waiter, waitress; attendant	029/306/331
服务生	server	029/306/112
服务	serve; service	029/306
公务	official business	221/306
家务	housework	053/306
事务	work; (political etc.) affairs	281/306
事务所	business office	281/306/290
事务员	office clerk	281/306/331
商务	commercial affairs; commerce	107/306
外务	foreign affairs	297/306
国务院	State Council (PRC); State Department (US)	036/306/161

Example Sentences

1/306	我去中国是因为公务，不是去旅游。 I'm going to China for work reasons, not for tourism.
2/306	这家宾馆的服务非常好，他们的服务员都很友好。 This hotel's service is very good, and their staff are very friendly.
3/306	别问了，这是我的家务事，我不想说。 Stop asking me. It's a family matter and I don't want to talk about it.
4/306	我在大学学的是商务汉语，希望会对两年以后我去中国做生意有帮助。 I'm studying Business Chinese at university; hopefully it will be very helpful for me when I go do business in China in two years.
5/306	现在中国的孩子大多不帮爸爸妈妈做家务，因为在他们的爸爸妈妈看来，所有的时间对孩子来说，都是要去学习的。 Nowadays most Chinese children don't help their parents with chores because from their parents' point of view all their time shoule be spent on studying.

希 HOPE/EXPECT/RARE xī 307 X

Chinese	English	Character codes
希 + 望 → 希望	hope + hope = hope; wish for	307/302
有希望	hopeful; promising; prospective	158/307/302
大有希望	very hopeful; stand a good chance	014/158/307/302
没希望	no hope; no chance	078/307/302
希望小学	Hope Primary School (Chinese rural education program)	307/302/143/150

Example Sentences

1/307	我希望明天不会下雨。 I hope it won't rain tomorrow.
2/307	因为他学习非常好，所以很有希望考上好大学。 He's doing exceptionally well in his studies, so he is very hopeful to be admitted to a good university.
3/307	我希望以后能有机会去中国工作。 I hope I will have the opportunity to go to China to work in the future.
4/307	我明年七月要去中国东北的一所希望小学教书。 I will go teach in a Hope Primary School in northeast China next July.
5/307	我昨天在球场看见你哥哥了，他的球踢得太好了！我真希望有一天他能为国家踢球。 I saw your older brother on the football pitch yesterday. He played really well! I hope he can play for the national team one day.

X | 308 息 BREATH/NEWS/INTEREST (on loan etc.)/STOP/REST xī

Chinese	English	Character codes
休 + 息 → 休息	rest + rest = rest; take a break	313/308
休息室	lobby; lounge	313/308/283
作息	work and rest	176/308
作息时间	daily schedule; daily routine	176/308/115/231
作息时间表	schedule; timetable	176/308/115/231/189
出息	future prospects; grow up; yield interest	012/308
气息	smell; breath	098/308

Example Sentences

1/308	我们去休息室休息一下吧！ Let's go to the lounge to have a break!
2/308	桌子上的作息时间表是谁的？ Whose timetable is that on the table?
3/308	在中国，人们常常认为那些能上好大学的孩子都是有出息的人。我觉得这个看法有问题。 In China, people tend to think that those children who can go to good universities are sure to get on in life. I think this opinion is questionable.
4/308	我听妈妈说，你每天晚上都十二点以后睡觉，这样的作息时间有问题，对身体很不好！ I heard from mum that you don't get to bed till after midnight every night; following that kind of daily routine could be a problem — it's very bad for your health!
5/308	你看起来很累，休息一下吧，工作是做不完的。身体第一，没有好身体，什么都做不了。 You seem very tired. Have a rest. There's always work to do anyway. Your health comes first. Without good health, you can do nothing.

洗 WASH/BATHE xǐ 309 X

Chinese	English	Character codes
洗 + 手 → 洗手	wash + hand = wash one's hands	309/284
洗手间	toilet; bathroom; restroom	309/284/231
洗衣服	wash clothes	309/153/029
洗衣机	washing machine	309/153/051
洗衣房	laundry room	309/153/213
洗衣店	laundry	309/153/018
洗钱	money laundering	309/100

Example Sentences

1/309	先洗手，再吃饭。 Wash your hands first and then eat.
2/309	水果不洗不可以吃，吃了会生病的。 Fruit can't be eaten without washing; otherwise you could get ill.
3/309	中国人家里的洗衣机都在洗手间里吗？ Do all Chinese families keep their washing machine in the bathroom?
4/309	这件衣服我本来很喜欢，很想买，可是它只能手洗，不能机洗，最后我还是没买。 I liked this item of clothing at first, and really wanted to buy it, but it has to be handwashed and can't be put in the washing machine so I didn't buy it in the end.
5/309	这个大卖场的洗手间离大门很远。得从这儿往右走一百米，然后在卖洗衣机那儿再往左，你就看见洗手间了。 The toilets for this hypermarket are a long way from the entrance — you need to turn right, walk 100 metres, then turn left where washing machines are sold and you'll see the toilets.

X | 310 笑 SMILE/LAUGH xiào

Chinese	English	Character codes
笑 + 话 → 笑话	smile; laugh + speech = joke	310/046
说笑话	tell a joke	122/310/046
玩笑	joke; jest	299/310
可笑	funny; ridiculous	242/310
好笑	laughable; funny; ridiculous	039/310
大笑	laugh heartily	014/310
欢笑	joyful laughter	047/310
说笑	laughing and joking; banter	122/310
冷笑	humourless laugh or smile; sneer	068/310

Example Sentences

1/310	弟弟很会说笑话。 Little brother is very good at telling jokes.
2/310	什么事情让你们那么高兴，有说有笑的？ What made you so happy, all talking and laughing?
3/310	别开玩笑了，还是说真的吧！ No more joking please. Tell the truth.
4/310	你的笑话太没有意思了，一点儿都不好笑。你还是说一个别的笑话吧。 Your joke is boring, and not funny at all. You'd better tell another one.
5/310	小孩子常常不会说笑话，可是有的时候他们说的话很有意思，让人听了就想笑。 Children normally can't tell jokes, but the things they say can sometimes be amusing, and make you laugh when you hear them.

新 NEW xīn 311 X

Chinese	English	Character codes
新 + 年 → 新年	new + year = New Year	311/090
新近	recently; lately	311/236
新房	bridal chamber; brand new house	311/213
新手	novice; beginner	311/284
新生儿	newborn baby	311/112/024
最新	latest; newest	347/311

Example Sentences

1/311	你知道新生儿一天得 * 睡多少个小时的觉吗？ Do you know how many hours a day newborn babies sleep?
2/311	你的新学校离新家近吗？你喜欢你的新学校和新同学吗？ Is your new school near your new home? How do you like the new school and your new schoolmates?
3/311	我得 * 买些新衣服了，现在的这些衣服穿了很多年，都过时了。 I need to buy some new clothes; I've been wearing the ones I've got for years, and they're all old-fashioned.
4/311	这是最新的电脑，因为现在是新年，所以现在买便宜二百元。过了新年就贵了。 This is the latest computer, and because it's New Year you can buy it for 200 yuan cheaper. After New Year it will be more expensive.
5/311	A: 看！你看得到前面的车上写着什么吗？太好笑了！ B: "新手上路，让让我吧！"真的很有意思！ A: Look! Do you see what's written on the car in front? It's so funny! B: "Beginner on the road, make room for me." That's really amusing!

注释 Note

* 得 děi = have to; must

X | 312 姓 SURNAME xìng

Chinese	English	Character codes
姓 + 名 → 姓名	surname + given name = full name	312/082
百姓	common people	181/312
老百姓	ordinary people	066/181/312
贵姓	May I ask your (honourable) surname?	224/312
同名同姓	having the same given name and family name	130/082/130/312

Example Sentences

1/312	A: 请问您贵姓？ B: 我姓牛。 A: Excuse me, may I ask what your surname is? B: My surname is Niu.
2/312	《百家姓》里一共有多少个姓？ How many surnames are there in total in *Hundred Family Surnames*?
3/312	中国的姓大多是一个字，不过也有两个字的。 The majority of Chinese surnames are one character, but there are some that have two characters.
4/312	我不喜欢我的名字。因为只有两个字，和我同名同姓的人太多了！ I don't like my name that much. Since it only has two characters, there are too many people with exactly the same name as mine!
5/312	我看到过很多中国老人早上和晚上在一起跳舞，我觉得中国老百姓的日子过得太有意思了。 I've seen many elderly Chinese dancing together in the mornings and evenings. I think the lives of ordinary Chinese people are very interesting.

休 REST/STOP (doing something)/DON'T xiū 313 X

Chinese	English	Character codes
休 + 息 → 休息	rest + rest = rest; take a break	313/308
午休	lunch break	134/313
休会	recess; adjourn	313/049
休想	don't get the idea that…	313/142
休学	defer study	313/150
不休	endlessly; ceaselessly	007/313

Example Sentences

1/313	已经晚上十点了，早点儿休息吧。 It's already 10 pm. It's better to go to bed earlier.
2/313	我上大一的时候，因为身体不好，所以休学了一年。 During my first year of university my health was poor, so I took a year out.
3/313	中午了，我们现在休会一个小时，午休后再开。 It's midday. We'll recess for an hour and continue the meeting after the lunch break.
4/313	午休的时候，我常常去离我们公司很近的一家咖啡馆买一杯黑咖啡。 When it's lunch break I often go to the coffee shop near the office to buy a cup of black coffee.
5/313	她常常在我面前说个不休，让我不能休息。我很想告诉她“可不可以别说了”，可是我不希望她觉得不好意思，所以我从来没说过。 She often talks non-stop to me, not letting me get any rest. I really want to say to her "Can you stop talking?", but I don't want her to feel embarrassed so I haven't said it yet.

X | 314 雪 snow xuě

Chinese	English	Character codes
雪 + 人 → 雪人	snow + person = snowman	314/104
下雪	snow	139/314
大雪	heavy snow	014/314
小雪	light snow	143/314
雪球	snowball	314/272
白雪	white snow	180/314
雪白	snow white	314/180
雪亮	bright as snow; shiny	314/070

Example Sentences

1/314	椅子上那个雪亮的东西是什么？ What is that shiny thing on the chair?
2/314	你听过一个叫《雪人》的歌吗？非常好听。 Have you heard the song “Snowman”? It’s a really sweet song.
3/314	我的小狗雪白雪白的，所以叫“雪球”。 My little dog is pure white, so he’s called Snowball.
4/314	看！你雪白的衣服上怎么有个黑点？你得洗洗了。 Look! How did you get that black spot on your white shirt? You have to wash it.
5/314	这些不是新雪，是上个星期下的。已经不白了，是黑雪了。 This is not new snow; it’s last week’s snow. It’s not white any more. It’s black now.

颜 COLOUR/FACE yán 315 Y

Chinese	English	Character codes
颜 + 色 → 颜色	colour + colour = colour	315/277
五颜六色	multi-coloured	133/315/072/277
颜面	face; prestige	315/081
喜笑颜开	beaming with happiness; all smiles	137/310/315/061
红颜	beautiful woman; rosy cheeks	229/315

Example Sentences

1/315	你最喜欢什么颜色? What's your favourite colour?
2/315	这是我第一次在这个国家看到五颜六色的公共汽车。 This is the first time I've seen such a colourful bus in this country.
3/315	你眼睛好，帮我看一看，开过来的黑颜色的车是不是出租车? You have good vision, so help me have a look. Is the approaching black car a taxi?
4/315	告诉你，我妹妹上个星期生了一儿一女，这回真的让我们的爸爸妈妈喜笑颜开了。 I tell you, my little sister gave birth to a son and a daughter last week, and it had my parents absolutely beaming with happiness.
5/315	我哥哥喜欢红颜女子，他认为和漂亮的女人在一起很体面、有颜面。所以女孩子要想做他的女朋友，第一个条件是得漂亮。 My older brother likes pretty women. He thinks that being with a beautiful woman gives him dignity and prestige. Therefore, if a girl wants to be his girlfriend, the first requirement is that she's beautiful.

Y | 316 眼 EYE yǎn

Chinese	English	Character codes
眼睛	eye	316/238
眼红	covet; envious; jealous; furious	316/229
眼看	on the point of; look on idly or helplessly	316/062
眼明手快	sharp-eyed and dexterous	316/083/284/244
眼色	wink; signal with one's eyes	316/277
眼前	before one's eyes; any moment now	316/099
眼下	at present	316/139
眼药	eye ointment or drops	316/318
眼中/里	in one's eyes	316/168/069
不起眼	unremarkable; insignificant	007/097/316
白眼儿	disdainful or contemptuous look	180/316/024

注释 Note

* 上 shàng = use; apply

Example Sentences

1/316	你怎么了？为什么眼睛这么红？ What happened to you? Why are your eyes so red?
2/316	这个眼药每天上 * 两次：早一次，晚一次。 You need to use these eye drops twice a day: once in the morning and once in the evening.
3/316	我儿子的眼中只有他的老师，没有爸爸妈妈。 In my son's eyes, it's only his teachers that count, and not his parents.
4/316	你在哪儿呢？怎么还不来？火车眼看就要进站了。快点儿！ Where are you? How come you aren't here yet? The train will be at the platform in a moment. Hurry up!
5/316	妈妈常常为弟弟做很多事情，可是从来不问我要什么，我觉得妈妈眼里只有弟弟，没有我。 Mum often does many things for my little brother, but she has never asked me what I want. I feel like she only has eyes for little brother, and not for me.

羊 RAM/SHEEP yáng 317 Y

Chinese	English	Character codes
羊 + 肉 → 羊肉	sheep + meat = lamb; mutton	317/276
一只羊	a sheep	152/340/317

Example Sentences

1/317	这只羊真白！ This sheep is really white.
2/317	我最喜欢吃羊肉，所以每天晚上都吃羊肉面。 Lamb is my favourite food, so I eat lamb noodles every evening.
3/317	怎么有只羊在路上跑，它是从哪儿来的？ How come there's a sheep running on the road? Where has it come from?
4/317	眼下牛羊肉都很贵，鸡肉比牛羊肉便宜多了。 Both beef and lamb are expensive at the moment; chicken is much cheaper than beef or lamb.
5/317	这家羊肉馆儿只卖羊肉。想吃牛肉的话 * 去旁边的牛肉馆儿吧！ This lamb restaurant only sells lamb. If you want beef, go to the beef restaurant next door.

注释 Note

*……的话 = if (after conditional clause)

Y | 318 药 MEDICINE yào

Chinese	English	Character codes
吃 + 药 → 吃药	eat + medicine = take medicine	011/318
服药	take medicine	029/318
药店	chemist (shop); pharmacy	318/018
药房	pharmacy; dispensary	318/213
药水	liquid medicine	318/120
中药	Chinese medicine	168/318
西药	Western medicine	135/318
医药	medicines; medical	154/318
火药	gunpowder	050/318

Example Sentences

1/318	我在一家医药公司上班。 I work for a pharmaceutical company.
2/318	我不想吃药，不好吃。 I don't want to take medicine. It doesn't taste nice.
3/318	国外有中药店吗？买得到中药吗？ Are there any Chinese medicine shops abroad? Is Chinese medicine available for purchase?
4/318	我的老师病了，已经吃了一个星期的药了，可是还没好，所以我已经一个星期没看到她了。 My teacher is ill. She has been on medication for a week but still hasn't recovered, so it's been a week since I've seen her.
5/318	医生说你每天得服三次药，不能饭前服，都要饭后服。 The doctor said you must take this medicine three times a day, and only after meals, not before.

要 WANT/NEED/WILL/MUST/ASK FOR/IMPORTANT yào 319 Y

Chinese	English	Character codes
不 + 要 → 不要	not + must = do not; must not	007/319
要不 + 然 → 要不然	otherwise; or else	319/007/273
要是 A (的话) 就 B	if A then B	319/117/015/046/239
要么 A 要么 B	either A or B	319/077/319/077
要不得	unacceptable; intolerable	319/007/207
要点	main points; essentials	319/016
要饭	beg (for food or money)	319/026
要好	be friendly with; (of a relationship) close; better	319/039
要面子	anxious to keep up appearances; prideful	319/081/172
次要	less important; secondary; minor	200/319
就要	will; shall; be going to	239/319
快要	soon will	244/319
只要 A 就 B	as long as A then B	340/319/239

Example Sentences

1/319	我是一个要面子的人。 I'm keen on face-saving.
2/319	我和姐姐从小就很要好。 My older sister and I have been very close since we were little.
3/319	这些是我们今天学习的要点。 These are the main points that we're going to learn today.
4/319	只要 * 能做我喜欢的工作我就 * 高兴，钱多钱少是次要的。 As long as I can do a job that I like, I'll be happy. The salary I earn is less important, either high or low.
5/319	飞机快要 ** 起飞了 **，准备好了吗？飞到北京要两个小时。 The plane is taking off soon. Are you ready? It takes two hours to fly to Beijing.

注释 Note

* 只要 A 就 B as long as A then B

** 快要……了 soon (it) will

Y | 320 也 ALSO/TOO yě

Chinese	English	Character codes
一点儿 + 也 + 不 → 一点儿也不	a bit + also + not = not at all	152/016/024/320/007
也就是说	in other words; that is to say	320/239/118/122
也好	may as well	320/039
再也不	never again	163/320/007
不但 A 也 B	not only A, but also B	007/203/320
说的也是	indeed; it's true	122/015/320/118

Example Sentences

1/320	我喜欢喝咖啡，也喜欢喝中国红茶。 I like to drink coffee and I also like to drink Chinese red tea.
2/320	我一点儿也不想早起。 I really don't want to get up early.
3/320	我女儿今年上高三。也 * 就是说，她明年就上大学了。 My daughter is in her third year at senior high school. That is to say, next year she'll be going to university.
4/320	我再也 * 不想找服务员的工作做了，钱不多不说，每天的工作时间也 * 太长了。 I would never want to work as a waiter again. The pay is low without saying, and the hours are far too long as well.
5/320	不去就不去吧，这样也 * 好，你可以在家好好休息一下。 Don't go if you don't want to, and that's OK. You can get some rest at home.

注释 Note

*Unlike the English words "also; too; either", 也 cannot appear at the end of a sentence and must come before the verb or adjective it refers to. If using another adverb such as 都, it is placed immediately after 也. Example: I'm going, and my friends are all going too. 我去，我的朋友也都去。

宜 PROPER/SUITABLE/PLEASANT yí 321 Y

Chinese	English	Character codes
便 + 宜 → 便宜	convenient + suitable = cheap	264/321
宜人	pleasant; charming	321/104
不宜	unsuitable; inadvisable; inappropriate	007/321
少 * 儿不宜	not suitable for children	109/024/007/321
时宜	timely; appropriate to the occasion	115/321
事宜	matters; arrangements	281/321

注释 Note

* 少 shào= young

Example Sentences

1/321	这么宜人的天气，我们在外面多走一会儿再回家吧。 It's such pleasant weather. Let's walk a while longer outside before we go home.
2/321	下午场电影比晚场便宜。 Films in the afternoon are cheaper than evening ones.
3/321	生病的时候不宜过多运动，要多休息。 When you're sick, it's not advisable to exercise much. It's better to get more rest.
4/321	我们今天晚上看的电视里有少儿不宜的那些东西吗？要是有，就让儿子玩儿电脑去。 Is there anything on TV this evening that's not suitable for children? If so, we can ask our son to play on his computer.
5/321	我们明天下午三点在休息室见好吗？我们得说一说明年去中国工作的事宜。 Shall we meet in the lounge at 3 pm tomorrow? We need to talk about the arrangements for going to China to work next year.

Y | 322 已 ALREADY/STOP yǐ

Chinese	English	Character codes
已 + 经 → 已经	already + pass through = already	322/237
不得已	reluctant; have no alternative but to; unavoidable	007/207/322
早已	long since	334/322
不已	endlessly; incessantly	007/322
为 * 时已晚	already too late	303/115/322/300
年事已高	advanced in years; aged	090/281/322/030
已知	known (maths/science term)	322/341

注释 Note

* 为 wéi = in terms of, see 303 为

Example Sentences

1/322	我已经回国工作三年了。 I've been working for three years since I came back from abroad.
2/322	我早已不打篮球了。老了，打不动了。 I gave up playing basketball a long time ago. I'm too old to play.
3/322	妈妈，我为什么不可以和朋友出去，大家已经说好要去看电影了。 Mum, why can't I go out with my friends? We are going to watch a film.
4/322	我的奶奶年事已高，很多时候和她说话她都听不到。 My grandma is very old, and frequently she can't hear what you're saying when you talk to her.
5/322	因为中国新年的时候常常买不到火车票，所以很多人不得已，只好坐汽车回家。 During Chinese New Year it's often impossible to buy a train ticket, so many people have no choice but to take the coach home.

以 BY MEANS OF/ACCORDING TO/IN ORDER TO/AT yǐ 323 Y

Chinese	English	Character codes
以 + 上 → 以上	at + above = at or above; the above	323/108
以下	at or below; the following	323/139
以前	before; former; previous; ago	323/099
以后	after; later; in the future	323/044
以外	apart from; beyond; outside	323/297
以来	since (a past event)	323/065
可以	can; may; be able to; possible	242/323
因为……所以……	because... ; therefore	325/303/290/323
以为 *	think (take something to be true)	323/303
不以为 * 然	dismiss as mistaken; disapprove of	007/323/303/273
足以	enough to…	346/323
习以为 * 常	be accustomed to; take for granted	136/323/303/195

注释 Note

* 为 is pronounced in second tone wéi.

Example Sentences

1/323	我今天下午很忙，两点以后再给我打电话吧。 I'm very busy this afternoon. Please ring me after 2 pm.
2/323	我以前吃肉，现在不吃了，以后也不会再吃了。 I used to eat meat, but I don't now, and I don't plan to eat it again in the future.
3/323	在中国要想开出租车，只能在 21 岁以上，50 岁以下期间考试，再小再大都不可以。 To drive a taxi in China, only people aged between twenty-one and fifty can take the exam; anyone younger or older is not allowed to (drive a taxi in China).
4/323	你每天都睡得太少了，你得多休息。别不以为然，你这样会累病的。 You're not getting enough sleep each day; you should rest more. Don't dismiss it — tiredness will affect your health if you carry on this way.
5/323	你怎么来了？我知道你生病了，所以以为你今天不能来了。 Why have you come? I knew you were sick, so I assumed you wouldn't be able to make it today.

Y | 324 意 IDEA/MEANING/THINK/THOUGHT/INTENTION yì

Chinese	English	Character codes
意 + 思 → 意思	idea + think = meaning	324/286
有意思	interesting; enjoyable	158/324/286
有意	intend; intentional; deliberate	158/324
大意	careless; general idea; tenor	014/324
同意	agree; consent; approve	130/324
得意	proud of oneself; pleased with oneself	207/324
在意	care about; mind	164/324
乐意	be happy to do something	246/324
意外	unexpected; accident	324/297
意识	consciousness; be aware of; realise	324/116
意中人	ideal partner; object of one's affections	324/168/104
意气	spirit; temperament; personal feelings	324/098
意见	idea; opinion	324/054
生意	business; trade	112/324

Example Sentences

1/324	中国的爸爸妈妈都很在意孩子的学习。 All Chinese parents care about their children's study.
2/324	学汉语对和中国人做生意很有帮助。 Learning Chinese is very helpful for doing business with Chinese people.
3/324	对这件事，大家有什么意见？都说说好吗？ Regarding this matter, what's everyone's opinion? Shall we talk it over together?
4/324	那个中国电影我只看懂了一个大意，这一点儿都不意外。 I could only get the general idea of that Chinese film, which was just as expected.
5/324	我不是有意的，这也不是我的意思，请别太介意。 It was an accident. I didn't mean it. Please don't be offended.

因 CAUSE/REASON/BECAUSE yīn 325 | Y

Chinese	English	Character codes
因为……所以……	because... so; therefore	325/303/290/323
因果	cause and effect; causality	325/037
前因后果	cause and effect	099/325/044/037
病因	cause of disease	192/325
起因	cause; origin	097/325

Example Sentences

1/325	因为天气太热了，所以我不想吃东西。 Because it's so hot, I don't feel like eating anything.
2/325	妈妈常说有因就有果。做事情真的有因果关系吗？ Mum often says that everything you do has a consequence. But do your actions really determine your future?
3/325	因为弟弟比我小五岁，所以我比他高得多。 (Because) My little brother is five years younger than me, so I'm much taller than him.
4/325	这件事都是因为我，让我来跟大家说明一下起因吧。 This matter was all because of me, so let me to explain to you all how it came about.
5/325	我已经病了很长时间了，可是医生还没找到病因是什么。 I have been ill for a while, but the doctors still don't find what the cause is.

Y | 326 阴 CLOUDY/NEGATIVE yīn

Chinese	English	Character codes
阴 + 天 → 阴天	cloudy + day; sky = cloudy day; overcast sky	326/128
阴冷	gloomy and cold	326/068
阴雨	cloudy and rainy	326/159
阴影	shadow; shade	326/156
阴间	the netherworld; hell	326/231

Example Sentences

1/326	明天先晴后阴。 Tomorrow will be sunny at first and then cloudy later on.
2/326	今天是阴天，好在没有雨。 It's cloudy today, but luckily there's no rain.
3/326	我不喜欢阴雨的天气，这样的天气让人高兴不起来。 I don't like cloudy and rainy weather. It dampens people's spirits.
4/326	明天是晴天还是阴天？要是天气不好，我们就不出去了吧！ Will it be sunny or cloudy tomorrow? If the weather's not good, then let's not go out.
5/326	我听老人说，要是人没了，就是去阴间了。我觉得不可能，谁都没去过阴间，怎么知道有阴间？ I've heard old folk say that when people die they go to the netherworld. I don't think that's possible; nobody (alive) has been to the netherworld, so how do we know there is a netherworld?

泳 SWIM yǒng 327 Y

Chinese	English	Character codes
游泳	swim	328/327
泳衣	swimsuit	327/153
游泳衣	swimsuit	328/327/153
游泳运动员	(competitive) swimmer	328/327/333/212/331
游泳馆	indoor swimming pool	328/327/035
游泳课	swimming lesson	328/327/243

Example Sentences

1/327	妈妈给我买的黑色泳衣很漂亮。 The black swimming suit my mum bought me is very pretty.
2/327	中国有很多出名的游泳运动员。 China has many famous swimmers.
3/327	你们班谁游泳游得最快？是最高的那个男学生吗？ Who swims fastest in your class? Is it the tallest male student?
4/327	你是几岁开始学游泳的？你现在游泳游得怎么样？ At what age did you start to learn to swim? How well can you swim now?
5/327	我们学校有一个很大也很新的游泳馆。我们班每个星期上一次游泳课，每次四十五分钟。 Our school has a big new indoor pool. Our class has a forty-five-minute swimming lesson every week.

Y | 328 游 SWIM/TRAVEL/(part of a river) yóu

Chinese	English	Character codes
游泳	swim	328/327
旅游	tour; travel	251/328
出游	go on a tour; have an outing	012/328
游客	tourist; sightseer	328/063
游乐	amusement; recreation	328/246
游乐场所	playground; amusement park	328/246/196/290
游玩	play games; outing; excursion	328/299
上游	upstream	108/328
中游	midstream	168/328
下游	downstream	139/328

Example Sentences

1/328	这里什么时候游客最多？ When do you get the most tourists here?
2/328	七八月不是去中国旅游的好时候，天气太热了！ July and August are not the best time to travel in China. It's too hot!
3/328	这个星期六是我儿子五岁的生日，我会和他去游乐场玩儿一天。 This Saturday is my son's fifth birthday. We'll spend the day playing at the amusement park.
4/328	想好新年的时候做什么了吗？想去国外旅游还是回家看望爸爸妈妈？ Have you decided what to do during New Year? Would you like to travel abroad or go back home to see your parents?
5/328	这里的水不好，别喝，喝了会生病，我们往上游走吧。上游的水没问题，可以喝。 The water here is not good, so don't drink it, or you may get sick. Let's go further upstream; the water there is fine and drinkable.

右 RIGHT yòu 329 Y

Chinese	English	Character codes
右 + 边 → 右边	right + side = right side	329/188
右面	right side	329/081
右上	upper right	329/108
右下	lower right	329/139
右手	right hand	329/284
左右手	right-hand man; capable assistant	348/329/284
左右	left and right; approximately	348/329
左思右想	turn something over in one's mind	348/286/329/142
男左女右	male left female right (traditional saying)	259/348/091/329

Example Sentences

1/329	你看看书的右下边是什么字？你认识吗？认得出来吗？ Can you see the character at the bottom right of the book? Do you know it? Can you recognise it?
2/329	他左手写的字和右手写的一样漂亮。 The characters he writes with his left hand are as beautiful those with his right hand.
3/329	我们公司的右边有一个羊肉馆儿，我每天都去那里吃午饭。 There is a lamb restaurant to the right of my office. I go there for lunch every day.
4/329	他上完大学就开始在他爸爸的公司工作了，现在已经是他爸爸的左右手了。 He has worked at his dad's company since he finished university, and now he's become his father's right-hand man.
5/329	还有半个月左右就要开学了，你还不早一点儿买飞机票？别只想着玩儿了！ School starts in half a month or so. Why don't you buy the flight ticket a bit earlier? Don't just think about having fun.

Y | 330 鱼 FISH yú

Chinese	English	Character codes
鱼 + 肉 → 鱼肉	fish + meat = fish (as food)	330/276
鱼子	roe (fish eggs); caviar	330/172
一条鱼	a fish	152/295/330
鱼水情	close relationship (as a fish with water)	330/120/270
打鱼	catch fish; to fish	013/330
打鱼为生	earn a living from fishing	013/330/303/112

Example Sentences

1/330	猫都喜欢吃鱼吗？ Do all cats like to eat fish?
2/330	现在水里的鱼比以前少多了。 Now there are less fish in the water than before.
3/330	我买了两条鱼，你想让我怎么做？ I bought two fish. How would you like me to cook them?
4/330	你看见过大鱼吃小鱼吗？我在电视里见过。 Have you seen big fish eating small fish? I've seen it on TV.
5/330	以前这里有很多鱼，星期日的时候爸爸常常来这儿打鱼。可是现在这里很少能打到鱼了。 There were lots of fish here before. My dad often comes here on Sundays to fish, but these days he rarely catches any.

员 PERSON/STAFF/MEMBER yuán 331 Y

Chinese	English	Character codes
运动 + 员 → 运动员	sport + person = sportsperson; athlete	333/212/331
服务 + 员 → 服务员	service + employee = waiter, waitress; attendant	029/306/331
员工	personnel; staff; employee	331/032
人员	staff; crew; personnel	104/331
动员	mobilise	212/331
会员	member	049/331
球员	player	272/331

Example Sentences

1/331	我是这家商店的会员，在这儿买东西可以便宜一点儿。 I have a membership with this shop, which makes shopping here a bit cheaper.
2/331	你们国家最有名的足球运动员是谁？ Who is the most famous footballer in your country?
3/331	这里员工的服务太好了。我们下次还会再来的。 The service from the staff here is really good. We will come back again.
4/331	学校动员我们老师在休息的时候去帮助希望小学的孩子。 During the holidays, our school mobilised the teachers to help the Hope Primary School students.
5/331	运动员是不是从早到晚都得运动？他们是不是每天都很累？ Do athletes have to exercise from morning till night? Don't they feel tired every day?

Y | 332 远 FAR/DISTANT yuǎn

Chinese	English	Character codes
远 + 近 → 远近	far + near = distance	332/236
远大	forward-looking; ambitious	332/014
远道	long journey	332/206
远东	the Far East	332/019
远见	foresight; vision	332/054
长远	long-term; long-range	194/332
远视	long sightedness	332/117
远足	excursion; hike	332/346
远离	far away from; keep away from	332/248
远走高飞	go far away	332/345/030/027

Example Sentences

1/332	我爸爸是一个有远见的人。 My dad is a far-sighted person.
2/332	我家离公司不远，可以走路去上班。 My office is not far from my home. I can walk to work.
3/332	要是你坐公共汽车去就会觉得不太远，二十分钟吧。 It's not very far if you take a bus, about twenty minutes' ride.
4/332	去中国工作得远离家人，你会不会想家？ You'll be a long way from your family when you're working in China. Won't you be homesick?
5/332	我们一家都喜欢远足，上个星期日我们走了八个小时，是我们走得最远的一天。 All my family like hiking. We walked for eight hours last Sunday, which was the furthest we walked.

运 MOVE/TRANSPORT/LUCK yùn 333 Y

Chinese	English	Character codes
运动	sport	333/212
运动会	sports meet; game	333/212/049
运动场	sports field; playground	333/212/196
运气	luck (good or bad)	333/098
好运	good luck	039/333
走运	have some good luck; lucky	345/333

Example Sentences

1/333	我会的运动不太多，你呢？ I can't play many sports. How about you?
2/333	这个新运动场和以前的哪里不一样？ What's different between this new sports field and the previous one?
3/333	每天别只坐着，多运动对身体好。 Don't just sit there every day. Getting more exercise is good for your health.
4/333	我们学校每年都有校运动会。很多人都喜欢那天，因为可以和朋友在一起，还可以不上课。 Our school holds a sports meet every year. A lot of people enjoy that day as they can be with their friends, and don't have to go to lessons.
5/333	真走运！我在我最想去的公司里找到了工作。希望你找工作的时候也有好运气。 I am so lucky! I found a job at the company that I most wanted to work for. I hope you also have good luck with your job search.

Z | 334 早 MORNING/EARLY zǎo

Chinese	English	Character codes
早 + 上 → 早上	morning + on top = early morning	334/108
早期	early stage	334/096
早点	light breakfast	334/016
早饭	breakfast	334/026
早年	one's early years	334/090
早日	at an early date; soon	334/275
早晚	morning and evening; sooner or later	334/300
早先	previously; in the past	334/140
早已	long since	334/322
一早	early in the morning	152/334
一大早	early in the morning; first thing in the morning	152/014/334
早就	long since	334/239
早早儿	as soon as possible	334/334/024
早起	get up early	334/097
过早	premature	225/334
早报	morning paper	334/184

Example Sentences

1/334	（你）一大早就开始学习了？真是好孩子。 You've already begun studying so early in the morning? What a good kid!
2/334	我今天早上起得太早了，所以现在很想睡觉。 I got up too early this morning, so I really want to get some sleep now.
3/334	你没听说过这件事吗？我早就知道了，所以以为你也知道。 Haven't you heard about this? I knew a long time ago, so I presumed you knew as well.
4/334	我每天早上都去那家小饭馆儿买早点。不但很便宜，也非常好吃。 I go to that small restaurant to buy breakfast every morning. It's not only cheap, but really tasty too.
5/334	今天的早报我还没看呢，里面有什么你觉得有意思的，快给我说说。 I haven't read the morning paper. If there's anything in there you think is interesting, tell me about it.

丈 HUSBAND/MEASURE zhàng 335 Z

Chinese	English	Character codes
丈 + 夫 → 丈夫	husband + man = husband	335/216
大丈夫	true man; real man	014/335/216
丈人	father-in-law (wife's father)	335/104
男子汉大丈夫	real man; he-man	259/172/038/014/335/216
一丈	one *zhang* (3.3 m)	152/335

Example Sentences

1/335	我丈夫是中国人。 My husband is Chinese.
2/335	一丈是多长？和一米比，哪个长？ How long is one *zhang*? Compared to a metre, which is longer?
3/335	我丈夫的姓是他妈妈的，不是他爸爸的，这不太常见。 My husband took his mum's surname rather than his dad's; this is not very common.
4/335	我听说“丈人”是妻子的爸爸的意思。那你怎么叫你妻子的爸爸？叫“爸爸”还是“丈人”？ I heard that *zhangren* means wife's dad. How do you address your wife's dad then, dad or *zhangren*?
5/335	弟弟说要做男子汉大丈夫，不做小男人。 Little brother said that he wants to be a real man, not a little man.

Z | 336 找 SEEK/LOOK FOR/CALL ON SOMEONE/GIVE CHANGE zhǎo

Chinese	English	Character codes
找 + 到 + 了 → 找到了	seek + arrive + grammatical code = find	336/205/067
找工作	look for a job	336/032/176
找事儿	look for a job; look for trouble	336/281/024
找上门	call at someone's door	336/108/257
找出路	find a way out; seek an opportunity	336/012/250
不好找	not easy to find	007/039/336
找钱	give change	336/100
找出	find; seek out	336/012
找不着北	confused and disoriented	336/007/337/005
找机会	look for an opportunity	336/051/049

Example Sentences

1/336	姐姐很爱生气，常常一天生四五回气。爸爸说这是她没事儿找事儿。 Older sister gets angry very easily, often four or five times per day. My dad says that she likes to look for trouble.
2/336	哪里不对？我怎么找不出来？你能帮我看看吗？ So where is the mistake? How come I can't find it? Can you help me have a look?
3/336	现在所有的工作都不好找，没事的，慢慢找，会找到的。 It's not easy to find any type of job nowadays, but it is OK. Take your time and you'll find one eventually.
4/336	北京太大了，一下火车我就找不着北了。 Beijing is so big that I was lost as soon as I got off the train.
5/336	我的钱怎么少了？想起来了，昨天买东西的时候没找给我钱。 How come I've so little money left? I remember. I wasn't given change when I was shopping yesterday.

着（著）-ING (particle) zhe; Resultative Code zháo 337 Z

Chinese	English	Character codes
穿＋着→穿着	to wear + (ongoing action particle) = is wearing	198/337
雨下着	it's raining	159/139/337
别站着	don't stand	190/166/337
天还亮着	it's still light	128/226/070/337
天还黑着	it's still dark	128/226/228/337
走着去	go on foot	345/337/102
笑着说	say with a smile	310/337/122
忙着准备考试	busy preparing for the exams	254/337/344/185/241/282
着*火	catch fire	337/050
着*车	start the car	337/010

Example Sentences

1/337	昨天，一家有名的饭馆着*了一场大火。 There was a very bad fire in a famous restaurant yesterday.
2/337	他工作了一天，累得很，所以一上床就睡着**了。 He has worked all day long that he fell asleep the moment he got into the bed.
3/337	等着我，我现在就下来。 Wait for me. I'm coming down now.
4/337	开着车不可以打手机！ Don't use your mobile phone while driving.
5/337	还早着呢，我们可以晚点儿出门，坐下一班火车。 It's still early. We can leave a bit later and take the next train.

注释 Note

* 着 zháo = verb

** 着 zháo = resultative code to a verb

Z | 338 真 REAL/TRUE/GENUINE/INDEED zhēn

Chinese	English	Character codes
真 + 事 → 真事	real + matter = true story	338/281
真人真事	real people, real events; true story	338/104/338/281
真话	truth	338/046
真情	the truth	338/270
真是	indeed; truly	338/118
真正	genuine; true; real	338/339
真知	genuine knowledge; true wisdom	338/341
认真	conscientious; earnest; serious	105/338
天真	naive; innocent	128/338
真的	really; real	338/015
果真	if indeed; as expected; sure enough	037/338

Example Sentences

1/338	做我女朋友吧，我真的很喜欢你。 Would you be my girlfriend? I really like you.
2/338	我真的很喜欢孩子，因为他们都很天真。 I really like children because they are all so innocent.
3/338	他从小到大都是一个认真的好学生。 He's always been a conscientious student, ever since he was little.
4/338	你为什么这么看着我？我说的都是真话。 Why are you looking at me like that? I'm telling the truth.
5/338	真正的好朋友会在你做错的时候告诉你，不会只看着你做错事但什么都不说。 A real friend will tell you if you're going about something the wrong way; they won't just watch you getting it wrong and say nothing.

正 STRAIGHT/PROPER/MAIN/CORRECT/JUST (now) zhèng 339 Z

Chinese	English	Character codes
正在	in the process of (doing something)	339/164
正好	perfectly; exactly	339/039
正常	normal; regular	339/195
不正常	abnormal	007/339/195
正比	directly proportional	339/186
正点	on time; on schedule; punctual	339/016
正事	the real business; serious work	339/281
正经事	real work; serious business	339/237/281
正面	front; obverse; positive	339/081
正气	integrity; righteousness	339/098
正午	noon	339/134
公正	just; fair; equitable	221/339
正＊月	first month of the lunar calendar	339/162

注释 Note

＊正 is pronounced in the first tone as zhēng.

Example Sentences

1/339	我正在试穿衣服，这件衣服我穿正好。 I'm trying clothes on at the moment. This item of clothing fits me perfectly.
2/339	今年的天气很不正常，一天冷一天热，很多人都生病了。 This year's weather is abnormal: one day it's cold, the next day it's hot. Many people have become ill.
3/339	因为下大雨，今天的火车都不能正点到。 Because of the heavy rain, none of the trains were on time today.
4/339	对人也好，做事也好，我们都要公正。 Whether it's how people are treated, or how things are done, we all want fairness.
4/339	我正找你呢！是你的电话！你到哪儿去了？我叫了半天都不见你的人影。 I was just looking for you! There is a phone call for you! Where have you been? I've been calling you for a while but there was no sign of you.

Z | 340 只 ONLY zhǐ; MW zhī

Chinese	English	Character codes
一只 * 猫	a cat	152/340/076
一只 * 狗	a dog	152/340/033
只 * 身	by oneself; alone	340/279
只有	only (have)	340/158
只好	have to; have no choice but to	340/039
只是	merely; simply; only; but	340/118
只不过	nothing more than; it's just that...	340/007/225
只能	can only; is obliged to	340/088
不只	not only; not just	007/340
只得	have to; have no choice but to	340/207
只要……就……	as long as... then...	340/319/239
只说不做	all talk and no action	340/122/007/178

注释 Note

* 只 zhī = MW. (All other examples are pronounced as zhǐ.)

注释 Note

** 只要 [A] 就 [B] = as long as [A] then [B]

Example Sentences

1/340	我有一只 * 猫和两条狗。 I have one cat and two dogs.
2/340	只要 ** 认真学习，就 ** 能学好。 As long as you are diligent in your studies, you can learn well.
3/340	要是明天下大雪的话，我就只好后天走了。 If it snows heavily tomorrow I will have to leave the day after tomorrow.
4/340	别介意，我只不过是问问。再说，这件事我也只能问你，不是吗？ Please don't take offence, I'm just asking. And besides, you're the only person I can ask about this. Isn't that right?
5/340	不只是我，我们班的同学都考上了好大学，所以我们的老师非常高兴。 Not only me, but all my classmates as well got admitted to good universities, so our teacher is extremely happy.

知 KNOW/BE AWARE OF zhī 341 Z

Chinese	English	Character codes
知道	know	341/206
知识	knowledge	341/116
不知	not know; be unaware; unknowingly	007/341
告知	inform	217/341
得知	find out, learn of	207/341
知名	well-known; famous	341/082
可知	knowable	242/341
明知	be fully aware of; know perfectly well	083/341
知情	be in the know; have inside information	341/270
不为人知	not known to anyone; secret	007/303/104/341
知足	be content with one's lot	341/346
知足常乐	satisfied with what one has	341/346/195/246

Example Sentences

1/341	谢谢告知。 Thank you for informing me.
2/341	我是从同事那里得知的这件事。 It was from my colleague that I learned of this matter.
3/341	这里是一家中国的知名公司。 This is a well-known Chinese company.
4/341	她读了很多书，所以懂很多知识。我有问题的时候最喜欢问她。 She's read many books so she knows a lot. When I have questions, I prefer to ask her.
5/341	不知不为错，可是你明知这样做是错的，为什么还要做？ It's not your fault if you don't know, but actually you know very well that it's wrong to act this way. So why do you persist in doing it?

Z 342 纸 PAPER zhǐ

Chinese	English	Character codes
报 + 纸 → 报纸	report + paper = newspaper	184/342
白纸	plain paper; blank sheet of paper	180/342
红纸	red paper	229/342
纸条	slip of paper; note	342/295
纸杯	paper cup	342/004
手纸	toilet paper	284/342

Example Sentences

1/342	那红纸上写的是什么？ What was written on that red paper?
2/342	你有白纸吗？给我点儿好吗？ Do you have any blank paper? Could you give me some?
3/342	谁给你的纸条？上面说了些什么？ Who gave you the note? What does it say?
4/342	有了电脑和手机以后，看报纸的人少多了。 Now that we have computers and mobile phones, there are much fewer people reading newspapers.
5/342	明天是弟弟的生日，他的很多好朋友都会来，我们多买些纸杯吧。 Tomorrow is my little brother's birthday, and lots of his friends will come. We'd better buy more paper cups.

助 HELP/ASSIST zhù 343 Z

Chinese	English	Character codes
帮 + 助 → 帮助	help + assist = help	183/343
助手	assistant; helper; aide	343/284
助教	teaching assistant	343/233
助兴	add to the entertainment; liven things up	343/149
助听	hearing aid	343/129
助长	encourage	343/194
助学	(financial or practical) help with study	343/150
助人为乐	pleasure from helping others	343/104/303/246

Example Sentences

1/343	姐姐经常帮助我。 My older sister often helps me.
2/343	你的工作做得非常好，来做我的助手吧。 You do your job very well. How about coming to be my assistant?
3/343	虽然我只是助教，但是我每天的工作也非常多。 Although I'm only a teaching assistant, I have a lot of work to do every day.
4/343	我的手机不见了，是我姐姐帮助我找到的。 I misplaced my mobile phone, and it was my older sister who helped me find it.
5/343	大家看起来都很累，我来唱个歌给大家助助兴吧。 Everyone seems very tired. How about I sing a song to liven us all up?

Z | 344 准 STANDARD/ACCURATE/CERTAINLY zhǔn

Chinese	English	Character codes
准 + 备 → 准备	accurate + prepare = prepare; to plan	344/185
准时	punctual; on time	344/115
准点	right on time; on the dot	344/016
不准	not allowed to	007/344
对准	aim at; point at	022/344
水准	horizontal plane; level; standard	120/344
以……为准	take ... as the standard	323/303/344
准儿	certainty	344/024
准星	gun sight	344/148

Example Sentences

1/344	火车能准点到吗？ Will the train arrive on time?
2/344	考试以前我妈妈不准我看电视。 My mum doesn't allow me to watch TV before exams.
3/344	明天请八点准时到。 Please come tomorrow at eight o'clock sharp.
4/344	明天就考试了，你准备得怎么样了？ Your exam's tomorrow. How prepared are you?
5/344	他已经晚了一个小时了，没准儿不能来了。 He's already an hour late; maybe he's not coming.

走 WALK/GO/LEAVE zǒu 345 Z

Chinese	English	Character codes
走 + 路 → 走路	walk + road = walk; go on foot	345/250
走动	walk about; move around; visit each other	345/212
走过	walk past; pass by	345/225
走红	rise to fame; gain popularity	345/229
走运	have good luck; lucky	345/333
走样	lose original shape	345/151
出走	flee; run away	012/345
走来走去	move from place to place; walk up and down	345/065/345/102
走开	go away	345/061
走走	go for a walk	345/345

Example Sentences

1/345	天晴了，我们出去走走吧？ The weather's cleared up now. Shall we go out for a walk?
2/345	他现在是走红的歌星了。 He has how become a very popular singer.
3/345	因为很近，我天天都走路上班，不比坐车慢多少。 I walk to work every day as it is close. It's not slower than taking the bus.
4/345	虽然我们是多年的老朋友，但是因为最近都很忙，所以没怎么走动了。 Although we've been friends for years, because we've both been very busy recently, we haven't been able to visit one another.
5/345	谁的狗在吃我的午饭？快走开！ Whose dog is that eating my lunch? Go away!

Z | 346 足 FOOT/ENOUGH/AMPLE zú

Chinese	English	Character codes
踢 + 足球 → 踢足球	kick + foot ball = play football	292/346/272
不足	insufficient; deficiency; not worth	007/346
十足	ample; complete; 100%	114/346
足以	enough to…	346/323
足足	no less than; a full…; a good…	346/346
远足	hike; excursion	332/346

Example Sentences

1/346	昨天太累了，我足足睡了十个小时的觉。 I was so tired yesterday that I slept for a full ten hours.
2/346	我们学校有一个很大的足球场。 Our school has a very big football pitch.
3/346	小学生都要学怎么踢足球。 Primary school students all need to learn how to play football.
4/346	他考试考得这么好，足以说明他是一个很认真的好学生。 His performance in the exams was so good that it was enough to prove he is a very able and conscientious student.
5/346	对不起，我没有太多时间准备，所以准备得不足。 Sorry, I didn't have much time to prepare so I didn't prepare sufficiently.

最 MOST zuì 347 Z

Chinese	English	Character codes
最 + 喜欢 → 最喜欢	most + like = favourite	347/137/047
最后	last; final; at last	347/044
最后一天	final day	347/044/152/128
最近	recently; lately	347/236
最多	the most; at most; maximum	347/023
最少	the least; at least; minimum	347/109
最好	best; (it would be) best (to)	347/039
最新	latest; newest	347/311
最先	first; earliest	347/140
最高	tallest; highest; supreme	347/030

Example Sentences

1/347	这是最新的手机吗？为什么这么贵？ Is this the latest mobile phone? Why is it so expensive?
2/347	我真得走了，最多只能再等你三分钟。 I really have to go; I can only wait another three minutes for you at the most.
3/347	今天是这个学期的最后一天。 Today is the last day of this term.
4/347	今天是谁最先来教室的？看到桌子上的书了吗？我新买的一本汉字书不见了。 Who was the first to get into the classroom? Did you see a book on the table? The character book that I only just bought is gone.
5/347	我们最好现在就走。因为一会儿就是下班时间，那时候路上的车会很多，我们就不能准时见到他了。 We'd better go now because it will be rush hour soon and there'll be lots of traffic on the road, and we might not meet him on time.

Z | 348 左 LEFT zuǒ

Chinese	English	Character codes
左 + 边 → 左边	left + side = left side	348/188
左面	left side	348/81
左手	left hand; left-handed	348/284
左上	upper left	348/108
左下	lower left	348/139

Example Sentences

1/348	坐在你左边的人是谁？ Who is the person sitting to your left?
2/348	你的左手里有什么？给我看看好吗？ What is that in your left hand? Can you show me?
3/348	我明天晚上六点左右能到。 I can get there around 6 pm tomorrow.
4/348	你家左边的茶馆怎么关门了？我还想今天晚上和你一起去那里坐坐呢。 How come the teahouse to the left of your house is closed? I was thinking of going there with you this evening.
5/348	一共要写五千字，现在我已经写了三千个字左右了，后天就能写完了。 I need to write 5,000 characters altogether. I've already written about 3,000 and will be able to finish it the day after tomorrow.

跋：

酝酿数年　一朝面世

自从我提出“‘序法’是汉文语法”的理论，到如今能出版这套教材，前前后后经历了二十个年头。

二十年来，我一直用这段话给自己和我们的老师们鼓气：“不要羁绊于西方语言学家对我们语言下的定义；作为中国人，对汉语‘自性’的研究是我们义不容辞的责任。”

正源于此，我要诚心诚意地感谢外文局麾下的华语教学出版社，感谢他们的见识与勇气；也要感谢成立于 2006 年的英国子午文院（Meridian Chinese Studies）对“序法”理论的研究、开发以及长达 14 年的课堂实践，正是这些因素使得这套教材日趋成熟。

这里给“序法”冠以“范氏”做一个注脚：我是苏州范家的子孙，苏姓是家父北迁后作为艺术活动的“艺姓”。我家祖上有范蠡、范仲淹，序法这一点点小成就当属祖宗的福荫，为此称之为“范氏序法”。再，百多年前，清人马建忠首次以印欧语系解构汉文，著《马氏文通》，汉文在马氏西语“他性”的解释下流行至今。“范氏序法”力求返璞归真，重新回到汉文本身，尝试以其“自性”诠释语法规律。

整套书并非学术大著，又是针对外国学生，所以亦庄亦谐，以学习效果为主，学术依据为辅。每次碰到需用古字（甲骨文和篆体）的字符解构简化字体时，我都尽量寻找源头，但牵强乃至穿凿附会依然在所难免，还请读者和老师们谅解。

作者、主编　苏立群

2020.10 于英国伦敦

出版策划：王君校　韩　晖
统筹协调：付　眉　韩　颖　彭　博
策划编辑：陆　瑜
责任编辑：陆　瑜
英文编辑：韩芙芸

图书在版编目（CIP）数据

60 小时突破初级中文．课本．下册 ：汉英 / 苏立群主编．— 北京 ：华语教学出版社， 2021.4
ISBN 978-7-5138-2062-2

Ⅰ．①6… Ⅱ．①苏… Ⅲ．①汉语－对外汉语教学－教材 Ⅳ．①H195.4

中国版本图书馆 CIP 数据核字（2020）第 264881 号

60 小时突破初级中文．课本（下册）
LIQUN SU（苏立群） 主编
*

华语教学出版社有限责任公司出版
（中国北京百万庄大街24号　邮政编码 100037）
电话：(86)10-68320585　68997826
传真：(86)10-68997826　68326333
网址：www.sinolingua.com.cn
电子信箱：hyjx@sinolingua.com.cn
北京虎彩文化传播有限公司印刷
2021年（16开）第1版
2021年第1版第1次印刷
ISBN 978-7-5138-2062-2
008000